Thomas George Lawson

Thomas George Lawson

African Historian and Administrator in Sierra Leone

David E. Skinner

HOOVER INSTITUTION PRESS
Stanford University, Stanford, California

PHOTOGRAPHS

All photographs are by the author (1969).

ILLUSTRATIONS

The author gratefully acknowledges the permission of the Public Record Office for use of these illustrations:

Documents (photo section)

An Arabic letter written by Fode Ibrahim Tarawali of Gbile to the governor of Sierra Leone (Sir Arthur Edward Kennedy) in 1870. I have made very few changes in the accurate translation by Alfa Mohammed Sanusi, who later became the first Arabic writer and translator for the Aborigines' and Native Affairs' departments (PRO: CO 267/305, desp. 81, 1870, end.).

The Ordinance naturalizing Thomas George Lawson as a British citizen in Sierra Leone (PRO: CO 269/2, no. 4, 1860).

The Hoover Institution on War, Revolution and Peace, founded at Stanford University in 1919 by the late President Herbert Hoover, is an interdisciplinary research center for advanced study on domestic and international affairs in the twentieth century. The views expressed in its publications are entirely those of the authors and do not necessarily reflect the views of the staff, officers, or Board of Overseers of the Hoover Institution.

Hoover Institution Publication 208

To Christopher

Son, Friend, and Scholar

CONTENTS

Foreword

Imperial studies, once held in high academic esteem, have lately fallen out of favor. Yet whether for good or for ill, European empire builders helped to lay the foundations of modern Africa. Their record, and the role of their African assistants, remain to be fully evaluated. This gap the Hoover Colonial Studies series attempts partially to fill. The present series is a collection of monographs on a variety of related subjects—individual administrators like Sir Donald Cameron, African politicians like Eliud Wambu Mathu, the general history of relatively ill-documented territories like Togo, or specific socioeconomic problems such as the urban history of Elisabethville in the former Belgian Congo. To complement this project, the Colonial Studies series will provide edited versions of primary sources (diaries, letters, journals, and so on). In addition the Hoover Institution is supporting a multivolume study of the colonial military and civilian elites who ruled Africa.

David E. Skinner's work on Thomas Lawson is an important addition to the Hoover Colonial Studies series. Lawson belonged to that underdocumented and underappreciated group of Afro-Victorian civil servants and pioneers without whose insight and abilities the British could hardly have sustained their African empire. Lawson, a British-educated African, acted for more than four decades as the primary adviser to the governor of Sierra Leone on African affairs and as the effective head of the African service in that colony. His official correspondence and reports, beginning in 1846 and ending in 1889, fill thousands of pages; they provide scholars with valuable information on a vast array of political, economic, social, and administrative affairs in Sierra Leone and Guinea. Skinner's study is both a narrative and an analytical account of Lawson's family, his career in the imperial service,

and his place in African history. A sample of the
letters, reports and memoranda written by Lawson for
the colonial government is also included. These documents contribute information both on the role of the
emergent black elites and on West African history in
general.

Peter Duignan

L. H. Gann

A. H. M. Kirk-Greene

Preface

This study of the career and writings of Thomas George Lawson has been undertaken for three reasons. First, I felt that it was important to interest historians in the Lawson family, whose members are located in many coastal towns in West Africa; many of them have played important roles during the nineteenth and twentieth centuries. Second, I wanted to examine the career of Thomas George Lawson as a colonial civil servant whose role was vital to the development of British authority in Sierra Leone during the middle decades of the nineteenth century. Third, I intended to use some of the historical documents Lawson compiled to illustrate a short history of the Northern Rivers region of coastal Guinea/Sierra Leone. This region was important in the political and economic development of the Sierra Leone colony, and its leaders were influential in spreading Islam among the peoples of Sierra Leone.

A number of excellent studies have examined different aspects of colonial administration in Sierra Leone and other areas of British West Africa.[1] This study differs from others in two respects. First, it focuses on an *African* colonial official who was devoted to the expansion of British influence and control in West Africa during his long career (1846-1889). In fact, Thomas George Lawson had been recruited as an official member of the colonial service before 1846 by his employer and patron, John McCormack, a businessman who carried out missions for the government of Sierra Leone from 1815 to 1864.[2] Second, the study examines the steady, purposeful activity of British officials to extend colonial influence and control over the Sierra Leone hinterland during the nineteenth century. From the time the Colonial Office first assumed authority over Sierra Leone in 1808, British officials began expanding the role of the colony

in the interior.   McCormack and his protégé Lawson
played a crucial part in this process of expansion.

Historians and anthropologists working in Sierra
Leone have long recognized their debt to an African
colonial administrator who became intimately acquainted
with many African leaders and political systems in the
interior.   Thomas George Lawson, who was born at New
London, Little Popo (Anecho) in 1814, arrived at
Freetown, Sierra Leone in 1825 (see Map 1).   Educated
in Sierra Leone mission schools, he spent more than
forty years in the colonial service and provided invaluable data for government officials, traders, and
the Colonial Office.   His written reports amount to
tens   of   thousands of pages and contribute important
insights and background information for historians.
Lawson was particularly adept at collecting information about ruling families in the interior, much of
it based on oral traditions dating from the early
eighteenth century.   Although Lawson was a particularly valuable colonial officer, he was by no means
the only African working for the colonial government;
others were police constables, clerks, teachers, missionaries, village headmen, interpreters, judges, and
ambassadors.   The important role of Africans in colonial administration has not received the attention it
merits.   The expansion of European rule in Africa
could not have been accomplished without the services
of many African administrators and political leaders.

This study of Lawson and the colonial system is
divided into two parts.   Part one briefly describes
the development of the colony of Sierra Leone, the
history of the Lawson family, relations between
British and African leaders, and the role of T. G.
Lawson in the colonial administration.   Part two presents a very small sample of the letters, reports, and
memoranda written by T. G. Lawson for the colonial
government during his administrative career.   Most of
the documents selected focus on the states of the
Northern Rivers, an area between the Kaba (Small
Scarcies) River and Rio Nunez that was of great economic importance to the Sierra Leone colony.   They
deal with matters of trade, political relations, kinship and social life, and military affairs, and demonstrate Lawson's ability to synthesize data and provide
a basis for colonial policy and action.   Many of
Lawson's letters and memoranda focus on specific
events or matters of immediate interest to the

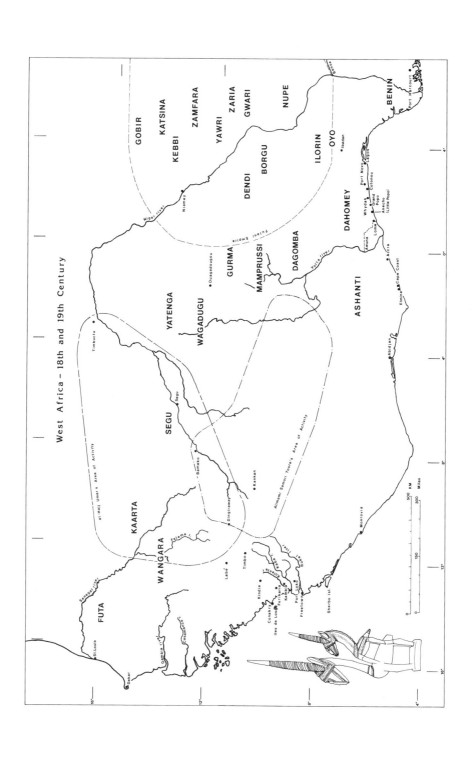

West Africa – 18th and 19th Century

government, while others are lengthy expositions on
the history of a region or an important ruling family.
Lawson provided extensive data on the founding of
states and dynasties and on political and military
conflicts in the interior. Although he did not write
a comprehensive history of the colonial hinterland,
another African civil servant, J. C. E. Parkes, in
1886-1887 summarized Lawson's political memoranda in
a report submitted to the Colonial Office by J. S.
Hay, the administrator in chief of the colony (Public
Record Office: CO 879/25/African No. 332). Printed
under the title "Information Regarding the Different
Districts and Tribes of Sierra Leone and Its Vicinity,"
the report itself is a valuable historical resource.

The present study was made possible only by the
assistance of many individuals and organizations.
Several colleagues and friends have provided inter-
views, documents, references, and advice that helped
me greatly with the study. Among those to whom I
extend my thanks are La Ray Denzer, Humphrey Fisher,
Christopher Fyfe, C. M. Fyle, Ray Ganga, Barbara
Harrell-Bond, Allen Howard, Jonathan Hyde, Marian
Johnson, Kenneth Kirkwood, Martin Klein, J. S. Koroma,
Abdul Labi, Ira Lapidus, Peter Mitchell, John Peterson,
Gladys Sheriff, M. B. Skinner, A. K. Turay, and
Alusine Yilla. I also thank the personnel of the
library, the archives, and the Institute of African
Studies at Fourah Bay College, Freetown, Sierra Leone,
for their remarkable assistance on my various trips to
Sierra Leone. I am grateful to the staffs of the
Ministry of Internal Affairs, the Ministry of Tourism,
and the District Headquarters at Kambia for their help.

I should like to express my gratitude in particular to Katherine Lincoln Bradner for making the excellent maps.

For financial assistance I am indebted to the
following institutions: The American Council of
Learned Societies, the National Endowment for the Hu-
manities, the Hoover Institution, the Social Science
Research Council, and the University of Santa Clara.

A final note of special thanks goes to Dr. Peter
Duignan of the Hoover Institution and Dr. Anthony
Kirk-Greene of St. Antony's College for their en-
couragement and guidance.

PART ONE

HISTORICAL BACKGROUND TO THE DOCUMENTS

Introduction

Sierra Leone holds a unique position in Great Britain's colonial African history. Members of the abolitionist movement in Great Britain wanted to return Africans residing in London to their native land, and the northern end of the Sierra Leone peninsula was selected as a site for their resettlement. The first colonists, who numbered 411 including British officials, embarked in 1787 and arrived at the peninsula during the summer. The initial settlement did not prosper, but its population was augmented by almost 2,000 emigrants from North America in 1792 and from Jamaica in 1800.[1] These settlers were put under the authority of the Sierra Leone Company, which had been organized by the British abolitionist movement. The colony of Sierra Leone became the center for the resettlement of all Africans taken from captured slave ships in West African waters after Britain's unilateral abolition of the trade late in 1807. At the same time the British government decided to transfer administrative authority from the company, which had governed the colony since 1787, to the Colonial Office, and Sierra Leone became a Crown colony administered by a governor and other appointed officials.

From the beginning the colony was not only a refuge for expatriate Africans and former slaves, but also a center of Christian missionary activity. The Church of England was the Established Church during the nineteenth century, and the Church Missionary Society (C.M.S.) was virtually a branch of the colonial administration. The C.M.S. was especially active in the villages of the colony and in the operation of educational facilities.[2] Many other Christian sects were also represented in the colony. The Nova Scotians (who had fought alongside the British in the North American colonies) and the Jamaicans (Maroons)

brought Christian beliefs with them, and the Wesleyans
from London and the North American Baptist missionaries were also active in Sierra Leone. The Wesleyans,
in particular, had established many schools there by
the 1830s and had greatly expanded their educational
program by the 1860s.[3]

The peninsula of Sierra Leone was an excellent
location for an anti-slave-trade colony. It was located in the midst of an old, flourishing slaving
area, with the Gallinas and Sherbro territories to
the south and the Northern Rivers up the coast. (Tasso
and Bence islands in the Sierra Leone River had had
slave factories more than a century before the settlement of Sierra Leone was established. The Sierra
Leone River provided an excellent natural harbor with
several good bays for loading and unloading ships.
The Sierra Leone Company was able to negotiate with
African rulers for land on which to locate the settlement, which was named Granville Town after Granville
Sharp, the British abolitionist. The company expected
to establish the original colonists as farmers who
would provide food for the new settlement, and they
intended the colony to become a center for trade with
African societies nearby and in the interior. Tobacco,
coffee, cotton, and rice were thought to be likely export crops, while gold, cattle, hides, and timber
could be brought from the interior for export.

Not unexpectedly, the slave factors, ship captains, and African slave traders were hostile to this
antislave settlement. These traders refused to cooperate with company officials and turned African rulers
against the settlement; this hostility often resulted
in the use of violence against company traders. The
French also perceived the location of an unofficial
British colony on the peninsula as a threat to their
operations along the coast, and their navy bombarded
Granville Town in 1794. It was rebuilt during the
same year and renamed Freetown. Local Africans who
objected to the expansion of the settlement attacked
it in 1801 with the aid of disaffected colonists and
African slave traders.[4] Despite these setbacks and
problems caused by disease and climate, the colony
gradually increased in population and began to attract
trade. The population increased dramatically after
1808 with the addition of Africans taken from captured
slave ships. Freetown, the administrative and economic center of the colony, also increased in area

and population. Growth was gradual but steady throughout the nineteenth century, as the population table
shows.

Table		
Population of Sierra Leone, 1811-1901		
Year	Freetown	Colony (including Freetown)
1811	1,917	---
1818	4,430	9,450
1826	5,790	17,354
1833	9,937	32,011
1840	13,741	42,765
1850	16,679	45,472
1860	18,035	41,624
1871	14,830	38,936
1881	21,931	60,438
1891	29,673	74,121
1901	34,284	76,237

The early settlers on the peninsula discovered
that the land was not especially suitable for the
cultivation of crops, and as the population increased,
more people turned to crafts and trade to survive.
After the early years of the nineteenth century only
a minority of the settlers were exclusively engaged
in farming, and many left the colony. Some settled
in adjacent areas, such as Sherbro or Koya. Others
went to the interior to participate in the long-
distance trading system. Many settlers, mostly those
from nearby territories but some from as far away as
Nigeria, returned to their homelands. A few were re-
enslaved, and some even became slave traders themselves. As educational and professional opportunities
increased with the development of colonial institutions, many colonists chose one of the professions
for their livelihood: the developing society required

government clerks, teachers, lawyers, and church officials. The European population of the colony remained
a very small proportion of the total throughout the
entire colonial period, so most of the professional
positions were filled by African settlers.

Most of the early colonists were Christians (but
not Anglicans) who had been exposed to the English
language. After 1807, however, the majority of settlers, who were Africans from the slave ships, were
neither Christians nor English-speakers. About 10 percent of these were of the Muslim faith, and the rest
were described by the Christian missionaries as "pagan." None of the new settlers, except those from
coastal trading societies, spoke any English. The religious and linguistic tone of the colony, however,
was set by the early colonists, the company and colony
administrators, and the Christian establishment. The
colonial institutions established early in the nineteenth century were based on English-Christian models.
The primary mission of the colony was to provide an
English-speaking, Christian environment for the liberated African population, and the principal agents in
this endeavor were the Christian missionaries.

The Christian missionaries—primarily C.M.S. and
Wesleyan ones at first—not only provided the personnel for the churches but also supplied the educational
facilities and played a major part in the administration of the liberated African villages. As the population table indicates, the majority of Africans taken
from the slave ships did not settle in Freetown. More
than eleven thousand Africans were liberated during
the first decade of the Crown colony's existence, and
Governors Thompson, Maxwell, and MacCarthy settled
most of them in villages of liberated Africans that
were located on the outskirts of Freetown or on the
hillsides of the peninsula. These villages had their
own governing institutions, churches, schools, and
farms, although they were under the direct authority
of the governor and his council.

The colony was also used as a base for Christian
missionary activities in nearby African societies. In
1799 the Christian Missionary Society was founded, and
in 1803 the C.M.S. began sending missionaries to learn
about the Susu language and culture in Dalamodiya, a
Susu town on the eastern boundary of Freetown. In
1806 the C.M.S. launched a series of mission stations

in the Northern Rivers region among the Susu, Baga, and Mandingo peoples, but that endeavor was abandoned after about thirteen years.[5] C.M.S. activities then shifted from the Northern Rivers to the Temne and Bullom territories just to the north and east of the colony, but without much better results.[6] Many mission stations were established, struggled along for a few years, and were finally abandoned, restarted or shifted to new locations without major impact on the local societies. In the colony and in the Sherbro territory to the south, on the other hand, Christian missionary work achieved positive results. There churches and schools were erected in the villages, and preachers and schoolmasters vigorously pursued missionary activities.

The majority of the "pagan" liberated Africans, who came under constant Christian influence as settlers in the Christian villages or apprentices to the colonists, were converted to Christianity. The children were sent to study in British-style schools where they learned English and received a Christian education. Although some missionaries complained about backsliders and the existence of "pagan" practices—"fetish worship," magic, ritual sacrifice, and so on—Freetown and the peninsula villages developed into strong centers of Christian worship, and many young men and women continued their religious instruction through the college level to become missionaries. From the early years of the nineteenth century, the great majority of Christian preachers, teachers, and lay officers in the colony were Africans. The demand for locally trained missionaries was recognized by the Church of England with the foundation of the Fourah Bay Institution (seminary) in 1827. This institution produced many of the colony's Christian leaders during the nineteenth century.[7]

The colony fulfilled the function assigned to it by the founders of the Sierra Leone Company by becoming a symbol of the antislavery movement. In addition to being the site of the courts of mixed commission, which from 1819 on judged the legal status of recaptured slaves, the government of the colony actively pursued an anti-slave-trade program. The governor and his agents consistently put pressure on African rulers in the interior to suppress the trade in slaves. They argued that these Africans could obtain more wealth through the promotion of legitimate trade with the

colony and with Great Britain than through the slave
trade. The colony government also brought numerous
criminal actions against suspected slave traders, who
were either liberated Africans residing in the colony
or African traders who were in the colony on business.[8]
As a result, the slave trade became more difficult to
operate, and some African rulers, who wanted to maintain good relations with the colony, suppressed or
restrained it in their territories.

The great increase in legitimate trade from the
interior and along the coast to the Colony was clearly
a factor in the development of an alternative economic
system that attracted many African traders and migratory workers. The expansion of trade during the nineteenth century was largely a result of the interest
taken by African economic and political leaders in
promoting trade with the colony. The long-distance
caravan trade was dominated by Muslim leaders to the
north and northeast of the colony, and many of the
colony's new residents, particularly between 1820 and
1880, were representatives of families who operated
the interior trading networks. Increases in population and trade required greater numbers of dockers,
laborers, craftsmen, shopkeepers, and security personnel, and Freetown became an important center for
education and employment in administration. These
factors caused additional migrations of Africans from
the hinterland to the city. By the middle of the
nineteenth century, therefore, Freetown had developed
into a small urban center that attracted increasing
numbers of migratory and permanent residents in search
of educational and employment opportunities.[9]

The settlement of more liberated Africans in
Freetown and the increased migration of Africans from
the hinterland added to the complexity of the urban
milieu. New communities evolved and urban institutions developed to meet the needs of the growing population. These communities had their religious spokes-
men, political leaders, wealthy families, professional
and economic notables, and social organizations that
functioned within the framework of the colonial system. New churches and mosques were constructed,
schools were provided for education and religious instruction, trade facilities and social services were
organized, and leadership networks were developed that
provided continuity for the communities. Sierra Leone
officials promoted contact with the leaders of these

institutions to facilitate the efficient operation of the colony's administration and economy.[10]

The expansionist colonial program that was consistently promoted by governors and other Sierra Leone officials was an important factor in the growth of population and trade. This program was clearly reflected in the elaboration of the local colonial service, especially from the mid-nineteenth century on, and in the development of a system of treaties with African rulers beginning in 1818 (this system will be discussed in Chapter two). The Colonial Office did not always sanction the aggressiveness of local officials but it usually acquiesced in the actions of governors and lesser officials. The expansion of British colonial activity and the elaboration of the local colonial service made it necessary to recruit African personnel as agents of the administration. Parliament would not allocate the tens of thousands of pounds that would have been needed to provide British personnel for the Sierra Leone Secretariat or for stations in the hinterland. British merchants or colony officials could occasionally be sent to the interior as ambassadors or mediators, but the day-to-day administrative and diplomatic functions had to be performed by African personnel who were familiar with African customs, languages, political systems, and social and economic networks. Africans thus became an integral part of the Sierra Leone colonial service. They performed many of the ordinary clerical tasks, but they also acted as ambassadors, mediators, intelligence officers, advisers, and policy makers. Sierra Leone represented the first purposeful extension of British authority over African territory, and colonial officials promoted the expansion of Christianity, the development of economic relations, the suppression of the slave trade, and the acquisition of more colonial territory. It was into this milieu that a boy named Thomas George Lawson was brought in 1825.

Chapter One

THE LAWSON FAMILY

The Lawson Family at Little Popo

George Acquatay Lawson was born in the Gold Coast area
of West Africa sometime after 1780. His exact place
of birth and the origin of the family name Lawson are
somewhat uncertain. Written sources dated from the
mid-nineteenth century identify George A. Lawson as
either a Fante from Accra or a native of Little Popo.[1]
A letter written in 1884 states that he was a nephew
of King Ashonbor Dajehu of Grigi and Little Popo and
that the king made him a captain and the protector of
English traders at Little Popo.[2] In this and another
letter in the same year George A. Lawson is called
Lattey or Lartey Aokoo. These two letters are somewhat suspect, however, for they were intended to establish that the Lawson family was subordinate to
another, more royal, family and thus to undermine the
authority of the Lawsons over Little Popo during a period of conflict over succession and control of the
political system.[3]

Linguistic evidence from the various names associated with the Lawsons indicates that the family
probably came from an area between the Accra plains
and Little Popo, and that it derived from the Ga people mixed with various other ethnic groups near the
Little Popo area.[4] Whatever the origins of the family, a number of things about George A. Lawson's life
are clear. As a boy he was taken (or sent) to England
for education. It was there that he undoubtedly acquired the name Lawson, and he may have been the
protégé of William Lawson, who was a merchant in the
Gold Coast region.[5] It was not unusual for Africans

to study in England during the eighteenth century. In
1788 there were fifty Afro-European and African children studying in the Liverpool area, while others went
to school in London and Bristol. Most of the children
were sent to England from the Windward or Gold Coasts,
and in most cases they were placed in the care of a
British captain. Other African adults and children
also made their way to England to obtain an education
or to gain an economic advantage, or simply out of
curiosity. Such exposure to English culture was
viewed as a positive experience by the merchants on
the Coast. "It has always been the Practice of Merchants and Commanders of ships trading to Africa, to
encourage the Natives to send their Children to England, as it not only conciliates their Friendship
and softens their Manners, but adds greatly to the
Security of the Trader; which answers the Purpose both
of Interest and Humanity."[6]

After receiving his formal education in England,
George A. Lawson became a steward on a slave ship. He
also acted as an interpreter for the ship's physician,
receiving a bonus for this special work. Through his
service on the ship Lawson was able to save money and
to gain a firsthand knowledge of the techniques of
trade. In about 1812 he took his savings and settled
in Little Popo. Through his knowledge and contacts he
was able to establish himself there as an important
middleman, and he built a town which he called New
London. Shortly after arriving in Little Popo he married a daughter of the king of Awuna (see Map 1) and
they had at least three sons: George Lattey, Thomas
George, and Edmund. James Lawson, a prominent merchant and leader during the mid-nineteenth century,
was probably one of several other children produced by
the couple.[7]

For about a decade George A. Lawson developed his
economic position and political authority at Little
Popo, and in 1821 he conquered the territory and established himself as king. His grandson, William T.
G. Lawson, wrote about the conquest more than sixty
years later: "I have, moreover, discovered that my
grandfather, by conquest, became the independent Sovereign of this town and the surrounding country. The
King of Gliji [Grigi], on whose signature the French
attach so much importance, and whose ancient predecessors were truly owners of the soil, is only a Lieutenant of the King of Little Popo."[8] Contemporary sources

refer to George A. Lawson as chief or king of the area,
and it is clear that the Lawsons had become the dominant trading and political family in Little Popo by
the 1840s. As traders in slaves and palm oil they became wealthy, and George Lawson raised his children to
live in a European style. Two European travelers,
John Duncan and Frederick Forbes, said that Lawson and
two of his sons lived as Englishmen, while the other
children were living as Portuguese. Duncan mentioned
that in addition to the wealth the Lawsons had accumu-
lated through slaves and palm oil, Little Popo produced
cotton and earthenware, had good farm land, and was
plentifully provided with stock.[9] Because of his early
education and experiences, George A. Lawson maintained
close ties with the British. The town of New London
flew the British flag, and British traders were favored
there. In 1852 Lawson signed an agreement with Admiral
Bruce, who was acting on behalf of the British government, to end all trade in slaves within his territory.

George Acquatay Lawson died in 1856. He was succeeded as king of Little Popo by his eldest son, George
Lattey, who continued the close ties between his family and the British until his death in June of 1860.
His successor should have been Thomas George Lawson of
Freetown, but Thomas was not interested in returning
to Little Popo; instead, he undertook the role of king
maker.[10] He was responsible for overseeing the political affairs of Little Popo until the territory came
under German control late in the 1880s.

A series of regents or temporary rulers evidently
followed George Lattey's death. A Major Lawson and an
Alexander Lawson ruled successively,[11] but after a few
years a younger son of George A. Lawson's, Edmund,
became king and provided strong leadership until his
death in 1882.[12] He may have taken the title King
George Acquatay Lawson II. King Edmund and another
Lawson, Richard, were prominent merchants during this
period, and many of the Lawson "houses" continued to
be active in trade.[13] The political autonomy of the
family was gradually eroded, however, by European com-
petition for territory. France and Germany claimed
sections of the coast as protectorates, and while the
British recognized their long-standing relationship
with Little Popo, there was little they could do to
prevent the Germans from taking control of the area.[14]

After Edmund's death in 1882 there was no immediate

successor, and political manipulation by the French
and Germans intensified political divisions. For several months the Lawson family was leaderless until the
British sent William T. G. Lawson, the eldest son of
Thomas George and an assistant colonial surveyor, to
represent his father. The family selected William as
the regent of Little Popo in the summer of 1883.[15]
Within a few months he had reunified the family, who
chose Prince Daniel C. Lawson to become the new ruler.
Daniel assumed the title King George Acquatay Lawson
III (some sources say IV) and was crowned on October 27,
1883.[16] William Lawson continued to act as the King's
principal adviser until February 1884, when the Germans forced the king to sign a trade agreement and removed William and two other counselors of the king
from the mainland, keeping them prisoners on a German
ship. Because of British intervention, the Germans
released William Lawson (a British subject) at Lagos
on the condition that he not return to Little Popo.[17]
This series of incidents terminated the direct connection betweem the British and the Lawson family of
Little Popo.

The Lawson Family in Sierra Leone

Thomas George Lawson, who was born in October
1814 at New London in Little Popo, was the second son
of George Acquatay Lawson. His mother was a member of
the royal family of Awuna.[18] At the age of eleven
Thomas George was sent by his father to England for
his education. He was entrusted to an English merchant and sailed on a British ship that made the usual
port of call at Freetown. Instead of continuing with
the ship when it sailed, however, Thomas was placed
under the care of John McCormack, a principal timber
merchant in the colony. McCormack had already lived
in Sierra Leone for eleven years and had performed
several missions for the government. He became Thomas
Lawson's patron and saw to it that the youth received
a good education in the colonial school system. After
completing his formal education Thomas was employed as
an agent and interpreter in McCormack's timber company.[19]

During his long association with McCormack, Lawson
became acquainted with many African leaders in the colonial hinterland, and he learned several of the languages spoken in their territories. He also learned
to read the Arabic script that was used for writing

many African languages and for communication between
literate Muslims. His familiarity with nearby small
states, notably Koya, Port Loko, Kafu Bullom, Loko
Masama, Marampa, and Masimera, was intimate; but he
also had dealings with merchants and leaders further
north and in the Sherbro territory to the south (see
Maps 2 and 3). On one of his visits to Koya he met a
young woman named Sarian, who was a granddaughter of
the Nem Gbanna of the kingdom. (The Nem Gbanna had
been the regent of Koya during the late eighteenth
century and head of one of the three royal families of
the kingdom.) Lawson married her and thus established
strong ties with a prominent ruling family in the
interior.

Thomas George Lawson's linguistic abilities and
his knowledge of, and contacts with, African rulers
led John McCormack to rely more and more on his judgment and services. McCormack used Lawson as his interpreter and personal representative on his missions
for the colony administration. As the colony became
increasingly involved in African affairs, a more regular system of administration was required, and
McCormack recommended his protégé to Governor Norman
William Macdonald. In 1846 Governor Macdonald began
to use Thomas Lawson as his personal messenger to
Port Loko rulers and to other African territories.[20]
Between 1846 and 1851 Lawson proved his value to the
colonial administration, and in 1851 Governor Macdonald
proposed to employ him as the first official government messenger and interpreter in the colonial secretary's office at Ł100 a year. "His duties will be to
proceed on missions to Native Chiefs at seasons of the
year when it would be impossible to send Europeans
into the Rivers, and to translate and explain to them
the contents of the letters of which he might be the
bearer. . . . also to act as Interpreter when any
Chiefs or their messengers pay official visits to the
Colony, or as occasion might require."[21] The governor
also praised Lawson highly for his honesty and good
character and for the high esteem in which African
rulers held him. Thomas George Lawson officially began receiving his salary as government messenger and
interpreter on May 1, 1852, and in one capacity or
another he was a colonial official until January 1889.
From 1854 until the end of 1860 he was also an inspector of police, and from January 1, 1861, he carried
the title, government interpreter. After 1872 he was
head of a developing African affairs bureau, and in

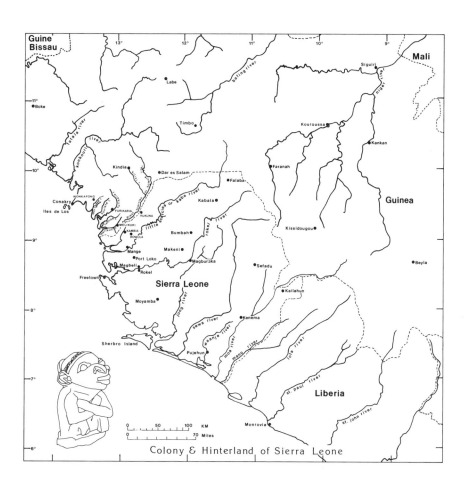

Colony & Hinterland of Sierra Leone

1878 he became the protector of government strangers
(guests) with the responsibility of providing Africans
visiting the colony on official business with food and
housing and of seeing to it that they came to no harm
from harassment or physical attack.[22] Lawson was entrusted with many important missions as the government's representative. He accompanied the many governors under whom he served on missions to the interior
where he acted as principal interpreter; he provided
the government with intelligence reports that were
based on firsthand knowledge about African territories
and families; he was the mediator between the government and African delegations who visited the colony;
and for more than forty years he was the primary adviser to the governor on African affairs and de facto
head of the African service.[23] His official reports,
letters, and memoranda, which began in 1846 and ended
in January 1889, amount to tens of thousands of pages,
and provide scholars with valuable data about many aspects of political, social, and economic affairs in
Guinea and Sierra Leone. Thomas George Lawson's activities, attitudes, and influence will be fully analyzed in Chapter two.

Thomas George Lawson's Family

Thomas George and Sarian Lawson had at least five
children. The eldest was William Thomas George Lawson,
who was born around 1840. He studied at schools in
the colony and was sent to England on a government
scholarship to complete his education. On his return
to Freetown in 1867 as a qualified civil engineer, he
was appointed to the colonial service.[24] He served as
assistant colonial surveyor in Sierra Leone beginning
January 1, 1868, and later held the same post in Lagos.
Just before his retirement to Lagos, he served as
civil engineer for the Gold Coast colony.

William T. G. Lawson was active in Sierra Leone
affairs for more than forty years. He was a strong
supporter of British colonial rule, English education,
and Christian missionary work. He made several attempts to gain control of the political system of Koya
kingdom. Between 1886 and 1890 he called himself a
chief or regent of the kingdom and made a claim for
the kingship himself. In his letter to the governor,
William Lawson described himself as a "prince" of Koya
who had been selected regent after the death of Bai

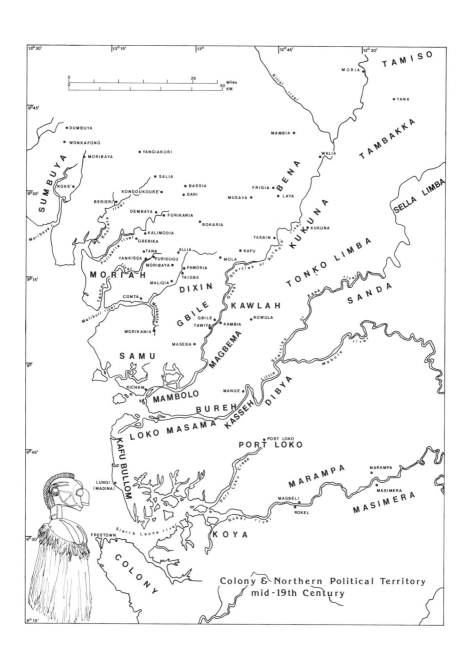

Colony & Northern Political Territory
mid-19th Century

(King) Kantah in 1872, and he claimed to be the rightful "king of Quiah." He ended his letter with a statement of loyalty to Great Britain: "I hope in the above
service to manifest that loyalty and attachment to the
British Crown which my father has done throughout his
official career and which I have always had as an example before me during my time in the Colonial service."[25] In 1890 William Lawson still claimed to rule
part of Koya by authority of the colony government,
but during that year a new king was selected and recognized by the governor. This king, who took the
title of Bai Kompa, was a bitter rival of Lawson's,
and he asked the governor to remove Lawson from Koya.

> I may inform Your Excellency that this is not
> the only instance that Lawson has attempted
> to usurp the crown of a country, he did it at
> Little Popo on the Gold Coast a few years ago
> and caused such an agitation there that the
> German Government had to remove him on board
> one of their men of war with a view to trans-
> port him to some distant place but was re-
> leased through the interference of the then
> Governor of the Gold Coast. He was at that
> time Assistant Colonial Surveyor of Lagos
> and left there and went to Popo where his
> father was born to assume the Government but
> failed.[26]

After 1890 William Lawson spent a great deal of time
in Lagos, but he visited the colony frequently and
continued to travel to Koya, where his maternal kin
resided. He often wrote letters to the *Sierra Leone
Weekly News* about colonial affairs, and in 1903 he was
still claiming ownership of villages in Koya by right
of inheritance.[27]

Another of Thomas George Lawson's sons was named
Moses Thomas George Lawson. Probably born in the late
1850s, he was educated in colony schools and at the
Fourah Bay Institution. He became the pastor of the
Church of God, a small American Baptist church that
had been founded in Freetown by John McCormack. Thomas
George Lawson had left the West African Methodist
Church to become a member of the Church of God in 1848,
and in 1864 he began serving as its manager. In May
1886 Moses Lawson married Miss Lucretia During, a
daughter of the Reverend J. During of the Niger Mission. The wedding took place in St. George's Cathredal

with the acting colonial chaplain officiating.[28] Because the Durings and the Lawsons had long been active
in colonial social life, many prominent people attended
the ceremony. Moses Lawson remained active in Freetown society until at least the second decade of the
twentieth century. During the 1890s he was the secretary of the Sierra Leone chapter of the Congo Training Institute, an educational institution located in
North Wales and financed in part by King Leopold II of
Belgium and the Congo Free State.[29] Early in the twentieth century he was also the secretary of the British
and Foreign Bible Society chapter in Sierra Leone.[30]

One of Thomas George Lawson's grandsons, James
Glynn Lawson, was sent to the Congo Training Institute
(also known as the Colwyn Bay Institute) in 1896 and
returned three years later as a qualified printer.
Later, during the 1920s and 1930s, James Lawson was a
government civil servant.[31]

Thomas George Lawson's youngest child was
Catherine Sarah Ann. She was educated at Annie Walsh
Memorial School, the leading women's secondary school
in Freetown at the time. On July 6, 1887 she married
Nicholas J. Spain, the younger brother of the colony's
postmaster, J. H. Spaine. The wedding at St. George's
Cathedral was conducted by Bishop Ingham, Reverend J.
E. Taylor (the assistant colonial chaplain), and Reverend S. Spain (the bridegroom's brother). The wedding of two members of such influential and politically active Freetown families attracted most of the
elite of the colony.[32]

There were other children in the Lawson family,
although information about them is scarce. Another
son, probably the second eldest, was named Thomas
George after his father; he died in March of 1897.
A daughter died in October 1878.[33] Perhaps this was
the daughter who married John Parker, a liberated
African who was engaged in missionary work for the
Church of God in the interior.[34]

Thomas George Lawson and his family clearly were
members of the African elite in Sierra Leone. He,
his wife, and the children about whom definite information exists played important roles in the social,
administrative, and religious affairs of the colony.
For many years Thomas George and his son William were
the two senior salaried African officers in the Sierra

Leone civil service. Thomas George retired in 1888 at
a salary of Ł350 , while William reached an annual
salary of Ł500 before retiring in 1886. Thomas George
also received compensation from the government for
looking after African ambassadors in Freetown, in addition to income from his farms in Koya. His son
Moses enjoyed high status in the colonial community
and held several responsible positions in religious
and social organizations, as I have already noted.

From the time of Thomas George Lawson's employment by John McCormack in the 1830s until well into
the twentieth century, the Lawson family was influential in the Sierra Leone colonial system. This influence was based on the very important services rendered
to the Sierra Leone government by Thomas George Lawson
over a period of forty-three years. It is doubtful
that the British would have been nearly so successful
in promoting their interests among African rulers in
the colonial hinterland without the knowledge and
devotion Lawson contributed during the formative period of African-British relations in Sierra Leone.

Chapter Two

THE COLONIAL SERVICE IN SIERRA LEONE

Development of the African Affairs Service

At the foundation of the Sierra Leone colony in 1787
and throughout the following century, the governing
agencies (the Sierra Leone Company until 1807 and then
the Colonial Office) were faced with three interrelated problems: economic viability, physical security,
and suppression or control of the slave trade. Attempts by colonial officials to deal with these problems led the government to effect closer relations with,
and gain a measure of influence over, African rulers
of coastal and interior states. To carry out its ob-
jectives, the government used its substantial economic
and military resources and developed an African affairs
branch of the colonial service. The principal mani-
festation of African-British relations was an elaborate system of treaties that was evolved to advance
British interests and influence in the hinterland.

The primary objective of colonial officials was
to obtain enough land to provide for the needs of the
early settlers and to assure control over the Sierra
Leone River. The initial treaty between company officers and African rulers was made on August 22, 1788;
through it the colony purchased land on the peninsula
and up the shore of the Sierra Leone River to Gambia
Island. The principal African signatory, the regent
Nem Gbanna of Koya, swore to keep the peace in the
neighborhood of Sierra Leone. In 1792 the colony purchased additional islands in the Sierra Leone River
from Bai Sama, the king of North Bullom.[1] By these
treaties the colony was formally created and the British entered into permanent relationships with African
political leaders.

Colonial officials quickly learned that the viability of the settlement depended on the establishment
of strong trade connections with the African states in
the interior. In 1791 the directors of the Sierra
Leone Company knew very little about affairs in that
region, but in 1794 two company agents, James Watt and
Matthew Winterbottom, were directed to travel into the
interior and establish trade relations with African
states.[2] From the coast of Guinea they traveled
through Baga and Susu territories to Timbo, the capital of Futa Jalon, and they returned by a different
route through the states of Tamiso, Tambakka, Bena,
and Moriah (see Map 3). They were well received, especially by Alimami (King) Sadu of Futa Jalon and
Alimami Mustafa Ture of Moriah, and they were able to
set up trade contacts between the colony and the interior states.[3] Sierra Leone Company reports indicate
that by 1798 trade had become substantial: about two
hundred traders were coming to Freetown each day from
as far away as eighty to one hundred miles.[4]

As the population of the colony increased, so did
the trade between Freetown and the interior. Beginning in 1808, when the liberated Africans began to
arrive, trade became a significant aspect of African-
British relations. Not only was commerce needed to
maintain the domestic economy, it also became an important factor in export-import activities. Between
1817 and 1821 both the number and the total tonnage
of ships steadily increased, while the value of im-
ports rose from ₤75,715 to ₤105,060.[5] Exports also
increased during this period: important products included rice, beeswax, logs and shingles, hides and
mats, palm oil, elephant tusks, coffee, and gold.

As trade increased, African rulers took a greater
interest in the colony. In 1824 a delegation of more
than sixty traders from Timbo arrived bearing a letter
from Alimami Abdul Qadri. Between January and April
of 1824 several hundred Fula traders came to Freetown
and spent more than ₤5,000 in gold.[6] Many other trade
delegations from coastal and interior states had already visited the colony; Susu and Mandingo traders,
in particular, had been coming in large numbers for
years, and they had established communities in and
near Freetown. Susu, Mandingo, Fula, and Sarakuli
ethnic groups provided the principal long-distance
traders in the colony during the nineteenth century,
but Temne, Bullom (Sherbro), and other peoples in the
immediate hinterland also maintained commerce.[7]

British officials hoped that the slave trade would decline as trade relations between the colony and African states developed during the nineteenth century. The establishment of Christian mission stations was another method used to suppress this commerce. Christian missionaries played an important role in administering the colony and in extending the British presence into the interior. In 1799 individuals closely connected with the founding of the colony and with the antislavery movement formed the Church Missionary Society,[8] which launched missionary efforts among the Baga and Susu in the Northern Rivers early in the nineteenth century and was largely responsible for the administration of liberated African villages in the colony. The C.M.S., the Wesleyans, and other Methodist missions dominated the educational system of the colony during the nineteenth century.[9]

The export of African slaves declined, partly because of the efforts of the British navy, but the slave trade continued and attempts to reduce or control it were met with hostility and violence by Africans and Europeans who had been profiting from the enterprise. Colonial officials accused European and African slave traders of instigating attacks on the colony by African forces in 1801 and 1802,[10] and in 1806 a prominent African landlord and trader in the colony was expelled as a suspected slave dealer and as one of those who had encouraged the attacks.[11] In 1811 officials feared another assault on the colony, but it never occurred.[12] The treatment of European traders in the interior was also affected by the hostility of slave traders. In 1814 the king of Moriah, Alimami Amara Ture, had several colonists seized along with their goods; one of them, a European named Daniel Goshel, was killed. According to Governor Maxwell this incident was instigated by American and European slave dealers who wanted to undermine the influence of the colony in important trading areas. In retaliation for these activities Governor Maxwell sent 150 troops of the Royal African Corps by ship to the Rio Pongas, where they destroyed all the American and European slave factories.[13]

The presence of slave factories was also mentioned as a possible hindrance to the development of C.M.S. missions in the Susu and Mandingo territories north of the colony, although the strength of Islam in these areas was considered a more important impediment.[14] One missionary, Reverend Hartwig, estimated

that the Mandingo trader-missionaries would bring the
entire Susu territory under Muslim control within
fifty years, and the other C.M.S. missionaries who
traveled in these territories agreed with him.[15] In
1807 another C.M.S. missionary, Reverend Renner, com-
mented: "Upon the whole they [Muslim missionaries] are
zealous in what they know and strict in observing the
doctrine of their religion. Their zeal in promoting
the cause of God and their prophet is a lesson to any
missionary if not to every Christian. It must be allowed that a true Mandingo man contents not merely to
make profession with the mouth, but he requires heart
religion too."[16]

Expanded trade relations, increased Christian
missionary activities, and the need for military security led the Sierra Leone government to seek methods
by which to establish a formal system of political relations with African rulers and economic leaders. Relations had already become fairly extensive before
1808. Several missions had been sent to the Susu and
Mandingo territories to the north of the colony, and
Arabic correspondence had been received by the governors of Sierra Leone.[17] A stipend system began that
had its roots in the customary payments made by the
colonial government to kings and chiefs in return for
the rental or purchase of land or the protection of
traders. In 1807 the government obtained formal recognition of the colony by King Farima and King Tom,
two local African rulers, in return for an annual payment of one hundred bars in goods.[18] (A bar was a unit
of measurement for the value of goods.) To promote a
systematic foreign-affairs system, the colonial government established a fund to be used for the settlement of disputes with African rulers, to pay the expenses of African representatives in the colony, and
to send government messengers to the interior. In the
1810 budget ₺400 was reserved for these functions, and
the Temne king of Koya was allocated ₺45 for his assistance to the government.[19] Thus by 1810 a foreign-
affairs budget and stipendiary system had become part
of the colonial administration.

The Sierra Leone government continued to send ex-
ploratory delegations to the interior to gather information about the political and economic conditions
there. Between 1817 and 1821 four major expeditions
were sent, led by Lt. Hokoe, Major Gray, Dr. Brian
O'Beirne, and Major Laing. Each expedition enhanced

the colony's trade position in the interior and provided valuable information about ruling families, potential alliances, and products available for trade.[20] The government made extensive use of John McCormack after he became an established trader during the second decade of the nineteenth century, and it also began to use prominent Africans as ambassadors and mediators; for example, Alimami Dala Modu (Mohammadu) Dumbaya of Madina (Lungi, Kafu Bullom kingdom) is frequently mentioned in official documents as a traveling representative of the government.[21]

The governors of the colony, who were well aware of the importance of establishing good relations with influential African rulers, endeavored to build a more regular system of foreign affairs. From 1818 on the use of treaties to acquire additional territory and to build trade contacts developed into a systematic administrative technique. The extent of colonial interest in trade and political relations is indicated by the treaty of July 6, 1818. By this treaty, which was concluded between Governor MacCarthy and Manga Demba, a king of the Baga (in modern Guinea), and signed by his subrulers and advisers, Great Britain acquired the Isles de Los off the Guinea coast. These islands had been a site for factories and trade during the height of the slave trade and continued to be an important entrepôt. An annual payment of five hundred bars to be paid in goods was the agreed price. The payments were to be made through Manga Demba's agent and relative Alimami Dala Modu Dumbuya, whose family had a claim to territorial rights on the isles.[22] Between 1818 and 1825 several other treaties were made between the government and African rulers in territories adjacent to the colony. The British acquired land and trade rights in Koya, Sherbro, the Gallinas, Port Loko, and Kafu Bullom, and they gained control over the rest of the islands in the Sierra Leone River (see Map 3). For these territorial acquisitions the government agreed to pay annual stipends ranging from 50-100 bars to three hundred Spanish dollars.[23]

A succession of governors and acting governors participated in this process of colonial expansion. In 1824 Acting Governor Hamilton submitted a trade report and map to the secretary of state for the colonies in London. He emphasized the need for regularization of relations with African states and the establishment of a British post at Port Loko. He also

advocated the creation of a customary-payment system
to reward African rulers for keeping the trade routes
open and for facilitating trade activities. The governor called for the settlement of the interior by
Sierra Leone colonists and the development of experi-
mental schemes for growing cotton, coffee, and other
crops.[24] In the following year Governor Turner reported that traders were coming to the colony from
Segu and that he had received two delegations from the
alimami of Futa Jalon. He proposed to establish a
British resident at Timbo to facilitate trade and to
make treaties with African rulers in the interior.[25]
A few months later the same governor wrote to the secretary of state: "The relations of this colony with
the adjacent nations and with the Interior are extending themselves with a rapidity which I can hardly
credit myself, although I always took leave to express
my opinion that it would soon be so."[26] It was Turner's
intention to put down the slave trade by force or
treaty and to establish firm relations with the African states along the coast and in the hinterland: "I
have little doubt but I shall have the honor ere long
to announce to your Lordship the total abolition of
the Slave Trade for 1000 miles around me, and a ten-
fold encrease to the trade of this Colony."[27] To increase British influence and control in the interior,
the governor intervened in a succession dispute at
Port Loko located about forty miles northeast of the
colony. Port Loko had been for a long time a center
of trade and a key area where many families influential in the political and economic life of the colony
resided.[28] Several of the important long-distance
trading families—some of whom were interrelated by
marriage—not only dominated the political and economic affairs of Port Loko, but also were powerful in
many territories to the north and northeast of the
colony.

The Sankoh family had been politically dominant
at Port Loko since the 1760s, but in 1815 an alliance
led by the Kamara and Bangura families terminated the
Sankoh hegemony and established a new dynasty. The
Sankoh ruler was killed in the war, but the family was
allowed to retain possession of its main town, Sendugu,
and several villages. In 1815 one of the leaders of
the revolt against the Sankoh political domination,
Moriba Kindo Bangura, was chosen alkali of Port Loko
(alkali is derived from the Arabic word for judge,
alqādī). He was a devout Muslim who had studied in

Moriah and claimed to have earned the title alkali
through his Islamic education. Alkali thus became a
title superior to alimami in the Port Loko political
system. After the death of Alkali Bangura I in the
autumn of 1825, a succession dispute developed between the supporters of Fatima Brima Kamara, an associate of Alkali Bangura, and Pa Runia Gbana, a leader
of the local Temne ruling house. Governor Turner was
determined to settle the dispute to the government's
advantage. The colony had not been able to control
the actions of Alkali Bangura, as Governor Turner explained in a dispatch to the secretary of state:

> Repeated presents had been made to the
> Chief with the view to his keeping the
> path open, but without much advantage.
> Threats had also been used, but as it
> was considered that vessels could not
> approach nearer than 40 or 50 miles to
> the town, these threats were disregarded,
> and at last they blocked up the path al-
> together. . . . it was essential that a
> well disposed person should succeed him
> [Alkali Bangura]. I determined, in or-
> der to effect this object to go up there
> myself with an armed force in the Colo-
> nial vessels and in boats. . . . The pres-
> ence of these vessels with 100 white sol-
> diers had the best effect as they always
> considered themselves secure from our
> shipping. The party against whom so much
> complaint was made for plundering the
> Foulah traders set up a Chief of their
> own and before my arrival got him ap-
> pointed successor to the late Ali Karlie,
> but in a manner at variance with the
> usual custom. This Chief had rendered
> himself very obnoxious to the Foulah King
> [of Futa Jalon], as well as to the Govern-
> ment of Sierra Leona and it was important
> that he should not be permitted to rule
> the Country.[29]

In Port Loko Governor Turner informed the assembled notables that the government of Sierra Leone
would not acknowledge Pa Runia Gbana as the new alkali
and would not maintain friendly relations with Port
Loko unless another alkali were selected. Turner
stated in his dispatch that this pressure, plus the

threat of civil war between the rival factions, induced the notables to obtain the resignation of the
new alkali and to ask the governor to select and install his replacement. The governor's dispatch
continued:

> They sent to me a Deputation with the
> Turban (there the Emblem of power) to be
> placed by me on the head of the man I
> thought most proper—and as under encreased
> trade and population of the Country they
> considered themselves incompetent to main-
> tain good order and authority, they also
> requested that their Country might be taken
> under the protection of the Government of
> Sierra Leone; to both these propositions I
> considered it my duty to accede, placing in
> authority Fatima Brama nephew and Heir to
> the last Chief, and the person generally
> considered as the proper successor; and
> drawing out and signing the accompanying
> convention which I have the honor to transmit
> to Your Lordships favourable consideration.[30]

In the ceremony of installation Governor Turner
was assisted by Alimami Dala Modu Dumbuya, a close
ally of the Sankoh family and a powerful leader who
had extensive economic interests in territories adjacent to Port Loko and in the Northern Rivers. The
convention to which Turner referred was dated December
12, 1825 and was signed by the governor, two other colonial officers, two representatives of the Barra family (the rival faction), two members of the Sankoh
family, Alkali Fatima Brima Kamara, and Alimami Dala
Modu Dumbuya. It transferred the sovereignty of Port
Loko to Great Britain in return for protection.[31] Governor Turner went on in his dispatch to say that other
rulers had petitioned the government to guarantee
peace so that trade might flourish, and he cited this
economic goal and the opportunity to promote the power
and wealth of Great Britain as the most important reasons for assuming protection over the interior. He
advocated the establishment of a system of indirect
rule based on annual stipends: "I would respectfully
submit that a small yearly Salary be given each Native
Chief, placed in charge of these Provinces or districts, from Ƀ50 to Ƀ100 a year."[32]

A year later Governor N. Campbell traveled to

Port Loko, and the convention of 1825 was ratified. Fatima Brima Kamara was formally recognized as the alkali, and the governor agreed that Sierra Leone troops could be used to enforce the alkali's rule and to keep the peace. For his part, the alkali promised to allow peaceful trade and to provide facilities for all traders who passed through Port Loko on their way to the colony, as well as to provide land for a Christian school and for a governor's residence.[33]

By the mid-1820s the pattern of African-British relations had become established. The struggle against the slave (export) trade and the promotion of legitimate commerce (together with the acquisition of land if necessary) were interrelated goals of the government. Force was used only as a last resort, although a demonstration of it was often thought to be salutary. The primary mechanism for the creation of a foreign-relations structure, however, was the treaty-and-stipend system. Through direct intervention, the use of gifts, the sending of influential ambassadors, and the promise of aid and trade, the governors of Sierra Leone built up a structure of relations with friendly African rulers.

During the early stages of this development the government operated its part of the system on an *ad hoc* basis. At times the governor personally led delegations to the interior, but usually he appointed a colonial official or European trader to represent him when negotiation of a treaty was contemplated. For trade or political matters a junior officer, a European trader, or a prominent African leader (such as Alimami Dala Modu Dumbuya) was deputized by the governor to handle colonial affairs. Colonial records at the Public Record Office in London and at the Sierra Leone Archives in Freetown indicate that no elaborate foreign-affairs organization had been developed by 1840. The colonial secretary and the governor of Sierra Leone communicated directly with African rulers and relied heavily on the knowledge and advice of African informants.[34] From the governorship of Sir Charles MacCarthy (1815-1823) until that of John Jeremie in 1841, the most frequently mentioned African adviser and ambassador used by the government was Alimami Dala Modu Dumbuya. He was a member of a politically powerful and wealthy Muslim family that had settled in the Northern Rivers territories. His grandfather had been a trader there during the eighteenth

century, and his father, Fenda Modu, had established
a political and economic base there before the 1790s.
Fenda Modu had been the principal adviser to Mungo
Simba Bangura, the king of Sumbuya and headman of
Wonkafong.[35] He had ruled a large number of villages
and towns and operated several plantations, and had
been very active in trade and in relations with the
government of Sierra Leone. Several of Fenda Modu's
sons were prominent in political and economic affairs
and dominated key commercial centers. Dala Modu first
came to the colony in 1794 with his father, and in 1801
he was sent by the Dumbuya family to settle on the
outskirts of Freetown. His town, Dalamodiya, became
a center for trade and Susu migration, and Dala Modu
acted as the principal landlord for strangers (or foreign traders) from the interior. He took the title
alimami, which he claimed was bestowed upon him in the
Moriah slave rebellion of the 1780s and 1790s. (This
title invests a Muslim notable with important political authority and is often used to indicate the position of paramount ruler.)[36]

Dala Modu and his followers were expelled from
the colony in 1806 after a trial in which he was accused of slave dealing and other activities hostile to
the colony. He moved his settlement to Lungi and named
his town Madina (town of faith). There he continued
to act as landlord for large numbers of traders who
came to the colony via the Northern Rivers: he called
himself the alimami of all strangers in the colony.
He was the most active developer of plantations in the
vicinity of the colony, providing Freetown with large
amounts of rice and other produce; his plantations,
like those of his father in the north, were worked by
slaves.[37] He also became involved in the timber trade
as an agent for Macaulay and Babington, a European
firm. After he was firmly established as a political
and economic leader at Lungi and in the colony he became virtually the king of Kafu Bullom and Loko Masama,
but his influence in the territories of Koya and Port
Loko was also extensive.[38] His family, political, and
economic connections in these small states and among
the Susu, Mandingo, and Baga territories to the north
made him an excellent choice as mediator and ambassador for the colonial government. Alimami Dala Modu
was instrumental in convincing Lieutenant Governor
H. D. Campbell in 1836 that African rulers wanted to
communicate directly with the Sierra Leone government
rather than to deal with European merchants acting as

intermediaries. They preferred to come to the colony
themselves or to send trusted messengers to meet with
the governor and other colonial officials. The use
of African delegations to the colony became particularly important during the 1830s as the treaty-and-
stipend system developed, although resident landlords
such as Dala Modu continued to be useful representatives for African rulers.

The trade-and-stipend treaty system became well
established during the 1830s. In return for an annual
payment, several chiefs and kings agreed to protect
all Muslim strangers traveling through Temne territories on their way to trade in the colony.[39] In 1841
British involvement in African affairs was extended
when African rulers agreed to allow the British mon-
arch to appoint an agent to visit and reside in Temne
territory "in order to watch over the interests of the
English people and to see that the agreement is fulfilled." The 1841 treaty continued: "Such Agent shall
always receive honour and protection in the Timmanee
Country; and the Timmanee Chief shall pay attention to
what the agent says, and the person and property of
the agent shall be sacred."[40] The series of treaties
negotiated between 1831 and 1841 created a system of
mutuality between the British and the Africans. Under
the provisions of these treaties African rulers were
responsible for protecting traders who passed through
their territories, keeping the trade roads open and
free of bandits, providing porters and facilitating
trade contacts, allowing merchants who had been certi-
fied by the colony government to set up factories
without payment of rent or customs fees (which would
be fixed and collected directly by the colony government), and permitting Christian missionaries to establish schools and churches. In return for these services, each ruler received official government recognition and an annual stipend that varied from Ł5 to
Ł50 depending on his rank and influence. Lieutenant
Governor H. D. Campbell was anxious to establish a
treaty relationship with each ruler who controlled
territory on either bank of the Rokel River to facilitate regular trade contacts with African states beyond
Koranko territory to the east of the colony. In a
dispatch to London the governor summarized the value
of a treaty he negotiated in April of 1836:

> Opening of the communications with the in-
> terior, for the introduction of British

manufactures. The authority it will give
this Government over the Native Chiefs,
and consequent protection which it will
afford to British subjects, and their property, the immense increase in the shipping
of Timber for the home market . . . and
lastly the security obtained for the re-
covery of the Liberated Africans who may be
entrapped.[41]

Two things occurred in 1841 to alter the development of a foreign affairs service in the colony.
Alimami Dala Modu Dumbuya died late in the year, and
the British government commissioner, Dr. Madden, sur-
veyed the situation in the colony. Alimami Dala Modu's
death deprived the colony's government of its principal representative to African rulers. At the same
time, Dr. Madden's official report emphasized the increasingly important role of Muslim and other African
traders to the economic development of the colony, and
he advocated the forging of close relations particularly with Mandingo, Susu, and Fula leaders. Between
1842 and 1852 there was a great increase in direct
government intervention in African affairs both to the
north and south of the colony, and treaties similar to
those made with the Temne rulers were negotiated with
Susu, Baga, Mandingo, and Sherbro leaders. Governors
W. Ferguson and N. Macdonald were especially active in
these efforts. John McCormack, the Freetown merchant,
was a useful intermediary in this process, and in 1846
his personal interpreter, Thomas George Lawson, became
Governor Macdonald's emissary. For six years Lawson
fulfilled this role, and in May 1852 he officially became government messenger and interpreter: he was the
first person to hold that position. In this post
Lawson became essentially a director of foreign affairs
and intelligence. Except for assistance from a Mandingo police officer (Momodu Yellie) and clerks in the
colonial secretary's office, Lawson was at first a
one-person department, but between 1869 and 1872 a
more vigorous philosophy of colonial expansionism
developed.

In addition to Lawson, who had long advocated a
more dynamic colonial role for Great Britain, two advisers were primarily responsible for promoting expansionism in African relations. In 1869 W. W. Reade returned from a trip to the northeast interior, and in
his report he recommended the creation of an Arabic

translation bureau and an elaboration of the stipend
system. Both recommendations were directed at improv-
ing the system of trade and enhancing communication
with rulers in the interior. In 1872 another government agent, Dr. E. W. Blyden, made similar recommendations after a trip to the north. He was particularly
interested in exploiting the resources of several influential Muslim states with which the colony had already been in contact for fifty years or more. His
ultimate aim was to extend Anglo-Christian civiliza-
tion in West Africa by using Arabic-speaking Africans
as agents of the colony government.[42]

By 1872 the Sierra Leone government had already
greatly expanded its treaty-and-stipend relations with
interior and coastal rulers, and correspondence and
direct contact with these rulers had also increased
significantly.[43] For many years Thomas Lawson had
been compiling detailed and extensive reports on many
territories, and he was the principal mediator between
the government and African leaders.[44] During 1846
Governor Macdonald had instituted a procedure requir-
ing stipendiary chiefs to visit Freetown, where they
were housed and fed by the government. It was his intention to show African rulers that they were subordinate to the colony's government and that they were
being paid their annual stipend as agents of the government. His statement to the secretary of state makes
his administrative policy quite clear: "It is therefore high time . . . to shew him [Alimami Amara Modu
Dumbuya of Madina] and all neighbouring Chiefs that
the Government of the Colony is paramount and they
must bow to it."[45] The governor recommended that except in cases where matters could be settled by letter, African rulers should be summoned to Freetown for
discussions, a procedure that would demonstrate their
relationship with the colony. Although some rulers
did travel to Freetown from time to time (usually to
increase their influence with the government), they
normally sent special ambassadors to collect their
stipends and to deliver messages to the governor. The
government also continued to send ambassadors—both
European and African—to negotiate with African leaders and to pay stipends. Occasionally governors of
the colony would travel to the interior to settle
major disputes, install a king (as at Port Loko), or
make new treaties. By the early 1870s, however, relations had expanded to the point where a more regular, institutionalized system was necessary.

Regularization began with the appointment of an
official protector of strangers by Governor A. Kennedy
in 1871. The position went to a prominent Aku trader,
George Metzger Macaulay, who was also an assistant to
Thomas G. Lawson, the government interpreter. In 1872
the governor increased the African affairs staff by
appointing a Muslim scholar, Alfa Mohammed Sanusi, to
be government Arabic letter writer. In 1876 the
loosely structured African affairs staff was organized
into the Aborigines Branch of the Colonial Secretariat,
and from that time Thomas Lawson was de facto head of
an African affairs department, which consisted of Alfa
Sanusi as first Arabic writer, Momodu Wakka as second
Arabic writer and assistant messenger and interpreter,
G. M. Macaulay as assistant interpreter, and an office
clerk. Sanusi and Macaulay were both Aku (descendents
of liberated Africans), while Wakka was a Mandingo
whose family lived in Timbo, Futa Jalon. In 1878
Macaulay resigned his post and was replaced as messenger and assistant interpreter by Sanoko Maddi (Mahdi),
a Mandingo from Dingiraway: Lawson then became protector of strangers. Lawson began collecting his reports
and memoranda in leather-bound volumes in 1873, and
beginning in 1878 translations and copies of Arabic
letters were also maintained by the African affairs
department. The collection of Lawson's writing was
ended with his second retirement in January 1889, but
the Arabic letters were recorded until 1901.[46] After
Lawson's retirement, J. C. Parkes, a Sierra Leonean
with long experience in the colonial service, became
director of the Native Affairs Department, which was
responsible for the day-to-day relations with African
rulers until the creation in 1898 of the protectorate
administrative service, which used British district
commissioners.

Promotion of British Interests in the Interior

Government policy during the administration of
the Sierra Leone Company and the British colonial era
was directed towards the promotion of British interests and the legitimation of the British presence in
Sierra Leone and the interior. To achieve these ends
the African affairs service and the treaty-and-stipend
system were developed. The primary function of the
African affairs service was to gather intelligence information about African states. To promote British
interests it was necessary for the senior government

officials to have accurate information about African
political systems, kinship relations, economic resources, possible trade routes, and the potential for
conflicts or alliances between neighboring states, and
the reports submitted by government agents provided
the colonial government with invaluable data on African political and social affairs. A second key function of this service was to legitimize British political and economic activities. As I mentioned earlier,
the frequent missions sent by the Sierra Leone government to the interior often resulted in trade agreements, concessions for Christian mission stations, and
the acquisition of territory.

　　The mission of Dr. Brian O'Beirne, assistant
staff surgeon, is a fine example of both functions.
In January 1821 O'Beirne embarked on a trade mission
to Timbo via Port Loko, Kukuna, and the Kolente River
route (see Maps 2 and 3). At his first stop in Port
Loko O'Beirne informed Alkali Moriba Kindo Bangura I
that the governor "wished to consider him the Principal Agent between [the Fula] and the Colony of Sierra
Leone."[47] O'Beirne demonstrated the government's respect for the alkali by firing three volleys of shot
and presenting him with gifts of a piece of blue baft
cloth, eight bars of tobacco, and a keg of rum.
O'Beirne conferred with the alkali and other leaders
of Port Loko, and they approved his mission to the
interior. For the next stage of his journey O'Beirne
was entrusted "to Loosani [al-Husain], on who he [the
Alkali] laid strict instructions to conduct me safely
to his Brother Jacoba [Yaqub], a Chief of Kookoonah.[48]
In Kukuna O'Beirne was received by the headman,
Alimami Fasinneh, the leader of the powerful Dumbuya
family there, to whom he delivered an Arabic letter
from his kinsman Alimami Dala Modu Dumbuya of Madina.
O'Beirne was thus attempting to establish the government's credibility with powerful leaders in the interior. Kukuna was a large, prosperous, and important
Muslim town located on a key trade route to the northeast (see Map 3). Alimami Fasinneh's status required
O'Beirne to present him with a sword meant for the
prime minister of Timbo. As in Port Loko, an assembly
of notables was convened, and the meeting was opened
with a prayer and a reading from the Quran. O'Beirne
displayed the gifts to be presented to the Alimami and
his leading advisers. O'Beirne's mission was then explained and after discussion by the assembled elders
it was approved. Alimami Fasinneh's brother, Modi

Mohammadu, and his son, Brahma, were selected to accompany O'Beirne to Timbo. O'Beirne's party took the
route from Kukuna through Tambakka, but the passage
was not an easy one. Serious difficulty developed between the party and the king of Tambakka, Kande
Ansumana Bugaro. Three of O'Beirne's advisers informed him that Kande Bugaro was a close ally of
Alimami Omaru (Amara) Ture of Moriah, who was angry
because the trade mission had not passed through his
territory on its way to Timbo. After giving additional
presents to Kande Bugaro and others and with the assistance of O'Beirne's advisers, who included the
brother of the king of Tamiso, the members of the mission were able to leave the town of Yana in Tambakka
and pass on to Tamiso, a Susu territory within the
sphere of influence of Futa Jalon. Passing through
Tamiso presented no problems, and the delegation arrived safely at Timbo, where O'Beirne was received
graciously by the king, Alimami Abdul Qadri.

At a meeting between O'Beirne and Abdul Qadri,
the alimami very strongly supported the opening of
regular trade between his country (along with Bure
and Segu to the east) and Sierra Leone. He promised
to keep the route between Timbo and Kukuna open and
expressed the hope that the colonial government could
do the same for the route between Freetown and Kukuna.
At Timbo O'Beirne saw many traders from Segu and noted
that there were abundant cattle, rice, and gold there
for trade. The delegation stayed at Timbo from March
11-24, and O'Beirne had several audiences with Abdul
Qadri. To enhance the prestige of the government
O'Beirne gave Qadri several fine presents, including
a silk umbrella, a double-barreled fowling peice, a
fine trunk, twenty dollars, and a silver snuff box.
Before allowing O'Beirne to leave, the alimami sent
his messengers ahead with an Arabic letter to prepare
for the mission's journey back to Kukuna, and he sent
his nephew along on the return trip as his personal
representative, with an Arabic letter addressed to the
governor of Sierra Leone. The alimami gave O'Beirne
three gold rings as a departing gift, and in return
O'Beirne placed his watch and chain around the king's
neck. The journey back to Kukuna was not delayed by
hostilities and the mission arrived at Port Loko without incident, accompanied by a large caravan of traders (including approximately 150 Fula with horses,
cattle, and sheep for the Freetown market) that had
joined it along the way. At Port Loko O'Beirne held

a feast for Alimami Abdul Qadri's nephew and for
O'Beirne's advisers from Tamiso, Kukuna, and Port Loko.
At an assembly of notables he formally introduced them
to Alkali Moriba Kindo Bangura I of Port Loko. After
the festivities and the formal reception the party embarked in two boats for Freetown. O'Beirne, Lieutenant
Laing, and the principal African representatives sailed
in the governor's barge, which had been sent for them.
Captain Grant, the Honorable Kenneth Macaulay (the
senior member of the governor's council), and other
dignitaries met the party in Freetown, and the African
delegation was formally introduced. O'Beirne concluded his journal thus: "The path leading from Port
Loco to Teembo may always be considered as in our hands
as long as we possess the interest and protection of
those by whom the persons just named were sent to
Sierra Leone."[49]

O'Beirne's trade mission was not unlike many
others the government sent out between 1794 and 1872.
The elaborate ritual included recruiting guides and
advisers from the notable families along the route,
procuring Arabic letters of introduction (passports),
bearing gifts to pay the necessary *bunyah* (presents that
indicated the government's respect for rulers and notables), formally meeting with assembled rulers to present gifts and explain the purposes of the mission,
and obtaining permission and protection to undertake
the next stage of the journey. Some missions, including those of Governor Turner and Governor N. Campbell
to Port Loko in the 1820s, led to an extension of
British authority over political and trade affairs and
to the acquisition of, or control over, land. Pure
trade missions seldom involved the formal signing of
treaties, but the establishment of political relations
was recorded and acknowledged by the principal authorities. Trade missions were designed to obtain information about routes, products, and the state of politics and war.

Colonial missions were sent also to settle disputes that had been interfering with trade with Freetown, that had led to the destruction of property
owned by British subjects, or that were in violation
of treaty provisions. Such disputes set in motion a
regularized diplomatic process. The initial step was
to send a government messenger to the interior with a
letter from the governor or colonial secretary. In
serious cases the messenger might be an important

African leader, a military officer of the colony, or
an influential European merchant. Effective mediators
for the government included people like Alimami Dala
Modu Dumbuya who had close kinship ties and economic
contacts in the affected regions. John McCormack,
who had extensive experience and influence in the interior, was also very helpful to the colony, and African and European traders established in interior centers often aided the government as intelligence
officers or mediators. Later in the century, T. G.
Lawson and his assistants provided the government with
an institutionalized diplomatic service. When a show
of force was considered necessary by government officials, a military officer was often sent as messenger.

Not infrequently, the colonial government used
threats of force or actual force to settle disputes
or to punish Africans who had disrupted trade or harmed
the property or persons of British subjects. The attack by government forces on the Rio Pongas factories
in 1814 is an example of the use of force as a warning
to potential disrupters of trade; and Governor Turner's
precedent-setting political/military expedition to
Port Loko in 1825 was a not-so-subtle hint that the
colony could use force when it was needed to promote
British interests. As a key inland trading port, Port
Loko was vitally important to the economy of Sierra
Leone; from the crowning of Alkali Fatima Brima Kamara
in 1825 to that of Alkali Moriba Bangura III in 1885,
a colony governor or his representative was present
at every crowning ceremony in Port Loko during the
nineteenth century.[50] The government consistently insisted on claiming that area as part of the colonial
territory—bound to Sierra Leone by a series of treaties made with several alkali.[51] The government often
reminded the alkali of their responsibilities under
these treaties, used them and their forces to keep the
peace and protect trade routes, and threatened to withhold the annual stipend unless provisions of the treaties were fulfilled.[52] For example, in December 1836
Lieutenant Governor H. D. Campbell instructed the
alkali to take his army into Limba territory and attack a town where trade was being impeded. The governor sent the alkali powder and balls for his muskets
and told him to kill or capture all the men who were
involved in the banditry and "to clear the road of
troublesome people."[53] In another incident, in 1841,
the colonial secretary informed the alkali that interference with the C.M.S. missionaries at Port Loko was

contrary to the treaty signed by Governor Jeremie, Alkali Namina Modu Bangura, and other rulers in that year. The missionaries, he said, "are not to be interfered with or molested on any account whatever nor will the Government permit them to be troubled."[54] In his letter to the alkali, Namina Modu Bangura, Colonial Secretary N. Macdonald summarized the purpose of the treaty system:

> You cannot expect that the English Government will expend such large sums of money as it has done in making Treaties with you and other Chiefs, for your good and benefit, and for the improvement of your Country and people without receiving any benefit from such expenditure, and that it will tacitly permit the Treaties there entered into, to be broken whenever it suits your interest to do so. . . . The Government is determined to enforce due respect to the Treaties, and as it will strictly act up to whatever it is bound to do by these Treaties, so it will at any cost compel the other parties to them to respect them also.[55]

The alkali of Port Loko and the alimami of Madina (Lungi) were only two of numerous African rulers who were incorporated into this foreign affairs system.[56] Many Africans became strong allies of the colony and acted as its agents and ambassadors. Others, who impeded trade or began wars in key areas, were punished. When Alimami Momodu Sankoh of Sendugu in Port Loko territory attacked Port Loko with the aid of Alimami Kala Modu Dumbuya of Madina in 1858, the government assisted the alkali of Port Loko and his allies in expelling the Sankoh-Dumbuya forces. By order of the government Momodu Sankoh and Kala Modu Dumbuya were sent into exile in the Northern Rivers, Dumbuya to Sumbuya and Sankoh to Moriah (see Map 3). A government treaty effected in 1860, signed by Alimami Fenda Sanusi Modu of Madina for the Dumbuya family and by Sadu Kamara and Kindo Bangura as representatives of Port Loko, reinstated Momodu Sankoh at Sendugu.[57]

Direct or indirect intervention to promote British interests was not uncommon. During the period 1854-1859 the government became deeply involved in a serious trade dispute in Moriah. In November 1854 the ruler of Maligia, Alimami Mori Mina Lahai Tarawali,

ordered all trade between his people and European traders on the Melikuri River stopped because he suspected
that the Europeans were interfering with domestic slavery. Even before this act the Europeans had complained
about the loss of their goods through theft. As a result of their precipitous expulsion in November, several traders were unable to remove their goods from
the area and they were destroyed or stolen. The traders appealed to Acting Governor Dougan for relief.
His first step was to send a peaceful mission to con-
fer with Alimami Mori Lahai, who refused to meet with
Dougan's messengers. The acting governor next sent a
military force of about 450 troops on three ships to
Maligia, whereupon the alimami met with the messengers
and agreed to compensate the traders for their losses.
Dougan ascribed the success of the mission to the show
of force: "but for the imposing force brought to bear
on the King's Town a very different result would have
followed."[58] The Colonial Office in London approved of
Dougan's methods and results: "The expedition appears
to have been conducted with much discretion as well as
success, and I have learnt with satisfaction that the
objects of it were attained without any collision having taken place, and that it had led to a revival of
the trade which had been stopped."[59]

By May 1855, however, it was clear that Alimami
Mori Lahai was not going to abide by the agreement, so
Dougan sent another expedition of some two hundred
troops by ship to destroy Maligia. The town was attacked and destroyed by fire on May 22, but while the
troops were burning it, they were driven off by a surprise counterattack. Many were shot and others drowned
when a boat capsized. Altogether among the government
troops there were seventy-four killed, twelve wounded,
and one missing. This disaster was followed by another
expedition sent to explore the possibility of negotiating the release of prisoners of war and settling the
trade dispute by peaceful means. Dougan instructed
the commanding officer "to avoid overtures to [Mori
Lahai], and to be careful, lest, by an act of his, the
chief should be led in the slightest way to imagine
that he was seeking to conciliate him; a course, which,
while it might give him an idea of weakness on our
part, would also tend to lower the dignity of this government."[60] The result of this mission was an immediate reopening of trade, but Alimami Mori Lahai refused
to compensate the traders. Dougan's advisers argued
that Mori Lahai and his superior, Alimami Fode Wise

Ture, king of Moriah, wanted peace and trade because food was scarce, manpower was required for the planting season, the cost of keeping warriors was too high, and their slaves intended to flee to the British warships. A temporary peace was reached, but in 1856 Acting Governor Dougan was suspended "for having, when acting-Governor, on the 21st day of May 1855, without authority and on insufficient grounds, sent an expedition against the Moriah Chiefs in the Mellicourie River beyond the Colony with order to burn or destroy the town of Malageah, planned without foresight or judgment, disastrous in its termination, and disgraceful to the British power."[61]

Disturbances continued in the Northern Rivers, however, unassisted by Dougan's presence. The key trading center of Kambia on the Kolente River had long been a place of conflict between the Mandingo-Susu forces controlled by, or allied with, Moriah and those of the Temne king, Bai Farima, of Magbema. Sattan Lahai Ture, an important military official and ally of Alimami Amara Ture of Moriah,[62] had contended with the Temne for control of the lower Kolente River early in the nineteenth century. His son, Alimami Sattan Lahai, created a small kingdom known as Kawlah with its capital at Rowula. He also claimed authority over Kambia, and like his father he was allied with the king of Moriah, at that time (1852-1862) Alimami Fode Wise Ture. In May 1856 Kambia was attacked by the Mandingo-Susu forces, and the factories of British subjects were raided and their goods stolen. The attackers occupied Kambia. The main leaders implicated in the attack were Alimami Sattan Lahai, Alimami Fode Wise, Alimami Ansumana b. (in Arabic genealogies "b." stands for "ibn," which means "son of"), Sanasi Tarawali (the successor to Mori Lahai at Maligia), and Alkali Buru Lahai Sankoh of Taigbe (Melikuri), all of whom had treaty agreements with the government of Sierra Leone. As a result, Governor Hill withheld the stipends due each of these rulers and recommended that the British attack Furikaria, the capital of Moriah.[63] As an alternative to directly attacking Furikaria, the government sent a combined force of Temne warriors and former slaves led by Lamina Bilali (a powerful warrior chief and escaped slave who had been opposing the Mandingo-Susu forces since the 1830s) to destroy the army occupying Kambia and kill its leaders. War continued throughout 1857, and during that year a British trader was killed. Governor Hill went to the Kolente

River by ship in 1858, but no settlement was reached.
On February 1, 1858, a government attack was directed
against Kambia, and the town was destroyed by rockets.
Governor Hill felt that this would teach hostile African leaders that they could not break their treaty
obligations. "The unfortunate and disgraceful result
of the expedition sent to Malageah in the year 1855
engendered a feeling of contempt for British power on
this part of the Coast, and nothing less than the lesson they have now received would satisfy the Soosoos
of their weakness when contending against disciplined
men well armed and properly led."[64]

As in many previous government actions, however,
the attack did not resolve the war. It continued into
1859 and was viewed by Sierra Leone government officials as a threat to the colony's expanding sphere of
influence. Governor Hill linked the attack on Kambia
and its occupation to the Susu attack on Port Loko by
the forces of Momodu Sankoh and Alimami Kala Modu
Dumbuya in 1858. In March 1859 the British again bombarded Kambia and gave further military assistance to
the Temne forces. Although the Susu-Mandingo force
held Kambia for more than a year, the Temne gradually
gained the upper hand. The Sierra Leone government
was able to effect a peace treaty between the contending forces in 1861.[65]

This "Susu-Temne" war was only one of a series of
wars in the Northern Rivers that involved trade, territory, and domestic slavery during the eighteenth and
nineteenth centuries (see Chapter three for more information on the Northern Rivers). The Sierra Leone
government frequently took an interest in such wars
because it could support African rulers who were considered pro-British and thereby protect British trading interests. Acting Governor Dougan was suspended
not because he had used force to enforce the provisions of treaties with northern leaders, but because
he had failed so disastrously in the attempt. The
history of African-British relations in the interior
is marked by bold, aggressive action taken on the ini-
tiative of colonial governors during the nineteenth
century. Such action was not always in accord with
Colonial Office policy in London, but governors continued to forge their own policies and to carry out
decisions taken by previous governors. African rulers
were not informed when a treaty was rejected, in whole
or in part, by the Colonial Office; instead, governors

consistently reminded these rulers of their obligations and the rights of the British under the provisions of the—sometimes invalid—treaties.[66]

The Role of Thomas George Lawson
in the African Affairs Service

One of the most dedicated, forthright colonial
expansionists in the Sierra Leone service was T. G.
Lawson, who was a colonial official from 1846 to 1889.
He came from a strongly pro-British family, and his
education and experiences in Sierra Leone reinforced
this attitude. He was emotionally attached to John
McCormack, his patron and mentor in the colony. When
McCormack organized the Assembly of God (American
Baptist) Church in Freetown in 1848, Lawson left the
Methodist Church to become a member. In 1862, two
years before McCormack's death, Lawson became the man-
ager of the Assembly of God; he was also a lay preacher.

By 1860 T. G. Lawson had decided to become a
naturalized citizen of Great Britain, and in 1861 he
offered his family's territory at Little Popo as a
colony for Great Britain.[67] Although Lawson continued
to refer to himself as an African, he clearly thought
of himself as an agent of Christianity and of the
British empire. His attitudes are expressed unambigu-
ously in the many reports and letters he wrote between
1846 and 1889 (see the documents in Part two for selec-
tions of his reports written between 1873 and 1888). In
1863, for example, he was sent by Governor Blackall to
the Moriah kingdom to free a young nephew of Bai
Farima (the king of Magbema) from slavery. In his report to the governor, Lawson wrote:

> I then stated that Your Excellency did not
> send me up to make a bargain or arrange-
> ment with them for the boy . . . . I then
> brought to their recollections many past
> acts of kindness and friendship done for
> them and their country by Your Excellency's
> Predecessor as well as yourself, in recov-
> ering not less than 24 of their principal
> Chiefs and principal heirs of their Coun-
> try from slavery (some of whom were pres-
> ent at the Meeting) from the Timmanees,
> Kossohs and Limbahs, and that for all this
> Your Excellency's Government never asked

of them so much as a farthing; and that
simply to give up one boy to Your Excellency they thought hard to do![68]

A few years later, in 1868, when he was sent on a mission to the Gold Coast, he said to his mother's brother,
the king of Awuna, "that he should thank the Whiteman
for having sent me his sister's son to see him; and
that the Whiteman came for the good of his Country.
The King then said that he would believe what the
Whiteman would say to him as they have brought with
them his own sister's son, who would not deceive him."[69]
Lawson was proud of his position in the government
service, and frequently emphasized his role as an
African agent of the British empire sent by the government to deal with African leaders.

He also felt that his opinions and activities
were well regarded by governors and other colonial
officials, and he was confident that his proposals
concerning colonial policy would be given serious
attention. In 1872 he was sent on one of his fact-
finding missions to the Northern Rivers to investi-
gate the possibility of negotiating a peace there
and to revive trade contacts that had been severed
because of the long period of conflict between the
Mandingo-Susu states and the Temne and Limba territories. His report concluded:

I may further observe that what has been
reported in the petition of the British
Traders in the Great Scarcies River has
been confirmed entirely by the movements
of Bey Farrimah and Allimamy Bokarry [of
Moriah]. Although they spoke well and
pleasingly yet I could not see any thing
by which I can confidently say that they
have no intention to fight, but the immediate and necessary steps which His Excellency has taken, if pressed and supported,
will prevent the war and thus save for the
benefit of Commerce about 600,000 bushels
of Ground Nuts and 200,000 to 300,000 bush-
of Benni seeds, besides other valuable produce and articles of trade, and to secure
the trade from the interior, I would strongly
and respectfully recommend that Treaties be
entered into without delay with the following Chiefs from whose Countries a large

> amount of trade comes to Kambia and to this
> Settlement and through which Caravans pass
> to Kambia and this Settlement with articles
> of trade independent of the Sierra Leone
> River.[70]

Lawson then listed the principal rulers of the region
and the amount of the stipend each of them should be
paid by the government, the total expense being £97.10.
As a matter of fact, governors who served during the
1870s did make a vigorous effort to incorporate the
Northern Rivers into the British colonial system (see
Chapter three).

Because of the close relationships Lawson developed with many governors, he was used more and more
during his many years of successful service to travel
in West Africa, to explain government policy, to medi-
ate disputes and maintain the treaty system, and to
make accurate and detailed reports for the governors,
who then forwarded them to the Colonial Office in
London. By performing these services over a long
period of time Lawson essentially became the foreign
secretary of the Sierra Leone government. Not only
did he travel throughout the hinterland of the colony,
he was also sent on two occasions to the Gold/Cape
Coast region on government business.[71] In addition, he
accompanied various governors and other high colony
officers on important missions to make treaties and
settle wars as their principal interpreter and political adviser (see Political Affairs in Part
two).

Another of his important functions was to receive,
and tend to the needs of, African rulers or their representatives when they came to Freetown. As the protector of strangers in the colony from 1878 on, he saw
to their housing, food, and safety; but he had already
become the official government link with African rulers
in the colony before that year.[72] Furthermore, Lawson
kept careful records of the number of caravans arriving in Freetown or nearby ports and provided a descrip-
tion of the types of goods brought for sale or trade.
He also collected information about trade and political conditions in the interior from the African notables who visited Freetown, and he was responsible for
sending his subordinates on government missions and
debriefing them upon their return to the colony.[73] Because of his extensive contact with Muslim rulers and

his knowledge of Arabic, he was also the government's representative to the Muslim communities in the colony, and he developed a good working relationship with them (see T. G. Lawson's Attitude and Role in Part two). Muslim leaders in Freetown usually directed their petitions or requests to Lawson and used him as a key mediator with the governor.[74]

From 1846, when he became Governor N. Macdonald's trusted messenger, until his retirement, Thomas George Lawson served in thirty-three government administrations. During that entire period he was very highly regarded by colony officials and African leaders. To the Africans he met in connection with his official duties he emphasized his African origins and his kinship (by marriage) with one of the royal families of Koya. To British officials he repeatedly demonstrated his loyalty and attachment to queen and empire. He was a consistent exponent of the expansion of British influence and authority in the interior, and he was always alert to the possibility of French inroads in the British sphere of influence. He opposed, for example, the establishment of a Catholic mission in Port Loko because he felt that the missionaries would be agents of the French government. Sierra Leone colonial officials highly valued Lawson's knowledge of the interior and his services to the government. In 1861 Governor Hill wrote to the secretary of state for the colonies: "Mr. Lawson bears a high moral character; he is a diligent zealous public servant, and most truthful, and I, therefore, beg to solicit Your Grace's favourable consideration of the enclosed petition."[75] The government administrator referred to Lawson in 1884 as "the Government confidential adviser in Native Matters."[76]

In 1886 Lawson decided to retire because of poor health, and Governor Rowe applied to the Colonial Office for his pension of £198.6.8 per annum and a gratuity of £100. In his dispatch the governor strongly praised Lawson's service to the colonial government:

> I have been in no hurry to get rid of his
> service. I should scarcely have completed
> the work I have lately done without his
> help and though other Interpreters will be
> found it will be long before anyone holds
> the position of confidence in the estima-
> tion of the neighbouring natives which he

has gained and which I believe him to
justly merit.

I do hope that Your Lordship may be
pleased to show some special mark of
appreciation of the services rendered
by Mr. Lawson. They stand, I believe,
alone and without equal in the history
of Her Majesty's Settlements on this
Coast.[77]

The Colonial Office granted Lawson his full retirement
pension, but the Ł100 gratuity was not allowed. Instead, a silver chain and plaque were sent as gifts
from Queen Victoria to be presented to Lawson at a
public ceremony. The presentation was made on September 24, 1886, at the Court Hall. Several hundred people attended the ceremony, including many important
African leaders, colonial officers, representatives of
the Christian and Islamic faiths, and businessmen.
Governor Hay presented the award and said:

During this period, I may say a life time,
he has by his strict integrity and unswerv-
ing loyalty combined with a most conscien-
tious discharge of his duties, deservedly
earned the respect and esteem of all with
whom he has come into contact. In addition,
he has won that which is always most pre-
cious to every loyal subject, the approba-
tion of his Sovereign, and Her Majesty has
been graciously pleased to sanction the presentation to him of a distinctive mark of
Her appreciation of his services.[78]

At the ceremony other colony officers also expressed
their opinions of Lawson's role in government:

His services and information are most valuable to all Governors and I can only hope
that in his retirement his long and great
experience in the service will be placed
still at their disposal and they will always be pleased to hear his opinion on
matters affecting the Colony.[79]

Since 1879 it has been my duty and pleasure
to associate myself with Mr. Lawson who has
been the referee and adviser on all matters

> relating to the Aborigines who visit this
> Settlement or are in any way connected
> with it. . . . Mr. Lawson has given each
> and all of us unalloyed pleasure, [and] we
> regard it as a fitting recognition and re-
> ward of long, staunch, and unwavering loyal
> service, and we are pleased and proud to be
> here today to witness this ceremony.[80]

To these accolades Thomas Lawson responded:

> I thank you for your kindness in being pres-
> ent here this afternoon. I was glad when
> the Administrator informed me of this recog-
> nition by Her Majesty the Queen of Her high
> approbation of my services. I wish to point
> to you all my children, the necessity of per-
> severance, obedience and submission in every
> thing you do, and not to be looking here and
> looking there. You all know I am now grey
> haired and it is now 61 years this year since
> I came to this Country and I have never seen
> such a thing done like the honor conferred
> on me today. We speak of celebrating the
> Centenary [of the colony] next year, and al-
> though the time is not yet come I believe we
> begin to feel its good. Do, my children and
> friends, I beg you to be obedient, persever-
> ing, faithful and submissive. And none here
> I think can doubt the success attending obe-
> dience, faithfulness and submission.[81]

After all the celebration, Thomas George Lawson
did not retire in 1886. He was too valuable to the
government and too wedded to his job. He continued
as government interpreter and African affairs adviser
for another twenty-eight months. Governor Hay wrote
to the Colonial Office that it would be impossible to
replace Lawson in his capacity as adviser and mediator
when he finally retired at the end of 1888. The position of government interpreter was abolished, and
J. C. E. Parkes, a young Sierra Leonean with prior
experience as a government agent in the interior, was
named head of the Aborigines (later, Native Affairs)
Department. Thomas Lawson did not end his connection
with the government. He continued to act as landlord
for Africans who came to Freetown on colonial business
or for trade, and he was an unofficial adviser to both
Africans and the government.

In 1888 Governor Hay summed up Lawson's value to Great Britain in his dispatch to London: "Mr. Lawson has expressed his willingness to give the Government the benefit of his advice and assistance [for] as long as he is spared [from death], an offer which might have been expected from this long tried and valued public servant, whose record from the year 1846 has been one of unimpeachable loyalty and devotion to his Queen and Country."[82]

SIERRA LEONE

IN THE TWENTY-THIRD YEAR OF THE REIGN
OF HER MAJESTY

QUEEN VICTORIA,

ALEXANDER FITZJAMES,
ACTING GOVERNOR.
(9TH APRIL, 1860.)

At a Council held on the Ninth day of April, in the year of our Lord One thousand, eight hundred and sixty.

AN ORDINANCE for the Naturalization of THOMAS GEORGE LAWSON, in the Colony of Sierra Leone.

WHEREAS THOMAS GEORGE LAWSON, a native of Little Popo, the son of the late Chief of that place. came to this Colony in the year 1826, is now Inspector of Police and Government Interpreter, and it being expedient that there should be removed from him (within the Colony) the disabilities to which aliens are by Law subject: Be it therefore enacted by the Governor and Council of Sierra Leone as follows:

I. That the said THOMAS GEORGE LAWSON shall be to all intents and purposes whatsoever, within the Colony of Sierra Leone and the Dependencies thereof, from the taking effect of this Ordinance, entitled to the rights of a natural born subject of Her Majesty, in like manner as if he had been born within the Realm of England.

2.

II. This Ordinance shall not come into operation until it shall have received the Royal confirmation, and the said THOMAS GEORGE LAWSON shall have taken the oath of allegiance to Her Majesty the Queen of England, nor until such confirmation shall have been notified by order of the Governor for the time being, Proclamation or other Public Notice.

A. FITZJAMES,
Acting Governor.

Passed in the Legislative Council this Ninth day of April, the year of our Lord, One thousand eight hundred and sixty.

ROWLAND DAVIES,
Acting Clerk of Council.

Freetown, Sierra Leone.
April 29th 1870.

Translation of a Letter written in Arabic to His Excellency
the Governor in Chief, from Fodey Talwaray [Tarawali] the Chief
High Priest of the whole of the Moriah Country, residing at
Gbeleh Great Scarcies; translated by Mahomed Sanasee, Native of
this Colony residing at Stephen Street, Fullah Town, Freetown;
received on the 28th instant.

Praise be to God, through his praise, and Praise and Peace
to the good creature of God, Mahomed, God's praise and peace be
to him.

This Letter [is] from me God's Servant, whose name is Fodey
Talwaray [Tarawali] of Gbeleh to the King (or Governor) of Sierra
Leone, the just [and] the good, and peace [be] among all people.

I wish to inform you that we are quite well and in good
health, and [I hope] you and all of your people are enjoying the
same. Praise be to God for this.

My reason of writing this letter is that you should know and
believe that the bearer of this letter is my son, whom I send to
pay my respectful compliments to you. When you went to Fouricaria to make the Peace between the Family [brothers] and all the
people of the Country, to cease from war and its evils, and you
never cease[d] till the whole of the land is now at perfect peace
and tranquility and in unity and love one with another, [and]
everyone returns to their Native residence because of you. [When]
we heard and have seen the same, [then] we love[d] and admire[d]
it very much and more; [and we would have loved to imitate that
again and again], but God has not given us the power.

At this time the whole of the country [has] joined and
agreed [on a single authority], except [for] very few. Take
notice, Oh King (or Governor) of Sierra Leone, that God has commanded us to make Peace among all people, and you have made
[peace in] our Country as God commanded [us to do]. This is the
reason I send this my son to express my Love, Honor and Thanks to
you that you may know that my heart is free towards [attached to]
you at all times, on account of your just[ness], goodness, and
quieting the Country [your making the country peaceful]; God
loves the Peacemakers instead of those who act to the contrary.
This is my [purpose of writing to] you.

[Also] I send by this my son to you as a present 4 sheep.
The name of this my son is Fodey Luseny [al-Husain], whom I sent
to be present with Allimamy Bocaria [al-Bukhari] at Fouricaria
when they shook hands [to help to settle things].

Left: Shaikhu Luseni Tarawali, a principal informant and political leader of Gbile; and a grandson of Fode Ibrahim Tarawali. *Right:* al-Hajj Muhammad Sanasi Fofana, a principal informant in Gbile.

al-Hajj Muhammad Sanusi Sesay, Imam of the Tawiya mosque, and his wife.

The town mosque at Tawiya.

A mosque in Rokupr, near Kambia.

The town mosque at Kambia.

The Njai family mosque in Kambia.

Chapter Three

THE NORTHERN RIVERS STATES AND
BRITISH COLONIAL EXPANSION

Introduction

Beginning with the foundation of the Sierra Leone
settlement in 1787 and continuing throughout the next
century, the British were economically and politically
involved in the region they called the Northern Rivers
(known by the French as Rivières du Sud). The region
between the Kaba (Small Scarcies) River and the Rio
Nunez had long been an intensive trading area not only
for the British but for other European merchants as
well,[1] and the settlement at Sierra Leone transformed
the area into an especially vital resource that contributed to the economic viability of the colony. During the nineteenth century the territories from Sumbuya
south to Kambia on the Kolente (Great Scarcies) River
were particularly important to the economic and political stability of Sierra Leone. This region, which
included states as far as ninety to one hundred miles
inland, has a complex political history that has not
been analyzed in detail.[2]

Unlike kingdoms such as Ghana and Mali, the Northern Rivers did not undergo political centralization,
even though the area had come under strong Mande influence by the eighteenth century. For a very long
period Mande migrations had been occurring as a result
of the disintegration of the political system of Ghana,
the expansion of the Mali empire, and the development
of the Atlantic slave trade. Mande traders, warriors,
craftsmen, Muslim missionaries, and their kinsmen had
been moving westward in small groups. Along their
migratory routes they built communities, intermarried
with (and sometimes conquered) indigenous peoples,
attracted additional migrants, and sent out agents

who continued the process. Gradually, an interlocking
trade network developed from the interior to the Atlantic. The Mande had certainly pushed to the coast
by the fifteenth century, and the increasing amount of
trade with Europe by the late sixteenth century provided further incentive for settlement.

Both trade and Islam were key factors enhancing
the influence of Mande groups. As the *jula* (*dyula* and
yula are variant spellings), clusters of kin groups
among the Mande who specialized in long-distance trade,
sought new markets, they extended their trade contacts
throughout West Africa. They brought new sources of
wealth into communities, acted as landlords and middle-
men, and became prominent in the political life of
their new settlements.[3] The jula were closely associated with groups of *marabūt*, traveling Muslim missionaries who were often called *mori* by the Mande, and some
jula kin groups produced both trading and religious
specialists. One Mande kin group, the Jakhanke, was
composed largely of Muslim clerics and traders. The
Jakhanke very likely was formed through intermarriage
between different Mande peoples during the latter period of the Ghana empire. Jakhanke informants trace
the homeland of their ancestors to Ja or Jakha in
Masina.[4] Muslim missionaries, however, were not necessarily connected with trading activities. They had
their own ideology that caused them to be fervent pros-
elytizers, and they frequently used their specialized
religious and literary skills to promote their own
well-being and obtain a livelihood. Their skills included specialized knowledge about medicine, spiritu-
alism, education, religious rituals designed to bring
health and wealth to the local population, political
mediation and advice, and letter writing. In addition,
trade caravans and trade centers operated by other
Mande increased the missionaries' financial possibili-
ties and provided them with bases for building up self-
sufficient Muslim communities. The traders encouraged
the settlement and activities of the mori because they
needed the religious guidance and services they provided; and the mori often assisted the traders to become members of the local political elite. Thus, the
jula and mori strengthened each other and enhanced
the position of Mande communities in areas removed
from their powerful political centers in the interior
of West Africa.[5]

This process of settlement and community building
led to the formation of many small states (as in the

Senegambia) that were located along the long-distance
trade routes. The existence of such communities in
the Northern Rivers by the late sixteenth century is
confirmed by the information of the Portuguese missionary Fr. Barreira, who visited the Kolente River in
1602. He found there the small Muslim Susu state of
Bena, located about forty-five miles inland and just
north of the river (see Map 3).[6] This Susu community
was a vanguard of the migrations that had been pushing
toward the Northern Rivers coast. Successive migrations of other Susu, Sarakuli, and Maninka groups supplanted or intermarried with the indigenous peoples,
and new oral histories of migration and settlement became dominant. Most of the families prominent in the
eighteenth and nineteenth centuries had settled in the
region after the mid-seventeenth century.[7]

Settlement of Mande Families, c. 1680-1750

Several Mande kin groups settled in the Northern
Rivers region during the late seventeenth and early
eighteenth centuries; developed economic, political,
religious, and military power; and formed a series of
small states of considerable importance in the region
until the French and British consolidated their colonial systems at the end of the nineteenth century.
Some of these kin groups migrated separately and established distinct communities, but as a result of
intermarriage and increased settlement many families
and communities contained representatives of several
Mande kin groups. Among the important Mande families
who have resided in the Northern Rivers for more than
250 years are the Ture, Fofana/Tarawali, Yansane,
Sankoh/Yilla, Konte, Bangura, Kamara, Suma, Kebe,
Silla, and Dumbuya/Koroma. Some of these—especially
the Fofana, Kebe, and Silla families—are known primarily for their Islamic scholarship and teaching,
while others have a long history of trading and political activity.

According to oral traditions and written sources,
the Ture, Fofana, and Yansane families arrived in the
Northern Rivers as a single immigrant group. The
three main leaders of this group are identified as
Fode Mamudu Katibi Ture, Fode Abu Bakari Yansane, and
Fode Abu Bakari Fofana. ("Fode" is a religious title
indicating that a person has been educated to teach
others about Islam.) It is said that these men—more

likely their forefathers—and their followers had migrated together from Hoummi via Futa Toro to Futa
Jalon and then to the kingdom of Tambakka southwest of
Tamiso. At Tambakka they became the guests of the
king, Mangaba Ninson Mambi Kamara. [8] According to tradition, their party contained a large number of families, amounting to "almost an army," and brought sixty
loads of books, many goats, sheep, cattle, and horses.
In Tambakka these Mande strangers built the village of
Moriadi (Small Moriah) on the Kolente River (see Map 3).
After residing there for some time the king of Tambakka
summoned them and asked who was their leader. Abu
Bakari Yansane named Fode Mamudu Katibi Ture as the
political leader and Fode Abu Bakari Fofana as the
marabūt. At a grand assembly of the notables of Tambakka, Tamiso, and Kukundia (small Kukuna, a small
state to the east of Tamiso), the king praised the economic assistance, the Muslim teaching, and the good
conduct of his guests. As a token of his appreciation
he gave his daughter in marriage to Fode Mamudu Katibi
Ture. The marriage prospered and the couple had many
children. [9]

Several years later the king, Mangaba Ninson Mambi
Kamara, died and was succeeded by his younger brother,
Ninson Manson. At this point Fode Mamudu Katibi Ture
led a westward migration of his family, some of the
disinherited children of Mangaba Ninson Mambi, and the
families of Fode Abu Bakari Yansane and Fode Abu Bakari
Fofana. Some of the children of Fode Mamudu Katibi
Ture remained in Tambakka and Tamiso. Along their
westward route the migrants founded or conquered towns
and settled in them. Sons of Mangaba Ninson Mambi
settled at the villages of Mambia (near the Kilissi
River), Wossoya, Frigia, Yangiakuri, Kiria, Dumbuya,
Walia (in Bena), Mola, and Kafu. Those who remained
with Fode Mamudu Katibi Ture traveled to Kuyeya and
Furidugu and drove out the Mandeyi. Before these conflicts occurred, the Yansane faction of the party had
settled at Laya in Bena and in Taigbe on the Melikuri
River, where they drove out the Mandeyi or Bullom
residents.

The Ture and Fofana factions continued their set-
tlement of the area they called Moriah or Kisi Kisi.
In their travels they entered what was then part of
Bena territory. Fulfilling a prophecy made by Fode
Abu Bakari Fofana, the party crossed the Furikaria
River at the place where the village of Koyandalu was

situated. There they killed a doe and offered its leg
to the head of the Yansane family at Laya who ate it:
according to the prophecy this meant that the Ture
would replace the Yansane as rulers of the area. The
village of Koyandalu was renamed Fode Katibia after
Fode Mamudu Katibi Ture; later it came to be known as
Furikaria. Fode Mamudu Katibi's sons and younger
brothers were installed in several towns in the region,
among them Moribaya, Gberika, Bassia, Dari, Tana, and
Dembaya. His eldest son and successor as head of the
family, Manga Abu Bakari Ture, had already established
his base at Yankissa.

        According to oral tradition, Laya had been founded
by Mori Lahai Saliu Yansane, a son of Fode Abu Bakari
Yansane. Other towns founded by the Yansane family
were Furidugu (by Salmata Modu Yansane) and Kalimodia
(by Kali Modu Yansane, probably a grandson of Fode Abu
Bakari). The family was also prominent at Taigbe and
Furikaria. Although the Ture and Yansane families became rivals for the economic and political control of
Moriah and adjacent territories, they also maintained
close personal ties, and marriages between the two
groups were frequent. One important marriage was that
between Famoro Ture, a son of Worogbe Demba (Fode
Mamudu Katibi's younger brother), and Mema Yansane
from Taigbe. The town in which they and their descendants settled is known as Famoria. A second prominent
marriage between the two families took place during
the mid-eighteenth century when a Ture from Furikaria
married a Yansane woman from Laya. Their son, Sattan
Lahai Ture, became a great warrior (*kelitigi*) during
the reign of Alimami Amara Ture, king of Moriah (1803-
1826), and his son, Alimami Sattan Lahai Ture, founded
a political dynasty at Rowula, south of the Kolente
River.

        The third kin group associated with this Mande
migration, the Fofana, also continued to play an important role in Moriah and nearby territories. The
missionary/scholar Fode Abu Bakari Fofana resided in
Furikaria, and many of his descendants continued to
live there as advisers to the Ture. A branch of the
Fofana family, led by Maligi Fantumany Tarawali,
founded Maligia, which became a major political center
in Moriah during the eighteenth century. Two other
members of the kin group became prominent leaders in
territories south of Moriah: Konditu Modu Fofana migrated to Port Loko, probably before 1820, and his

younger brother, Ibrahim Tarawali, was established at
Gbile, just across the Kolente River from Kambia, during the 1830s. Both the Yansane and the Fofana families were deeply involved in the political, military,
and religious affairs of Moriah during the eighteenth
and nineteenth centuries.

The migration of the Ture, Fofana, and Yansane
families occurred sometime between 1680 and 1720, and
Moriah was founded around 1720, with Fode Mamudu Katibi
Ture as its first paramount leader. There may have
been several migrations rather than the one mentioned
in the oral traditions. The Yansane may very well
have entered the region prior to the Ture, as the
prophecy of Fode Abu Bakari Fofana indicated. In any
event, it is clear that the migrants were moving into
territories occupied by other Mande and non-Mande
groups. Bena was already dominated by Muslim Susu,
perhaps by the Suma kin group, and the oral and written traditions show that wars of conquest against the
Mandeyi/Bullom and Baga/Temne coincided with the migrations. Many Bullom moved south along the coast
into Samu, and the Baga were forced to the north. Oral
traditions indicate that the Temne originally occupied
the Melikuri River area and that the Temne of Dixin
are a remnant of that group. In the nineteenth century the Temne attempted to regain territory in Moriah
that had been lost to the Mande settlers.

Besides the Suma, other Susu kin groups had probably settled in the Northern Rivers before the Ture-
Yansane-Fofana migrations. One such group, the Bangura,
settled in Wonkafong, which became the capital of the
small state of Sumbuya.[10] A second Susu kin group
that settled in the Northern Rivers before the eighteenth century was the Sankoh. Three members of this
jula family came to the coast from the interior of
Guinea; they and their descendants founded many towns
and villages in the region. One of the three, Bai
Fereh, settled at Taigbe, which the Ture-Yansane-Fofana
migrants found already in existence, according to tradition. Two of the important eighteenth-century headmen of Taigbe were Ibrahima Sankoh and Buru Lahai
Sankoh. Between 1750 and 1760 the Sankoh of Taigbe
imposed their rule on Port Loko, and three Sankoh alimami governed the area during the eighteenth century.
Around 1800 a son of Buru Lahai Sankoh, Brima Konkori,
became alimami, but he was overthrown by a combined
Temne-Susu army in 1815. The family was allowed to

keep its villages near Port Loko, however, and the
Sankoh retained considerable political influence and
economic power in the area.[11] Another of the original
Sankoh migrants, Fode Mamudu, settled in Magbema near
the Kolente River. His son, Bai Potho, and many grandsons founded several villages that became centers of
trade and Islam in the region: one of the most important was Tawiya, founded during the eighteenth century
by one of Fode Mamudu's sons or by a grandson, Fori
Sineh Sankoh. Other important towns where members of
the Sankoh family settled were Conta, Robissi, and
Masebah.

Another very influential jula kin group that migrated into the Northern Rivers during the eighteenth
century was the Dumbuya family. Its members have been
identified as descendants of Fa Koli Koroma, a nephew
of the Sosso leader Sumanoro, who nevertheless supported Sundiata Keita of Mali in the thirteenth century. Although they were originally Sarakuli, the
Dumbuya now identify themselves as Susu. There are
two distinct branches of the Dumbuya group in the
Northern Rivers. Although no precise genealogy indicating their relationship exists, both groups claim to
have migrated from Bambuk and a reconstruction of their
genealogical charts suggests that they were once part
of a common migratory group. A British colonial officer and an excellent historian, E. F. Sayers, collected
oral traditions of the Dumbuya at Kukuna in the 1920s
(see Map 1):

> Dumbwiya is one of the Susu appellations of
> the clan better known elsehwere as Koroma.
> . . . They are perhaps of Serakholé origin
> and go back to the days of the pre and post
> Islamic empire of Ghana or Walata which lay
> to the North of the upper Senegal and to
> the W[est] of the middle Niger [River]. . . .
> The known ancestors of Dumbwiya of Bramaia
> [Kukuna Chiefdom] were Koroma from Bambouk,
> the country to the south of Kayes, and
> bounded by the R. Faluné [Faleme River] to
> the West [and by] the Upper Senegal to the
> East. . . . They came down it would seem
> under the leadership of Faran Lahai, or per-
> haps an earlier ancestor, and kept at first
> to the West bank of the Kolente.[12]

Commissioner Sayers's report and oral traditions

recently collected indicate that Faran Lahai founded
the towns of Laya and Tassin in Bena territory.[13] Although these traditions conflict somewhat with those
of the Yansane, Dumbuya lineages are prominent in both
towns. According to the oral sources, descendants of
Faran Lahai continued their migrations to the Melikuri
River, where they found a headman named Ibrahima Sankoh
at Taigbe. From there some migrated to Tawiya, where
Sankoh were in residence, passed on to Kambia and built
a Dumbuya section of the town, and finally migrated
eastward to a heavily forested area inhabited by Mandeyi, whom they expelled. Two grandsons of Faran Lahai,
Wule Brahima and Wule Maligi, and their followers built
the town of Kukuna and several neighboring villages.
Genealogical dating and comparison with other oral traditions indicate that Kukuna was probably founded between 1730 and 1750.[14] The Dumbuya settlement at Laya
may be provisionally dated before 1700—roughly con-
temporaneous with the Yansane settlement there. Including the brothers Wule Brahima and Wule Maligi,
there have been fifteen or sixteen kings (entitled
alimami or *kandeh*) of Kukuna since the eighteenth
century.[15]

The second Dumbuya kin group that traces itself
back to Bambuk is the Dumbuya family of Bolobinneh
(near Conakry) and Lungi (in Kafu Bullom). The first
Dumbuya definitely associated with coastal Guinea near
Conakry was Fenda Muhammadu (Modu), who settled there
around 1770. Oral sources, however, state that Fenda
Modu's father, among other Dumbuya, was a prominent
trader in Sumbuya before Fenda Modu arrived and that
he died there. It is likely that these Dumbuya were
members of the Faran Lahai party which dispersed toward the coast around 1700. Fenda Modu, who was also
a trader, came to Sumbuya with several sons, the eldest of whom was Dala Muhammadu (Modu). By the 1780s
the Dumbuya were well established as traders and landlords in Wonkafong, Bolobinneh, and other villages
where they owned plantations serviced by slave labor.
Fenda Modu developed close relations with the Sierra
Leone Company during the 1790s, and Dala Modu became
the chief Dumbuya—and Susu—trading agent in the colony in 1801. He became one of the most influential
African leaders in the area of the colony during the
first half of the nineteenth century, and his successors continued to exercise considerable authority in
two small kingdoms, Kafu Bullom and Loko Masama, from
their base at Lungi. Fenda Modu raised the standing

of the family in the Northern Rivers. He became the
virtual king of Sumbuya around 1800 and was even suggested as a candidate for the kingship of Moriah, if
he wanted to usurp the Ture right of succession there.
Both he and his son Dala Modu are cited by European
sources as powerful leaders in the northern territories.[16] They and their successors maintained very close
contact with each other and cooperated in economic and
political matters. The Sierra Leone government used
the Dumbuya of Kukuna, Bolobinneh, and Lungi as primary economic and political contacts throughout the
nineteenth century.

The kin groups described above were only a few of
the many Mande families that settled in the Northern
Rivers region during the seventeenth and eighteenth
centuries. It is said that the Konte helped to found
Berieri, to the north of Furikaria, and that the Suma
settled in Musaya in Bena country. The Sise, Silla,
Kebe, Kamara, Traore, and Kaloko also founded villages
throughout the region. By the middle of the eighteenth
century a distinctive political system had been established that later developed close relations with the
Sierra Leone colony.

Society and Polity in the Northern Rivers

The migrants who settled in the Northern Rivers
were traders, Muslim missionaries, and warriors. Many
of the dominant kin groups there are identified as
jula (long-distance traders) or as belonging to the
yula "tribes."[17] The Kamara, Yansane, Fofana, Sankoh,
and Dumbuya are most frequently identified as yula by
informants. As the migrants entered the region, they
conquered, intermarried with, or settled among the indigenous peoples. Over time, several small states developed that supplanted or built upon the foundations
of previous petty states. A city-state system evolved
that was based on long-distance trade and agriculture.
Each of these small states was composed of a central
town and subsidiary towns and villages, and each was
dominated by one or two kin groups who formed the
aristocracy. This aristocracy, composed of primarily
traders and Muslim missionaries, possessed military
forces that were used to protect the migrants and their
trade caravans, and were useful in extending the migrants' control over new territory. Not all settlement,
however, was a result of war. Strangers often sought

the permission and protection of local rulers before settling in an area, and intermarriage of elite groups was not uncommon. The Dumbuya kin group of Bolobinneh in Sumbuya, for example, was related by marriage to the Baga king, Manga Demba, the Bangura family of Wonkafong, and the Bai Sherbro (Kamara) family of Kafu Bullom. The long-distance traders and Muslim mission-aries were highly regarded as possessors of wealth or special skills, and they were rewarded with grants of land, marriage into the elite families, and political positions.

These states were usually small in land area (from 150 to 1,000 square miles) and population (from ten thousand to more than sixty thousand), although the rulers of Moriah, as we shall see, attempted to create a fairly sizable kingdom north and south of the Kolente River after the mid-eighteenth century. They were centers of trade located on established caravan routes between the interior and the coast. Many were acces-sible from the coast via river boats or small sailing vessels. In addition, these states had an agricul-tural base, and they traded a considerable amount of their own produce, particularly rice, groundnuts, palm nuts and oil, benni seed, and some tobacco and cotton. They were also transit ports for livestock, hides, gold, ivory, and other items from the interior. Fenda Modu Dumbuya's plantations, for example, are reported to have yielded one hundred tons of rice and one hun-dred tons of salt each year. He owned nine towns and villages in Sumbuya and was the kingdom's most influ-ential political leader.[18]

The slave trade was an additional economic re-source in the region until well into the nineteenth century, and the majority of agricultural laborers in the states were slaves. Estimates of the slave popu-lation of Moriah run as high as 80 percent of the total population in the nineteenth century, although this figure cannot be verified.[19] Except for household servants, who often were integrated into the kin group, the slaves lived in farm-villages called *dakha* by the Susu. They farmed land for their masters and also had plots of land reserved for their personal use. The produce of the farms was transported to the owners for their own use and for trade to other Africans and Eu-ropeans. Some of this produce, particularly rice, was imported by the colony of Sierra Leone. Plantation slaves were bought and sold: there was a flourishing

trade in them between the Northern Rivers and the
Mende and Sherbro areas south of the colony. The
status of slave was inherited by the children, and
slaves were seldom freed. Household slaves, who were
often considered clients or junior members of the kin
group, were not sold. Furthermore, the children of a
slave concubine and a freeman usually were considered
to have the status of the father. It is not easy to
ascertain from the sources how slaves were treated in
these states, but several slave revolts were recorded.
A major revolt occurred in Moriah during the late
eighteenth century: the slaves established a refuge
at Yangiakuri for a time before they were defeated.[20]
Slaves also attempted to escape, particularly after
the Sierra Leone colony was founded, and many of them
fled to the slave sanctuary of Lamina Bilali in Tonko
Limba between 1838 and the 1880s.[21]

    Not all labor was carried out by slaves. Many
kin groups worked their own farms, particularly if
they were not members of the ruling elite. The crafts
were controlled by freemen who were organized into
guilds. Leatherworkers were especially respected because they were credited with Quranic knowledge and
skill in making Arabic charms. The important political, economic, military, and religious roles were dominated by a few kin groups. The main town and subsidiary towns of a state were usually ruled by a single
extended kin group, although specialized roles—such
as fode (religious leader or scribe), kelitigi (warrior chief), and santigi (subchief or adviser)—might
be filled by other kin groups. In some of these
states political power was shared by two kin groups,
as in Taigbe (Sankoh and Yansane) and Laya (Yansane
and Dumbuya). The town of Kambia, located on the
Kolente River, was also an exception: there several
kin groups vied for control. Kambia was a key center
of trade between the interior and the coast and between the Northern Rivers and Freetown, and it attracted and was settled by many jula and Muslim families. Its economic and strategic importance involved
the town in several wars during the eighteenth and
nineteenth centuries, as different political interests
attempted to gain control over the territory. In the
1750s, for example, the king of Moriah, Mangaba Abu
Bakari Ture, launched a *jihad* to promote Islam and to
extend his rule to include the Kolente River area.[22]
This pattern of conflict was often followed during
the nineteenth century.

The populations of these states were politically
and socially stratified. The central town of each
state was headed by an alimami or kandeh (roughly
equivalent to king). Subsidiary towns and villages
were led by alkali. The alimami were assisted by
santigi, ministers, kelitigi (warrior chiefs), and
fode, who formed a council of advisers. These were
hereditary positions, and the few kin groups who dominated them formed an aristocracy. Below this elite
were traders who were not members of aristocratic families, craftsmen, free peasants, household slaves, and
plantation slaves. Strangers who migrated into the
region (these were usually of Fula or Mande origin)
were integrated into the social system according to
their wealth, kinship status, and Islamic educational
attainment. The position of alimami was generally
passed down to the next eldest brother or to the eldest son, although in some states (see the king list
for Kukuna in the Appendix) two houses of two kin
groups held the position alternately. Sometimes, of
course, succeeding generations produced several candidates for the position, and civil war resulted in many
instances.

By the mid-eighteenth century the major centers
of political power in the Northern Rivers were Tamiso,
Tambakka, Bena, Kukuna, Sumbuya, Berieri, Taigbe, and
Furikaria (see Map 3). Port Loko to the south had
been an important trading port for some time. The
different centers were connected through kinship or
marriage, and they were closely tied into the long-
distance trade network, but they had their own dynasties, hierarchies, and sociopolitical institutions.
The migrations of the late seventeenth and early eighteenth centuries did not immediately alter the city-
state pattern of government, but they did cause an increase in the Mande population, and they ultimately
led to serious attempts to build centralized kingdoms
similar to Mande political systems found elsewhere in
West Africa.[23] Two holy wars reported to have occurred
during the eighteenth century were attempts at state
building. Lahai Salieu Yansane, the son of Fode Abu
Bakari Yansane, launched a jihad from his base at Laya
early in the eighteenth century in an attempt to promote Islam and gain more territory.[24] This evidently
occurred before the establishment of the Ture settlement at Furikaria; and the thrust of the jihad was to
the west, to incorporate the area around the Melikuri
and Furikaria rivers into the Bena political system.

Two informants related that the Ture had taken the
Moriah area from the Yansane early in the eighteenth
century, and another described the Yansane as the
"Ground Kings of Moriah," which would indicate that
they had settled there before the Ture.[25] Furthermore,
all written and oral sources agree that the Yansane
and other jula kin groups were responsible for crowning the new alimami of Moriah, and that when a Ture
candidate attempted to proclaim himself alimami without strong jula support, civil war inevitably ensued,
as was the case in 1862-1869.[26]

The second jihad mentioned in the sources was led
during the 1750s by Mangaba Abu Bakari Ture of Yankissa,
a son of Fode Mamudu Katibi Ture. This was probably
the war that extended the authority of the Ture
throughout the Moriah area between Sumbuya and the
Kolente River and encroached on the territory of Bena.
It is also undoubtedly the war to which the tradition
of usurpation of Yansane authority refers.[27] Although
Fode Mamudu Katibi may have founded the Ture dynasty
at Furikaria as early as 1700-1720, Mangaba Abu Bakari
may be considered the first of the Ture alimami of
Moriah, who exercised authority over that state from
the mid-eighteenth century until the consolidation of
French colonial rule during the 1880s. Political control by the Ture was not absolute during this period,
however, for three reasons. First, the transition
from a former alimami to a new one usually entailed
intense rivalry for the position among the different
branches of the Ture kin group. There were several
Ture centers of power in Moriah. Among the most important were Furikaria (the capital), Yankissa,
Gberika, Moribaya, Famoria, and Tana (see Map 3).
Furikaria and Yankissa provided the leading candidates
initially, but senior kinsmen from Gberika and Moribaya
also claimed a right to the position of alimami, and
in 1827 Ali Gberika Ture became alimami. Alimami
Mustafa Ture and Alimami Ali Gberika Ture were both from
Gberika.[28] Such rivalries allowed different factions
within Moriah (and even in neighboring states) to back
their candidates and to manipulate the political situation, weakening the power of the successful candidate.

Second, the pre-Moriah city-state system continued to limit the power of the Ture alimami. Within
Moriah, the towns of Taigbe, Kalimodia, Maligia, and
Berieri were political centers of non-Ture kin groups,
and they resisted attempts by the Ture to establish

absolutist rule. These towns were also the centers of
the yula tribes who had the responsibility of crowning
the new alimami. To protect their local authority and
defend their positions as king makers, the leaders of
these centers often led dissident movements to prevent
an uncrowned or autocratic alimami from exercising authority. In addition, the yula tribes were represented in neighboring states, and they often intervened in Moriah affairs when an alimami threatened the
autonomy of their territories.[29] Thus, the Dumbuya
families of Bolobinneh, Lungi, and Kukuna; the Sankoh
families of Tawiya and Port Loko; the Yansane family
of Laya; and the Tarawali and Fofana families of Gbile
and Port Loko were intimately involved in the affairs
of Moriah. Furthermore, the political leaders of
still other kin groups in neighboring states also intervened in the politics of Moriah. The kings and
town headmen of Tambakka, Bena, Tonko Limba, Kawlah,
Magbema, Samu, Dixin, Sumbuya, Mambolo, Bureh, and
Port Loko played a part, from time to time, in settling
political disputes there. These states were often directly or indirectly involved in the Moriah civil wars
or wars of expansion during the nineteenth century.[30]

Third, the French and British governments became
increasingly active in the Northern Rivers region during the nineteenth century, and they frequently interfered with or influenced the processes of succession
and intervened in disputes that caused property damage
or inhibited trade. The alimami of Moriah—along with
leaders of other states—found that their authority to
govern independently was becoming circumscribed by actions taken by European strangers. This occurred repeatedly from the 1840s to the end of the century—
whenever a civil war erupted or the Bilali-Susu war
started again. On several occasions the region from
the colony and Port Loko north to Sumbuya and Bena was
involved in such conflicts.[31]

Despite the wars of expansion—including the holy
wars mentioned above—trade and Islam provided the
basis for intercommunity and interethnic contact in
the states north of the colony. Trade brought wealth
into these states, and political leaders and trading
families encouraged the development of institutions
and agencies that would facilitate it. Factories,
goods, and caravan routes were protected from robbers;
landlords offered their services to strangers; bearers
and guides were provided from town to town; and the

political leaders and trading families established
close relations with the merchants in the colony and
with the Sierra Leone government. Many leading political and jula families had agents who resided permanently in the colony and acted as brokers, landlords,
and ambassadors.[32] It was to their advantage to promote peaceful trade and to help punish those who disrupted trading activities in the interior. A vast
trading network developed during the eighteenth and
nineteenth centuries that fulfilled these functions.

Muslim teachings and missionaries also played a
significant role in the development of interethnic and
intercommunal contact. By its very nature Islam in-
volves missionary activity. The concept of jihad means
not only holy war, but also zeal and exertion by a
Muslim to spread Islam, primarily through teaching and
preaching. Wherever the marabūt settled, he founded
a primary school for the study of the Quran, performed
the required rituals, and offered his specialized
skills to the indigenous population. His political
and economic connections, literary knowledge, and per-
formance of religious services (which included making
charms for protection from evil or disaster and performing ceremonies of prophecy or divination) made the
marabūt a valuable asset to the local notable, warrior,
and even the peasant. Muslim traders and missionaries
intermarried with local notable families, and the fode
were used by rulers as political and religious advisers, scribes, and teachers for their children.

To serve the growing Muslim communities, the rulers and marabūt established schools, mosques, and
prayer fields.[33] The daily prayers and Friday midday
sermon were observed, the fast of Ramadan and its feast
day and other important feast days were celebrated,
the religious tax (zakāh) was collected for the needy,
and special sacrifices were made to Allah for the welfare of the communities. In 1796 the Swedish botanist
Adam Afzelius observed the fast-breaking ceremonies
led by Sattan Tumany Tarawali at Maligia:

> Santantumany was not present at first, but
> as soon as he had arrived with his retenue,
> consisting of the high priest and some other
> eminent persons, to the place of assemblage,
> they formed a procession and proceeded two
> and two with the priest at the head taking
> a tour round the town to the large plain on

> the eastern side of it. . . . Here they
> made their prayer and performed all their
> religious ceremonies, customary upon this
> grand occasion, and which were really im-
> posing and in a certain respect also
> edifying. [34]

At these ceremonies about three hundred people were
assembled, and at the prayer field the high priest—
who was also described by Afzelius as "the School-
master of the district"—led the assembly in prayer
and delivered a sermon, after which all shared bread.
Then there were more short speeches and prayers, and
the congregation returned to the meeting house where
singing and dancing commenced. [35] James Watt, an ambassador for the Sierra Leone Company, was present at
a similar ceremony at Berieri on May 1, 1794. There
the people, dressed in their finest clothes, assembled
to pray at the *sallekene* (prayer field), after which
there was a feast and singing and dancing. [36]

An English naval officer, Lieutenant John Mathews,
who visited Moriah in the 1780s, observed Muslim
schools and religious ceremonies and noted that "Man-
dingos" were actively proselytizing among the indigenous people. [37] There were many missionaries among the
Mande migrants who settled in the region to serve the
communities. Several towns became well known for
their schools and marabūt, among them Maligia, Taigbe,
Kalimodia, Furikaria, Laya, Kukuna, Tawiya, and Dar
es-Salam (see Maps 2 and 3); and some of the notable
missionary families in the region were Yansane, Fofana,
Kamara, Kaloko, Silla, and Sise. Scholars from these
kin groups established traditions of Islamic education
that continued over many generations. For example,
Fode Ibrahima Tarawali b. Ibrahima Konditu b. Yusufu
b. Lahai Salim Fofana was descended from a long line
of Muslim scholars. Fode Ibrahima Tarawali was born
in Furikaria in about 1785; he was educated there and
in Tuba, a Jakhanke religious center. During the 1820s
or 1830s the alimami of Tawiya, Dura Tumany Sankoh,
asked Alimami Ali Gberika Ture of Moriah to send Fode
Ibrahima Tarawali to his territory to establish a
Muslim educational center. On land that was granted
to him, Fode Ibrahima developed the village of Gbile
and founded a *jāmiᶜah* (Muslim university) that had
about one thousand students at different levels of instruction. This university had an extensive library
of Arabic texts and attracted students from both

Muslim and non-Muslim families in the area. Although
Bai Yinka I, the king of Bureh, was not a Muslim, his
son and grandson—later to become Bai Yinka II and Bai
Yinka III—attended Fode Ibrahima's university and became Muslims. The university and most of its collection of books were destroyed by fire in the Susu-Temne
war of 1875, but when Fode Ibrahima died in 1880, he
left forty Arabic religious texts to his scholarly
sons, and the family has continued to teach there and
to govern several villages in the area until the
present. [38]

The C.M.S. missionaries who attempted to establish a base in the Northern Rivers between 1806 and
1819 were impressed by the level of religious knowledge and devotion displayed by the residents of
Moriah. [39] One of the strengths of the Muslim missionaries was their willingness to participate in tradi-
tional religious rituals and to incorporate Islamic
prayers into them; in this way, non-Muslims became
familiar with Islamic ideas and practices, and Muslim
missionaries became accepted as religious specialists
in non-Muslim societies. [40] By the early nineteenth
century Islam had made a very strong impact on the region from the Baga territory north of Sumbuya down to
the Rokel River states south of Port Loko. The process of diffusion and integration continued throughout
the nineteenth century, and the Sierra Leone government developed a positive policy towards Muslim notables and Islamic concepts and practices. In the
Northern Rivers Islam provided the basis for a common
culture and helped to promote interethnic and intercommunity relations, although these positive contribu-
tions were undermined to some degree by the expansionist military activities of some of the rulers of the
region.

British Relations with the Northern Rivers

By the mid-eighteenth century the Northern Rivers
consisted of a number of small states—centers of politics, commerce, and Islam—developed by Mande migrants
and located on key trade routes from the interior.
Initially, the Sierra Leone Company and later, the
colony on the peninsula found a flourishing economic
system in the Northern Rivers, and the British officials set about to establish political and economic
relations with the leaders of these states. Several

British delegations were sent to the region from the
1780s on. Lieutenant Mathews reported on the "Mandingo Country" in 1787, and two company officers,
James Watt and Governor Zachary Macaulay, visited the
Northern Rivers in 1794.[41] Watt, who passed through
Bena and Moriah on his return from Timbo, recommended
that the company establish a factory in Moriah. He
and the governor met with several important leaders in
Wonkafong, Furikaria, Moribaya, Maligia, and Laya. The
company's goal was to end the slave trade and to develop trade in African goods produced in the Northern
Rivers or imported from the interior. Two other company representatives, Smith and Bright, were sent to
the region in 1802 for the same purpose, and African
leaders also began to send their agents to the colony.[42]
The Dumbuya kin group from Bolobinneh was probably the
first to establish a permanent town near the colony
when Dala Modu settled on the peninsula in 1801 (perhaps as early as 1799).

With the parliamentary abolition of the slave
trade in 1807, the assignment of Crown colony status
to the company's territory in 1808, and the settlement
in the colony of Africans taken off slave ships by the
British navy, the viability of Sierra Leone became
even more dependent on the development of economic
contacts with African states. Sierra Leone Company
reports during the 1790s emphasized the economic importance of the Northern Rivers to the colony, and
Governor Thompson in 1810 and Governor Maxwell in 1814
noted that supplies from the region were necessary to
the colony's development.[43] Rice production alone made
the region valuable to the growth of Sierra Leone, but
other products, many of which were imported by caravan
from the interior, were also of great value. In 1826,
for example, the governor reported that a single caravan of gold worth Ⱡ12,000 to Ⱡ15,000 had been diverted
from Freetown to the Rio Nunez by Alimami Amara Ture
of Moriah.[44] In 1845 a French government report stated
that there was a daily shipment of cattle from the
Tannah River area by sea to Freetown.[45] In 1854 the
acting governor of Sierra Leone was afraid that war in
the Northern Rivers might disrupt the area's important
trade relations with the colony:

> The Native Chiefs in the neighbourhood of
> the Mellicourie, Scarcies [Kolente and
> Kaba] and Fouricaria Rivers are in a very
> unsettled and intractable state, and I

shall undoubtedly have to bring them to
their senses by sending up a sufficient
force to chastise them. They have been
plundering the property of British Subjects and maltreating their persons for
imaginary wrongs, and if I am not able
to take immediate steps against them, the
valuable Trade of those Rivers will be
lost to us entirely. The Mellicourie
River alone supplied groundnuts last year
to the amount of about £100,000 and unless
I am in a position to shew these Chiefs
that I have the power of punishing them,
the whole trade will be lost to the British and taken up by the French.[46]

As the population of the colony increased and
trade contacts intensified, the government became concerned not only about the supply of products but also
about the regulation of relations between colony merchants and African rulers and landlords in the interior. British involvement in the Northern Rivers
area's affairs led to misunderstanding and conflict.
As early as 1794 James Watt reported that Alimami
Mustafa Ture of Moriah was opposed to the passage of
the Sierra Leone delegation through his territory because the party was under the protection of Alimami
Brama Sayou of Bena.[47] The colony's assistant surgeon,
Dr. O'Beirne, also encountered difficulty on a trip
in 1821 because the delegation had bypassed Moriah on
its way to Timbo. Alimami Amara Ture claimed that
Kukuna was a territory subordinate to his, and that
therefore the delegation should have come to him before taking that route.[48] Although the 1794 dispute
was resolved when Alimami Mustafa graciously received
Watt and requested that a colony factory be established
in Moriah, the dispute in 1821 reflected a serious
conflict that had been developing for many years.

In 1809 or 1810 Governor Thompson had received
a letter from Alimami Amara Ture protesting the abolition of the slave trade.[49] By 1813, possibly earlier,
Alimami Amara was engaged in a dispute with colony
merchants and also with a political rival in Moriah,
Alimami Sanasi Tarawali of Maligia. In 1814 Alimami
Amara ordered an increase in the price of rice exported to the colony and the seizure of the property
of British subjects. A British trader was also killed,
evidently by order of the king. When Governor Maxwell

protested these actions, Alimami Amara responded:

> Governor, I and Solyman [Modi Sulaiman of
> Fangi] we tell you one thing, if you do not
> want to buy any Slaves please do let those
> people that want to buy them come unto us
> freely, and do not take their ships and
> property away from them. If you do, take
> care of yourself—don't think you will get
> any black man's thing [goods] in all this
> Country either to buy or to eat.[50]

The king then justified the selling of slaves according to provisions of the Quran, and he added:

> Governor we [do] not want war with any man—
> [when] first white people come [to] this
> Country for trade palaver—we all were very
> glad of it, and whatsoever they wanted we
> tried to get it, Bulls, rice, yams, oil,
> Slaves, Ivory etc. but today white people
> come to take the Country away from us and
> make Slaves of us in return. . . . We don't
> like war—don't force us Governor—this
> country is your country if you only will
> leave off taking these Slave trading Ships
> that come to this coast to bring us a lit-
> tle thing [goods]—you know this country
> belongs unto us the Natives of it. You are
> a Stranger here, we are the proprietors.[51]

Alimami Amara was upset by British interference
with the slave trade, but he was also concerned about
a challenge to his authority within the Moriah political system. Rivalry for trade contacts was one ele-
ment in the conflict, but internal dissension also
derived from the pre-Moriah state system and the at-
tendant political rivalries. Since 1813, or even earlier, Alimami Amara had been disputing with Alimami
Sanasi Tarawali, who headed the small trading state of
Maligia on the Melikuri River. The king of Moriah was
attempting to control trade, while Maligia and other
trading states desired to maintain autonomy in economic
matters. The conflict between Alimami Sanasi and
Alimami Amara continued until the latter's death in
1826, and generated a war that eventually involved
many of the political centers in the Northern Rivers.[52]
The two sides in the regional war, which lasted from
1825 to 1827, were led by Alimami Ismail (Smilah)

Bangura, the king of Sumbuya, and Alimami Amara Ture.
Those allied with Alimami Ismail included Alimami
Sanasi (Maligia), Bamba Musa (the king of Bena), some
leaders of Berieri, and Alimami Dala Modu Dumbuya
(Lungi and Bolobinneh), who provided Sumbuya with guns
and powder. Alimami Amara's allies were Alimami Namina
Lahai (the head of Moribaya, a Ture stronghold), Modi
Sulaiman (Fangi), and other leaders in Moriah including Ali Gberika Ture, who succeeded Alimami Amara as
king in 1827. After Alimami Amara's death, the new
alimami, Ali Gberika, called for peace; he was supported in his efforts by Alimami Dala Modu Dumbuya and
the governor of Sierra Leone. With the assistance of
the Sierra Leone government, a treaty of peace was
signed on May 25, 1827.[53]

Thus, during the twenty years after the abolition
of the slave trade the colony government became directly involved in the politics of the Northern Rivers,
including military intervention in 1814 (see Chapter
two). In 1818 the colony acquired the Isles de Los
(see Map 2) from the Baga king, Manga Demba, and his
nephew and his agent in the colony, Alimami Dala Modu
Dumbuya, in return for an annual payment of five hundred bars.[54] In 1826 two Sierra Leone government agents
obtained the rights to Matacong Island from Alimami
Amara,[55] and in the following year acting Governor
K. Macaulay extended British sovereignty to the rivers, landing places, and islands (including Matacong)
in Moriah and Sumbuya kingdoms and effected a temporary peace among the parties.[56] The ubiquitous Alimami
Dala Modu was also a signatory of the 1827 treaty, as
a representative of the ruling houses of Sumbuya.

Because of the colony's extensive trade interests
in the Northern Rivers, it was inevitable that its
government would become increasingly involved in the
politics of the region, and also that pre-existing internal rivalries would be exacerbated. The centralization of political power in Moriah during the eighteenth century, spearheaded by the Yansane and Ture
kin groups, did not destroy the small trading states
that had been incorporated into the Moriah system, and
these states constantly endeavored to maintain their
autonomy. Struggles for power also took place within
the Ture family, especially when a new alimami was to
be selected, and periodic slave revolts contributed to
the political instability. Furthermore, territorial
conflicts between the Susu, Mandingo, Temne, Bullom,

and Limba peoples caused extensive military action,
the use of mercenary and slave armies, and the destruction of trade products and closing of routes,
in addition to the intervention of the British and
French governments. Any conflict involving serious
political instability, loss of trade, or damage to
property of British subjects resulted in some kind
of protest or direct action by the colony.

In 1802 a dispute between Quia Bubakar b. Mustafa
and Amara b. Fode Imran over the succession to the
kingship of Moriah ended with the selection of Amara
Ture in 1803. The Sierra Leone Company watched the
process with interest, but did not attempt to influence the selection.[57] Alimami Amara ruled—with opposition, as we have seen—until his death in 1826, and
evidently no succession struggle followed. Ali Gberika
Ture ruled Moriah from 1827 until almost 1850, and
there is no record of serious internal conflict during
that period (see the Moriah king list in the Appendix.)
After 1850, however, numerous internal and external
conflicts occurred in which the British became involved.

The period from 1850 to 1883 was one of intensive
conflict in the Northern Rivers, eventually involving
military forces from Tonko Limba, Kukuna, Bena, Moriah,
Sumbuya, Samu, Magbema, Kawlah, Mambolo, Kasseh, and
Port Loko, and mercenaries from the Yoni and Mende
territories south of the Rokel River region. There
were three general causes of this outburst of military
activity. First, there was a series of succession
disputes in Moriah between 1850 and 1868. Second, the
central trading town of Kambia, nominally a part of
the territory of Bai Farima of Magbema, was coveted
by both Moriah and Kawlah. Third, the Susu-Mandingo
forces wanted to punish Lamina Bilali and his allies
for harboring escaped slaves. The wars these disputes
produced caused great disruption of trade, property
damage, and the deaths of a few British subjects. The
colony government took direct action on a number of
occasions to protect its access to products and trade
routes and to defend the interests of its residents.

Between 1842 and 1852 the Sierra Leone government
negotiated several treaties with rulers in the Northern
Rivers. Through these treaties the colony hoped to
extend British influence in the north, develop legitimate commerce, and suppress the slave trade. The
treaties added many African leaders to the list of

stipend chiefs,[58] and their provisions were used to
justify the government's interference in the political
affairs of the African states in the Northern Rivers.[59]
The government of the colony became directly involved
in the politics of the region and used its economic
influence, African allies, and military power to favor
one faction over another.

The relatively peaceful reign of Alimami Ali
Gberika Ture ended in 1849, and he was succeeded in
1850 by Quia Fode Ture, a grandson of Quia Modu Ture.
His succession, however, was contested by Fode Wise
Ture, and when Quia Fode died in 1852, Fode Wise re-
newed his claim. He was challenged by Ali Foray Ture,
and the succession was not settled until 1855 with the
crowning of Fode Wise, who ruled until his death in
1862.[60] His reign, however, was marred by a series of
serious wars and conflicts with the colony government,
caused to some extent by the existence of significant
internal dissension.[61] By 1856 Alimami Fode Wise was
active in a war that eventually involved the area from
Sumbuya to Bureh and from the coast to Tonko Limba.
The two principal leaders of the war, Alimami Sattan
Lahai Ture of Kawlah and Alkali Buru Lahai Sankoh of
Taigbe,[62] gave as its cause the need to punish Lamina
Bilali and the Limba who supported his freed-slave
state. It was a continuation of the conflict that
had erupted in 1837-1838 when Bilali, members of his
family, and other slaves had fled Kukuna and established a small state in Tonko Limba. Both Alimami Ali
Gberika and Quia Fode had participated in the conflict
as allies of Kukuna against Bilali.[63] Slave revolts
and escaped slaves were a serious problem in a region
where perhaps two-thirds of the population had slave
status and where most of the production was accomplished by slave labor. Control of the slave population no doubt concerned the leaders, but the war during the 1850s appears to have been rooted in a desire
to dominate trade routes and incorporate Kambia into
the Mande political system.

Kambia was founded as a fishing village, probably
early in the eighteenth century. It quickly developed
into a crossroads for traders from the north and east
on their way to the Guinea and Sierra Leone coast.
Its residents included Susu, Mandingo, Limba, Temne,
Fula, and later Sierra Leone traders. The area had
long been a center of trade, as Lieutenant Mathews
noted in the 1780s: "The Scarcies [Kolente and Kaba

rivers] are both rivers of great trade for slaves, rice, and camwood, and for the fruit cola, which they sell to the Portuguese traders from Bassou."[64] The Dumbuya family of Kukuna had a residential quarter in Kambia, and there was also a Mandingo town, headed in the early nineteenth century by Balay Brima Kamara. The Ture kin group from Moriah had representatives in the town, and members of important families from Tonko Limba, Kawlah, and Sanda lived there.[65] Kambia, located on the south bank of the Kolente River on the edge of Susu country, was under constant pressure from attacks by Mande forces. Alimami Mangaba Abu Bakari Ture in the eighteenth century and Sattan Lahai Ture (the war minister of Alimami Amara Ture) in the early nineteenth century had attempted to incorporate the territory into the Moriah system. The Sankoh kin group was settled at Tawiya and in several villages along the north bank of the river across from Kambia, and Alimami Dura Tumany Sankoh (Tawiya) and Alimami Ali Gberika Ture (Moriah) established Fode Ibrahim Tarawali in Gbile in the 1830s. Alimami Ali Gberika and later kings of Moriah considered Tawiya and Gbile part of their political system. Alimami Fode Wise used Gbile as a residence during the siege and occupation of Kambia between 1856 and 1859, and he maintained that Kambia was within his territory.[66]

Sattan Lahai Ture's son, Alimami Sattan Lahai of Kawlah, also attempted to bring Kambia under his control during the 1840s and 1850s. Alimami Lamina Bamoi, the headman of Kambia between 1840 and 1864, and Bai Farima of Magbema resisted Alimami Sattan Lahai's efforts for more than two decades. Alimami Sattan Lahai, however, convinced the Sierra Leone government that he was the king of Kambia, and he was so recognized by treaty in 1851; both the British and French identified Kambia as part of his territory.[67] His participation in the war against Bilali during the 1850s was designed to consolidate his claim to Kambia and to connect his territory with that of his Ture kinsmen in Moriah.

The Sierra Leone government, which had already been involved in the disastrous Maligia expedition, was furious that trade had once again been disrupted and property of British subjects destroyed. Thomas George Lawson was dispatched as a negotiator, and Alimami Fode Wise of Moriah was initially designated by the government as its official mediator. Negotiation

failed, primarily because Fode Wise was allied with
Alimami Sattan Lahai and with the leaders of Kukuna.
The governor of the colony stopped Alimami Wise's stipend and hoped that Bilali and his allies would defeat
the Ture forces:

> That Fouday Wise has acted with design and
> treachery there can be no doubt, and his
> detention and subsequent confiscation of
> Mr. Davison's property cannot be palliated.
> . . . Billarley [Lamina Bilali] is in the
> field, the Timmanee Chiefs are supporting
> Lamina Bamoi [of Kambia], and as far as I
> can foresee there is every probability
> that both Fouday Wise and Sattan Lahai will
> be defeated and captured or killed.[68]

The Bilali forces failed, however, and because Governor Hill considered Kambia the "frontier of the
Colony," he authorized British military action against
the Ture forces at Kambia, pursuant to instructions
from the lords commissioners of the Admiralty in November 1857.[69] Governor Hill viewed the attack against,
and occupation of, Kambia and the combined Sankoh-
Dumbuya attack on Port Loko as elements of a coordi-
nated effort by the Susu-Mandingo states to threaten
the independence of the colony and an attempt to control trade. He felt it was imperative, therefore, to
administer a lesson to these forces, and it was his
opinion that the second of two British attacks had
dispelled the threat to the colony, although the Ture
forces later recaptured Kambia and peace treaties were
not signed until 1861.[70] The treaties recognized Lamina
Bamoi as "governor of Kambia" and included the town
within the territory of Bai Farima of Magbema.

The firm British action at Kambia demonstrated
the government's determination to keep trade routes
open and to protect the colonial frontier. The government of the colony also acquired an important ally
in Moriah during the conflict. Alimami Ansumana b.
Sanasi Tarawali succeeded Mori Mina Lahai as head of
Maligia in 1856. He was the son of Sanasi Tarawali,
who had carried on a dispute with Alimami Amara of
Moriah between 1813 and 1827. Although the government
originally implicated Alimami Ansumana in the attacks
on Kambia, he refused to cooperate with Fode Wise and
Sattan Lahai. Instead, he sent messages to the colony
government about the prosectuion of the war, and he

also informed the government about a dispute between
Moriah and Sumbuya for control of Moribaya, which was
attempting to maintain its independence.[71] Through
such actions Alimami Ansumana was pursuing a policy of
independence that had been in effect since the eighteenth century. Maligia was consistently a center of
opposition to Ture/Moriah domination throughout this
period.

Another time of serious political instability
followed the death of Alimami Fode Wise Ture in 1862.
Maligi Gbaily Ture of Furikaria, with the support of
his uncle Lahai Sware, insisted that he was alimami,
but this claim was disputed by Alkali Bukhari Ture,
the headman of Yankissa and a descendant of Alimami
Quia Modu Ture. Even before Alimami Wise's death
Alkali Bukhari had contacted the colony government
about making a treaty directly between the two parties. He emphasized the extensive trade in groundnuts and other products that his territory conducted
with the colony.[72] He was, in effect, declaring his
independence of Fode Wise. Two years later, in 1862,
Bukhari claimed that he was the senior member of the
Ture family and had been chosen by Fode Wise to succeed him as alimami. In fact, both Bukhari and his
opponent agreed that Lahai Sware had the better claim
to succession, but he had declined because of old age
and had designated Maligi Gbaily as the successor. It
was improper, however, to succeed an alimami by means
of designation. Traditionally, the leaders of the
yula tribes had to agree on a new alimami and the senior member of the yula wrapped the turban of office
around the king's head during the formal crowning ceremony.[73] Both Gbaily and Bukhari claimed to have been
installed as alimami, but no crowning ceremony had
been held for Bukhari. Maligi Gbaily did have the
support of the majority of leaders and may have been
formally crowned before 1864, but Bukhari refused to
accept his rule and retreated to Gbile, Fode Ibrahim
Tarawali's town, in 1865; there he assembled a force
comprised mainly of Temne warriors, which he used to
obtain the position of alimami. The civil war began
in 1865 and continued for four years, even though
Maligi Gbaily was captured and killed in 1866 or 1867.
In 1868 the Sierra Leone government finally recognized
Bukhari as alimami of Moriah.[74]

Alimami Bukhari's reign, which lasted until late
1883, was marked by internal dissension, civil war,

and conflict with neighboring states. He never gained
the support of several prominent political figures in
Moriah. Those allied against him throughout his reign
included Alimami Musa of Koke, Alimami Sori Fikeh of
Berieri, Alkali Yallan Fode Ture of Famoria, Alimami
Fode Tumany Tarawali of Maligia, and Alkali Sipyana
Sankoh of Conta. His support came from his immediate
family in Yankissa and a few other Ture-controlled
villages, from the Yansane kin group (Fode Ibrahim
Yansane was one of his principal advisers), from the
Sankoh kin group at Tawiya, from Fode Ibrahim Tarawali
of Gbile, and from his distant kinsmen Alimami Sattan
Lahai I and his son Alimami Sattan Lahai III. He also
continued throughout his reign to rely on Temne mercenaries, who created grave problems in the region by
marauding and destroying several towns and villages in
the region.[75]

Alimami Bukhari's reign was also marked by a re-
surgence of the war against Bilali in the 1870s. Like
his predecessors, Bukhari was allied with Tawiya,
Kawlah, and Kukuna against the rebel slave leader. He
also pursued an expansionist policy and claimed that
Kambia was part of his territory. For his planned attack on Bilali and his allies, Alimami Bukhari used as
his base Rogberi, a Sankoh town on the north bank of
the Kolente River between Gbile and Tawiya. He attempted to gain the support of Alimami Sattan Lahai II
of Kawlah so that he could cross his territory and attack Bilali, but Sattan Lahai refused. No damage was
done to the slave state, but the military activities
set in motion another Temne-Susu war that lasted several years and caused extensive property damage.[76]

The interest of the Sierra Leone government in
the Northern Rivers intensified during the 1870s because the French had been making treaties with leaders
and increasing their trade north of the Kolente River.
The French government established a station at Binty
in the late 1860s headed by a Commandant de Circle.[77]
Thomas George Lawson, who was particularly alarmed
about French encroachment in what to him had always
been British territory, was sent in 1872 to collect
information about the state of affairs in the Northern
Rivers and to negotiate a peace settlement. During
his tour Lawson talked with many of the leaders in the
northern states. In his report he recommended that the
colony expand the treaty system, establish sovereignty
over the region, and collect customs on trade goods.

> I would further recommend that . . . a
> proper person with a sufficient staff of
> Officers, and a Boat and men should be
> stationed on a proper spot to watch Brit-
> ish interests, and should be furnished
> with a flag which is to be hoisted daily,
> as some foreigners (Europeans) appear to
> be creeping in gradually into those riv-
> ers, and I was informed by some of the
> Chiefs that some have offered to enter
> into Treaty agreements with them which
> the [Chiefs] have refused to do.[78]

The government agreed with Lawson, and in 1876 and
1877 Governor Rowe entered into treaty arrangements
with political leaders of Kawlah, Magbema, Bureh,
Mambolo, Dixin, Loko Masama, Tawiya, and Samu. The
treaties granted to Great Britain sovereignty over
both banks of the Kaba and Kolente rivers "so far as
She may require the same for the purpose of the collection of revenue or for other such purposes as to
Her shall seem good."[79] With these treaties a British-
French boundary in the Northern Rivers began to take
shape, but the British had not yet given up on the
territory further to the north, which Lawson described
as vital to the economic viability of the colony.[80]

Internal instability in Moriah adversely affected
trade and political relations in the Northern Rivers.
Alimami Bukhari's opponents continued to withhold their
support because Bukhari had not been properly crowned.
Furthermore, they complained that he was demanding
money from candidates for town-headmen positions and
that he was attempting to collect a tax for trade
rights.[81] They also argued that his use of mercenaries
had brought terrible destruction to the region and
caused a decline in trade. Alimami Bukhari, on the
other hand, accused his opponents of being unfaithful
Muslims because they violated the Islamic prescription
that subjects must support their lawful rulers. He
claimed that they opposed him because he was trying to
introduce orthodox Islamic practices to Moriah.[82] In
June 1878 Governor Rowe traveled to Moriah in an effort to reconcile the two factions, one led by the
alimami and the other by his nephew, Alkali Quia Fode
Dawda of Furikaria. The alkali of Furikaria was supported by most of the important leaders in Moriah, including those of Berieri, Koke, Taigbe, Famoria, Conta,
and Maligia, while the alimami still had the support

of the Yansane kin group and its leader, Alkali
Kadiatta Modu of Kalimodia, of Fode Ibrahim Tarawali,
and of the Sankoh family of Tawiya. The governor
gathered the important leaders at Kalimodia, near
Alimami Bukhari's town, and negotiated a peace among
them. Fode Ibrahim Tarawali delivered a sermon about
the necessity for subjects of kings to obey them.[83]

The peace was only temporary. Later in the year
a combined army from Dari and Furikaria attacked the
town of Bassia, which was allied with Alimami Bukhari.
The alimami accused the attackers of being impious and
called on them to make full restitution. A full-scale
civil war that lasted from 1879 to late 1883 followed
their refusal.[84] When his opponents counterattacked,
Alimami Bukhari retreated in 1880 to Rogberi, and with
the assistance of Alimami Sattan Lahai III of Kawlah
and Temne mercenaries he waged a vigorous war for three
years. Bena eventually entered the war on the side of
Alkali Quia Fode Dawda, while Kukuna, Sumbuya, and
Morikania (a Mandingo outpost in Samu) supported
Alimami Bukhari. The Sierra Leone government, with
whom Bukhari had had close relations for almost twenty
years, initially supported the alimami, and the French
favored Alkali Quia Fode Dawda and his allies. The
war dragged on, damage to property increased, and trade
declined. The Mandingo-Susu allies of the alimami
turned against him because of his reliance on Temne
mercenaries who did great damage in the region. The
French committed Tirailleurs Sénégalaises to the battle against him in 1882; and the Sierra Leone government, understanding that support for Bukhari was futile
and that the war had spread south of the Kolente River,
also abandoned him and effectively admitted that the
territory north of Gbile and Dixin was within the
French sphere of influence. Because of pressure by
the colony government Alimami Bukhari was forced to
flee his refuge in Magbema and go to Kukuna and eventually to Tambakka, where he died in 1885. Quia Fode
Dawda was confirmed by the French only as alkali of
Furikaria; although he used the title alimami, he
never regained the authority that had been exercised
by many of his predecessors. The Moriah kingdom re-
verted to a city-state system and then came under
French colonial rule in the 1890s.[85]

During the long period of conflict in the Northern Rivers the British consolidated their position in
the area of the Kolente-Kaba rivers. A treaty of

June 10, 1876, between Governor Rowe and principal African rulers was used as the basis for establishing a customs station on Kikonkeh Island at the mouth of the rivers. When the African rulers protested that they had not agreed to give up their sovereignty, and objected to the payment of customs, a major dispute ensued. The African rulers ordered colony traders to cease their activities and abandon their factories, and the government officer on Kikonkeh was harassed and then physically attacked. In May and June of 1879 a government messenger, Mr. Harding, was detained at Robat in Magbema by the recalcitrant leaders.[86] Late in June Governor Rowe traveled to Kambia to negotiate a settlement of the dispute.[87] The governor told the leaders assembled at Kambia that the government had a treaty signed by them that permitted the establishment of a customs station, but Alimami Sattan Lahai III argued that if the kings allowed their boats to be searched they were giving up their sovereignty over the river: the imposition of a tax was the same as selling part of their land, and they could not agree to it. Governor Rowe explained that government expenses, including the payment of stipends to African rulers, were high, and that he needed the revenue. The discussions continued for three days, and finally Rowe addressed the Africans forcefully: "[The kings] have told me their mind and say always the <u>duty</u> the <u>duty</u> [customs]—they talk of the old friendship but not of the way in which they have broken the old friendship. The Queen is a very good friend but a very bad enemy and if they want to try their strength with the Queen's strength they will find it so."[88] The governor stated that the duty was necessary to pay higher stipends, but the kings responded that they did not want higher stipends. If they had to pay a duty they would have no power in their states and would be kings in name only. Bai Yinka of Bureh said: "Every country has a law, as the white man has his law, so also the Timmanee man has his own law and if they don't keep up to their own laws, their kingship would not be respected."[89] The kings requested that they be allowed to renounce the treaty that had ceded land to the government, and the governor agreed to submit their request to the Queen. The treaty was not abrogated, and the customs station remained, to be followed ten years later by a police post.

A second major dispute involving alienation of land and British control over customs occurred in 1882.

In this conflict the *bai sherbro* (kings) of Samu and of
Mambolo both claimed ownership of the town of Kicham
on the north bank of the Kolente River (see Map 3).
The dispute was important to the British because the
bai sherbro of Samu had not signed the 1876 treaty
ceding the river banks to the government, and he refused to acknowledge Governor Havelock's authority
over the town. The governor spoke to the king at
Kicham, informed him that the land had been ceded to
Sierra Leone in 1876 by the bai sherbro of Mambolo,
and ordered him to leave, but the bai sherbro of Samu
maintained that the Kolente River and Kicham were
under his authority. After waiting on board his ship
for thirty minutes, the governor ordered three rockets
to be fired into the king's compound, destroying it.
The king was removed from Kicham and a new town chief
was appointed to rule as a British agent.[90]

These cases clearly illustrate the methods by
which British control was gradually extended over the
northern territories. The government established its
authority in the Kolente-Kaba rivers area as it had in
Port Loko during the 1820s. The northern kings correctly perceived that the inspection of their boats
and the payment of duty on river trade was, in effect,
recognition of British authority over their territories and loss of their political and economic independence. Throughout the nineteenth century British interests were vigorously promoted, a process in which
Thomas George Lawson played an important role. Before
his final retirement in January 1889, the influence of
Sierra Leone in the interior had been definitely established, and within five years after Lawson's death
in 1891 a British protectorate had been created over
the hinterland of Sierra Leone.[91]

PART TWO

SELECTED DOCUMENTS

The reports, letters and memoranda of Thomas George Lawson contained in Part two of this study were selected from eleven bound volumes compiled by Lawson between 1873 and 1889 while he was de facto head of the African affairs section of the Sierra Leone government.

The documents are not arranged chronologically; rather, they are presented under five headings: Political Affairs, Military Matters, T. G. Lawson's Roles and Attitudes, Trade Information, and Alimami Samori Ture. Lawson did not necessarily focus only on one topic in each of his reports; the reader will find two or more covered in many of the documents.

Lawson's reports were extensively used by colonial governors and by the Colonial Office in London; they offer insight into the important role that a West African played in Great Britain's colonial administration during the middle and late nineteenth century.

The eleven volumes are located in the Sierra Leone National Archives at Fourah Bay College:

The Government Interpreter's Memoranda (GIM), 1873-1876. 436 pages in one volume.

The Government Interpreter's Letter Books (GILB), 1876-1889. Ten volumes:

1. November 28, 1876-July 26, 1878 (451 pp.)
2. October 26, 1878-April 16, 1880 (335 pp.)
3. November 10, 1879-December 31, 1881 (420 pp.)
4. January 2, 1882-November 28, 1882 (528 pp.)
5. December 4, 1882-March 3, 1884 (438 pp.)
6. March 4, 1884-June 5, 1885 (434 pp.)

7. June 9, 1885–June 22, 1886 (334 pp.)
8. June 23, 1886–August 27, 1887 (334 pp.)
9. August 29, 1887–September 6, 1888 (262 pp.)
10. September 7, 1888–January 25, 1889 (175 pp.)

Again, I should like to gratefully acknowledge
the cooperation and assistance given me by the staff
of the Sierra Leone National Archives. In particular,
I should like to thank Mrs. Gladys Sheriff, head
librarian at Fourah Bay College, for her help and
encouragement.

POLITICAL AFFAIRS

Information relative to the neighbouring countries

1. Bulama a Country situated several hundreds of miles north of this Colony was once belonging to it but given up to the Portuguese in the year 1870 or 1871.

2. The Rio Nunez and Rio Pongas said at present to be under French Authorities are both in treaty with this Government see Treaties 49. 50. 57. pages 381. 384. 403 Ordinance Vol. 2. The Chiefs of the former do not receive a stipulated sum as stipend, only annual presents whenever it is necessary—The Chief of the latter receives an annual stipend of £15, there are several Merchants and Traders belonging to this Settlement who are residing in both places for commercial purposes.

The Nunez is divided into two parts inhabited by two distinct tribes called the Ky Kandies and Naloes and governed by two Chiefs viz. Dukar Chief of the Ky Kandies and Urah Towle Chief of the Naloes they have for several years been friendly with this Government— Dukar was here on a visit to His Excellency Sir Arthur Kennedy in 1871.

The Chief of the Rio Pongas is called John Catty recently appointed to succeed the late King Yangy Will— Sir A. Kennedy visited the Pongas in 1871.

The products are shelled groundnuts, Beniseeds, Coffee, Gum Copal, India Rubber, Agusi, Beeswax, Hides, Gold, Ivory—the Chiefs of Nunez and Pongas pay annual tribute to the King of Futah Jalon, he having conquered the country some years ago and no King can be crowned for either place without the approval of the King of Fulah, the interior natives resort [to] those countries to trade in greater number than at any other place.

3. The Kobah Bagga Country situated on the East of
the Rio Pongas is inhabited by a tribe called Bagga—
The country is not in treaty with this Government, but
the late King, who died a few months ago as well as
his Chiefs, was friendly disposed to this Government
and had applied to enter into treaty with it, which
application was forwarded to the Secretary of State
and a favorable reply sent to him—the King's wish not
having been carried out is owing to the constant re-
movals of Governors and the recent disturbance on the
Gold Coast; The people are very peaceful and harmless
and would not make slaves of one another—they make
good seamen. It is bounded on the North by mainland,
on the West by the Rio Pongas River, on the east by
the Bramaiah River and on the South by the sea—it has
about 60 miles Coast line—The products are Palm Kernels, Palm Oil, Groundnuts and Beniseeds.

4. The Bramaiah Country is inhabited by people from
Rio Pongas who resorted thither for independence. It
is not in treaty with this Government nor does it appear that the people wish to have any, the late Chief
was called Manga Lawry, the Chief town is called
Bramaiah, it is stockaded and fortified with cannons,
the people are peaceful but always in a defensive position—The products are the same as those of the
Pongas. The present Chief is called Will Fernando.
Captain Ruston of H.M.S.S. "Pandora" visited it in the
year 1863 by direction of the Governor in search of a
Slaver—I was ordered to accompany him—We did not
suceed in capturing the Slaver on that occasion, but
she was afterwards found aground beyond the Nunez on a
bank in the sea called the Alcatras—it appears that
the slaves murdered the crew except a white boy who
was spared to steer the vessel and was directed to
steer her to where the sun rises from, he did as he
was bid by which he got the vessel aground and they
landed on the adjacent shore Captain Ruston demanded
them but were not delivered—the white boy was taken
care of and sent back to his country—the vessel's
figure-head was brought here and laid before the Vice-
Admiralty Court—This country was formerly a notable
slave depot, it is bounded on the east by the Dubrika
River, on the West by the Bramaiah River, on the north
by the mainland and on the South by the Sea—thickly
populated.

5.   The Carlome Bagga Country is inhabited by another
tribe of Bagga having the same manners and customs as
the Kobah who are all pagans, except a few proselytes
of the Mahomedan religion, the natives are good seamen—The French Government has no influence in this
country—The King is called Balla Demba and is in
treaty with this Government see Treaties Nos. 5. 42.
47. pages 277-360-377.   The products are the same as
those of the Kobah—the trade at Isles de Loss is done
chiefly with the people of this Country, Bramaiah and
Kobah Bagga—a portion was ceded to this Government
see Treaty No. 5 page 277 Ordinance Vol. 2.   The people are friendly disposed to this Colony—It is bounded
on the East by the Mania River, on the West by the
Bramaiah River, on the north by mainland on the South
by the sea—thickly populated.

6.   The Sumbuyah Country including Moribiah is large
and inhabited by a tribe of Soosoos called Sumbuyah
(meaning mixture of people) who are Mohammedans but
indulge in intoxicating drinks as the Baggas, are warlike, the capital is called Wonkafong and is situated
about 20 miles up the river, it has many creeks and
riverlets—The products are Groundnuts, Beniseeds,
Coffee, Cattle, Hides, Gum etc.

The Chief Koota Modoo is in treaty with this Govern-
ment and receives an annual stipend of Ꮮ20 see Treaty
No. 58 page 406—It is bounded on the north by the
mainland, on the south by the sea, on the east by the
Berieri and Fouricaria River and on the West by the
Mania River—having Matacong Island adjacent—The
French does not seem to have any influence there—it
is thickly populated.

7.   The Moriah Country, comprising Fouricaria, Beri
Eri, Kokeh, Fanjay, Tannah, Forodugu, Yenkissa, Malaghea,
Mellicourie and various other towns is extensive, and
inhabited by a tribe of Soosoo called Moriah—They are
all Mohammedans very extensively engaged in the slave
trade with the neighbouring countries—The King Alimami
Bokharri is considered powerful and warlike, he was
crowned in the year 1865 in the presence of the officers of H.M.S.S. "Zebra" when a salute was fired.
Judge Huggins was subsequently directed to visit him
by the Governor—His Honor had previously visited that
country in company with Major Ireland by direction of
the Governor, to settle a serious disturbance I went

on both occasions as Interpreter. The King and some
of his Chiefs are in treaty with this Government see
Treaties Nos 36. 38. 44. 51. 55. pages 350. 366. 346.
387. 400. and are receiving annual stipends, the French
Government exercises authority, it appears, over a
portion of this country, it has a block house at Binty
on that portion of the Samo Country lying on the south
of the Mellicourie River, known as the entrance it is
fortified and contains a small number of Troops and
a Commandant.

The King and his Chiefs have been very friendly with
this Government and have always expressed their desire
to be under this Government rather than any other Foreign power, and have protested against the proceedings
of the French—Sometime in January or February last
the King visited the French Commandant at Binty (which
he had refused to do) and the grand reception that he
met with seems to impress him favorably toward that
Government which is obvious by the expression in the
latter part of his letter sent a few weeks ago in
reply to one from this Government relative to the
plunder said to be committed on the property of Messrs.
Ditchfield and French in the Great Scarcies River.

The Country has been in war with the Limbas for the
last three years with the view of subduing one Bilali
(a runaway slave) at the head of a large number of
runaway slaves who have made themselves free and are
under the protection of the Limbas a tribe in the
interior of the Timmannee Country which is powerful
and has always been friendly with this Government.
The Chief (Limba) is not in treaty but receives an
annual present. He visited Governor Hennessy at
Kambia in 1872 when His Excellency was there to settle
some disturbances and a handsome present was given
him—The [war] has been subsequently extended to the
Timmannees for having refused to allow King Bokharri
and his troops to pass through their country for the
purpose of carrying on their war. It may be well to
state that at the death of Fodey Wise the late King
there arose a contention for the throne between
Bikharri the present King and Maligi Gbeli his cousin
who had usurped it, and a serious war ensued in which
the troops of the latter were vanquished and himself
made prisoner and afterwards beheaded, the war however
lasted after the death of Maligi Gbeli till Sir Arthur
Kennedy arrived here, who put an end to it in the year
1870, when the two Cocoa nut trees in the garden north

of Government House were planted. The Timmanees were
supporting Bokharrie. The Country was in peace till
the above war was undertaken, which was after Sir
Arthur Kennedy left—The products are the same as
those of the other Countries but Groundnuts are more
abundant—The Country is nearer Matacong than it is
to Isles de Loss—It is bounded on the north by the
Beri Eri and Fouricaria River, on the South by the
Mellicourie River, on the east by the Timmanee and
Limba countries and on the west by the sea, it is
thickly populated.

8. Samo Country is in treaty with this Government
see Treaty No 37 page 347 ordinance No. 2. The King
Bey Sherbro and his head Chief Ceasay Saidoo receive
an annual stipend of Ł10 each, the people in the upper part are called Moricanians governed by Chief
Cearay Saidoo, they are Mohammedans and are more
powerful and warlike than those of the lower part (the
Aboregines) who are all pagans—The products are
Groundnuts, Palm Oil, Palm Kernels etc., it being near
the Mellicourie River the trade is done with the Merchants of that place, it is bounded on the north by
the Mellicourie River, on the South by the Great
Scarcies River, on the east by the Timmannee Country
and on the West by the sea—Thinly populated.

9. The Great Scarcies Country is accessible by a
large river named after it, it is divided into three
parts viz. the lower part commencing from Balansarah
creek to about 50 miles up the river on both sides is
governed by Bey Sherbro; he resides at Mambolo see
Treaty no. 66 page 426, Ord. Vol. 2. he is mild and
peaceful, the principal trading factories are built
on his territory and most of them are belonging to
French Merchants—He receives a yearly stipend and is
friendly disposed toward this Government—The Middle
division from Marinjah creek westward of the Village
of Ro-Pa Buncle which is the upper boundary of Bey
Sherbro's territory to Pinta Killie creek above the
town of Kambia, is governed by Bey Farima called in
the Treaty King of Magbatie and Kambia see Treaty No 3
page 272 Ordinance Vol 3 and receives an annual stipend—he is an ageable man and very intemperate, can
be induced by a small present to consent to any mischief, is powerful and always ready to join in war
with any who asks his aid as he did in 1865 in assisting Bokharri to distroy the Moriah Country.

The upper or interior part is contiguous to the Limbas
(Bilali's Protector) and is governed by Alimami AlHay
who is called in the Treaty King of RoWoolah see
Treaty No 2 page 269 Vol 3—he receives an annual stipend and is powerful and though peaceful, is always in
a defensive position—He and Bey Farima unite to fight
against Bokharri who is said to interfere with their
rights, the Country is extensive and thickly populated
—The people are Timmannees some of whom are pagans
and others Mohammedans—The Country is overrun by
Mohammedans who are actively engaged in proselyting
the people. The products are groundnuts, Beniseeds,
Agusi, Palm Kernels etc.

Caravans from interior with gold, Hides, Beeswax,
Ivory etc come direct to obtain conveyance for this
place some of which some times do their trade there
as at Mellicourie—There is a very large quantity of
produce bought yearly by the Merchants and exported
in exchange for which a large quantity of foreign
goods is given—the principal portion of the produce
comes from the Limba Country. There is a large portion of land on the right bank of the river (a considerable distance up the river) inhabited by the Digsaine
Timmannees another distinct tribe which is independent
of those of the left bank but are allied to one another
—The lower part was governed by Worikia Silimani (de-
ceased) and the interior part by Lunsenny—the people
of the former are Mohammedans and those of the latter
pagans—A great portion of this country, including
Mellicourie, is occupied by Soosoos whose injudicial
interference in the political affairs of the country
has created unpleasant feelings among the Timmanees
which resulted in their uniting with their allies who
had already been engaged in war to fight against them
(the Soosoos). The Kings and Chiefs of the Great
Scarcies Country are friendly to this Government and
if proper steps are adopted the rivers, bays, waters
etc. can be secured by this Government and duties collected—The River is navigable to Kambia by boats and
Canoes a distance of about 70 miles. The River is
navigable to Robatt a distance of about 40 miles by
large vessel. The water is fresh in the rainy season
and salt in the dry at which time the tide flows a
long way up the river. It was visited in 1873 by
Lieut. Stokes 2 W.I.R. and Commissary Blissett C.M.G.

10. The Ro Bureh or Small Scarcies Country is extensive and contiguous to the Great Scarcies, it is

accessible by the river named after it a branch of the
Great Scarcies River and navigable to the town of Ro
Bureh the former capital by boats or canoes, the en-
trance or barmouth is the same as to the great Scarcies.

I may take the liberty to mention that Yelboa and all
the islands at the entrance including Kaikonki occupied by Mr. Maillard a French Merchant and all the
banks on the South from Ki Polong Creek to a creek
above RoKon Macama a distance of about 40 or 50 miles
are British teritory see Treaty No. 45 page 369 Ordinance Vol. 2. ceded by the King of Locco Marsama whose
territory they had been. The King [of Small Scarcies]
is called Bey Yinka or Inga and resides at Ro Mangay.
His territory commences from Tappehtook on the north
bank to a considerable distance in the interior also—
The King is peaceful and friendly, and is in the treaty
with this Government, receiving an annual stipend.

The Country is inhabited by Timmannees who are pagans,
a few however embrace the Islam—the products are the
same as the Great Scarcies—Caravans occasionaly go
there to find conveyance to this place—There are
three or four distinct countries in the interior that
are not described here The Kings of which are not in
treaty with this Government but are friendly disposed
and presents are sent to them occasionally.

An agreement of friendship was entered into with them
by Governor Hennessy in 1872 of which a memo was made.
Stipends were allowed then, but nothing of it has been
heard since. The river is fresh in the rainy season
and salt in the dry. During the former season it runs
down rapidly and during the latter the tide flows a
considerable way up.

11.   The Bullom Country is devided into two parts,
each having its own King and Chiefs viz. the Kaffoue
Bullom and the North Bullom or Locco Marsama. The
Kaffoue Bullom commences from the South bank of Kipo-
long Creek round Leopard Island along the coast to
Magbogbo Creek near Tagrene point in the Sierra Leone
River.

The North Bullom or Locco Marsama commences from the
east bank of the Magbogho Creek including all the
islands in the Sierra Leone River viz. Tasso, Mayerber,
Bence, Pappel, Tombo, to a hill called Chainkaberreh
in the Port Lokkoh River and from Ripolong Creek on

the West round Baloh point past the South bank of the
Small Scarcies River to a creek a little above Rokon—A
portion of this country was ceded to this Government
see: Treaties nos. 12 & 45 pages 290 & 369.

The King of the former is called Bey Sherbro, he is in
treaty with this Government and receives an annual
stipend see Treaty No 46 page 373 Ordinance Vol 2.
The late Chief, father of the present, was a faithful
friend of this Government, for which particular respect
has always been shown to his people—the present Chief
was educated in this Settlement but is of such intemperate habits that he is almost possessed of no influence, for which reason I am always ashamed to introduce him to Governors—his elder brother who succeeded
his late father immediately was educated in England
but died shortly after he assumed the government of
this country—In the year 1818 a portion of land was
granted to the late Dalmodu, by the King, for his own
use which has been occupied by his people since, the
Chief town is called Longay or Madina—the late Dalmodu
was a powerful and wealthy man and rendered great assistance to the King in managing the affairs of the
country—the present Chief is called Alimami Fenda
Sanassi Modoo, he is also in treaty with this Government and receives an annual stipend, is very peaceful
and friendly and has always rendered assistance to
this Government in making peace among the neighbouring
tribes as his late father used to do—We returned from
the Sherbro in May last where he had been, for almost
two years engaged in settling some disturbances among
the natives on behalf of this Government. The King of
the latter is called Bey Mauro he is very friendly
disposed toward this Government and is ready whenever
called upon to assist in peace-making among the neighbouring tribes—He is in treaty with this Government
and receives rents, is peaceful and becoming very influential. The aborigines of Bullom are Pagans, but
Mohammedanism is fast gaining ground among them—the
Dalmodu people are all Mohammedans—the products are
the same as those of Scarcies—Several British subjects
reside there for agricultural purpose and supply our
market with provision—Bey Mauro and Alimami Sanassi
are two most useful native Chiefs.

12.   The Port Lokkoh or Bacca Locco Country is extensive and is about 60 miles distant from Freetown, it
is accessible by the river named after it, being a
branch of the Sierra Leone River, there are several

towns on both banks, those on the left as far as Ka
Capa Creek [a] little above Mafarree the eastern boundary between that Country and Locco Marsama are within
British jurisdiction though entirely inhabited by the
natives. Those on the right bank going up are not
within British jurisdiction—It is the landing place
of the interior natives viz: those from Falaba,
Sangara, Kankan, Sego and Timbuctoo and is much thought
of by the Government, there are several large and independent countries in the interior with which it is
allied and are parties to Treaty No 67 page 429 Vol 2.
The people are Timmannees—the Chief goes by the title
of Alikali, but there is a King called Bey Foki termed
Ground King in the Treaty, he resides about ten miles
inland and entrusts the management of affairs at that
place to the Alikali.

The second Alikali was crowned in the presence of
General Turner (Governor) who visited there for the
purpose attended by some of the white troops since
then no Alikali has been crowned without the sanction
of this Government, and upon the occasion of a coronation either the Governor goes himself or an important
official is deputed to represent the Government—the
important personages who have visited that country
after are—Sir John Jerremie (late Governor) in 1841.
Governor S. J. Hill in 1859.
Colonel Younge 1.W.I.R. in 1863
Sir Arthur Kennedy in 1871.

It is requisite and necessary that the official visit
be repeated as it serves to encourage trade and en-
liven the friendly feeling that is existing between
the people and this Government—and as it will perhaps
be inconvenient for your Excellency to go the vener-
able appearance of Major Doorly in his uniform will
make a very good impression not only among that people
but those in the Roquelle River also. Mohammedanism
was introduced among the people since 1816 which is
proposed by a great many and is therefore becoming the
religion of the country, they were pagans primarily—
Alikali Seckoo Camarra the present Chief and his sub-
Chiefs and people are peaceful but in a defensive position always are friendly toward this Colony, they
receive annual stipends as well as those in the interior as inducement to keep the roads to the interior
free, presents are annually sent to those in the far
interior with whom this Government is not in treaty
and who are not receiving stipends viz; The Kings of

Falaba, Kankan, Futah, Sangarra, Corankoh and Buré.
The Country is fertile and yields abundantly, the people are industrious and naturally intelligent—the
products are rice with which our market is supplied,
groundnuts, Beniseeds, the river is navigable by large
crafts to Bence Island and by boats or canoes to the
town of Port Lokkoh. Several British subjects reside
there for trading purposes—there is a mission station
there C.M.S.—thickly populated—it is situated north
of the Marampa Country. First Alikali crowned in 1816.
*see paragraph 19.

13. The Quiah is also an extensive Country of which
this Settlement was a portion, it commencees from the
eastern boundary of this peninsula and stops at
Rosolloh Creek, a distance of about 60 miles in the
Roquelle River, which devides it from the Masimerah
Country. British jurisdiction had extended to Benkia
and a considerable distance in the Quiah Creek to a
town called _____ but a great portion has been restored to the people see Treaty No _____ page ____
Vol ____ dated 29 January 1872. The country is fertile and thickly populated—Hardwood timber is abound-
ant. The people are peaceful and industrious, are
pagans—Mohammedanism is embraced by a few. The timber trade was extensively carried on there as well as
at Port Lokkoh from when the first shipment was made
in 1816 by the late John McCormack known as father
of that trade, and subsequently Police Magistrate of
this Colony. The titles of the Kings of Quiah are
Bey Farima, Bey Bureh and Bey Cantah—This Colony was
ceded by Farima father of Bey Cantah the last King
with whom we had war in 1860 to 1861—Since the death
of the late King a successor has not been elected, but
Ansumana Konkoh has been appointed Regent-Chief— until another King is crowned—The products are the same
as those of Port Lokkoh. Many British subjects reside
in the country some for trading and others for agricultural purposes.

The King receives annual rents see Treaties No. 1.
page 265 No 3 page 272—No. 6 page 280 Vol 2. and that
dated 29 January 1872.

The country has many Creeks and riverlets—the principal towns on the waterside are Ro Bagga, Ro Mangay,
Ro Toomba, Ma Cubitt, old and new Benkia, Kaigbelli,
Ma Kenke, Forodugu where Chief Alimami Lahai Bundoo
resides and several other towns, a mission station

C.M.S. is at Benkia—the people are friendly disposed
—the country affords a high way for the transpotation
of slaves by the Soosoos from the neighbouring countries to the Roquelle River [from] which they are embarked for their country. The boundary between this
Settlement and Quiah is defined in Map annexed to the
Treaty dated 29 January 1872.

14. The Marampa is another large Country thickly populated and not very fertile, a large quantity of produce is sent to our Market from that country it is
situated north of Masimerah Country from which it is
devided by the Sailoh or Roquelle River—It is inhabited by Temmannees who are pagans—Mohammedanism being
professed by a few—Several Fulahs and Mandingoes reside there as at Port Lokkoh—there are several large
towns on the frontier the principal of which is called
Magbelli where the interior natives bring their produce for sale and from whence Caravans embark for this
place. It is used to be visited by Governors formerly,
Governor Dundas Campbell visited it in 1836 and remained there for nearly three months. His Excellency
was accompanied by a few members of Council and principal Merchants and some troops—Governor S. J. Hill
visited it in 1857. There was a mission station at
Magbelli but was distroyed in 1860 by the natives—The
King resides in a town, named after the country in the
interior—he is called Bey Cobolo, a peaceful and up-
right man and friendly to all British subjects is in
treaty with this Government and receives an annual
stipend—At Magbelli the principal town on the waterside is Chief Pa Suba, appointed by the King to manage
the affairs of that place, he is very harmless, peaceful, & indolent and receives an annual stipend see
Treaty No 67 page 429.

15. The Masimerah is a very large country on the east
bank of the Roquelle River, it commences from the
Rosolloh Creek by which it is devided from the Quiah
Country to the Ma Bang Country a distance of about 80
or 90 miles—It is very fertile, a large quantity of
produce is sent to our market from there—The interior
trade comes through it—it is remarkable as a rice
country and as producing the best Cam wood with which
it abounds—there are several towns on the waterside
the principal is Roquelle after which the river is
named, the other is Rokon where the King resides at
present but his usual place of residence is Masimerah
a town named after the country.

The King is called Bey Simerah, he is civil but is
proud and conceited, is in treaty with this Government
and is receiving an annual stipend—The Slave trade is
extensively carried on with the Soosoos—The country
is continually at war with the countries in the interior no doubt for the purpose of making slaves of the
people to supply the Soosoos.

It is bounded on the north by the Mallal Country, on
the South by the Yonni Country on the east by the Ma
Bang Country and on the West by the Marampah Country,
the Yonni and Ma Bang Countries are all in treaty with
this Government see Treaty No 67 page 429 Vol 2.

16.   The Ribbee and Bompey are one Country accessible
by two rivers the one to the former is called Kates
or Ribbee River named after a town on the river, that
to the latter is by the Bompey the Capital and residence of the King—It is bounded on the east by the
Yonni and Quiah Country, on the west by the Yourah Bay,
on the north by the Quiah Country and on the south by
the Bago Creek by which it is devided from the territory of G. S. Caulker—The Chief of Quiah has right
over the Ribbee as far as the Camaranka Creek but the
Caulker family has been permitted to occupy it as well
as the Bannanna Island see Treaty No 8 page 283.   The
country is inhabited by mixed tribe of Timmannee and
Mendi (Kossoh) who are pagans.   The timber trade was
extensively carried on there but the principal products at present are rice and Kola nuts.   British jurisdiction extends to Masobul Creek in the Ribbee,
but the right bank going up is not within B. jurisdiction a few British traders are to be found in the
country, but the largest business is done by the firm
of Randall & Fisher, which has a large establishment
there in which there is a great quantity of goods on
which duties have not been paid—no customs officers
stationed there—The King is called Richard Canray
Bah Caulker—he is intemperate and powerless, was educated in the C.M.S. Grammar School at Government expense which does not seem to do him any good, is young,
and on returning to his country he retrograded, is now
a porroh-man an institution among the natives intended
to screen its members in their mischief—is in treaty
with this Government and receives an annual stipend
of £20. He would make war if he had power to do so.

17.   The Cockboro is in the jurisdiction of George S.
Caulker son of the late Thomas Stephen Caulker Chief
of Shaingay and Plantain Island—It commences from the
Bago Creek by which it is divided from the territory

of the King of Bompey to Yaltucker or Samo River which
form the Western boundary of British Sherbro—it is
bounded on the north by Bompey, on the west by the sea,
on the east by the Bagroo and on the south by Sherbro
River—It is inhabited by a mixed people as Ribbee and
Bompey who are pagans—the products are the same. The
Chief is called George S. Caulker, was educated in England, is very civil and intelligent and resides at
Shaingay a very decent and healthy town in which there
is an American Mission station, and several traders are
scattered in the country—The Mission was established
in the year 1850 which is progressing. The Chief is
averse to war, is in treaty with this Government and is
receiving an annual stipend—He visited this place in
June last—there was a family dissention among them in
April last which has been settled—There are many towns
on the frontier, the principal of which is Bompatook.

18. British Sherbro, comprising the Turtle and Sherbro
Islands, Bagroo, Manna Bagroo, Bayleh, & Bendoo, was
ceded to this Government in November 1861 during the
administration of Governor S. J. Hill further particulars can be obtained from the Commandant.

*19. The Quiah Country has a custom of crowning three
sub Kings and three Queens beside the King—the titles
of the sub Kings are Pa Nain Banner, Nain Sogo and Pa
Cappre, and those of the Queens are Bome Marrah, Bome
Rufa, and Bome Cappre who have entire control over the
idols and fetish of the country, they are supposed to
have intercourse with departed spirits of their ancestors
—the King can do nothing without consulting the sub-Kings
and Queens—The first of the sub Kings is to take charge of
the Country whenever the King dies until another is crowned
see Treaty No 1. page 265 in which Nain Banner a Sub King signs
Treaty for the Country, the King Bey Farima having died then.

20. There resides in the interior of Bompey a Mendi
(Kossoh) Chief called Gbanyah Lango who is a friend
and faithful ally to this Government—He came to the
assistance of the Government during the late Quiah war
in 1860 and supplied Kussoh recruits for the late
Ashantee Expedition among whom was his son.

> (Sd) Thos. Geo. Lawson
> Govert. Interpreter

Sierra Leone
24th July 1875.
(The above is not entered in the rough book No. 4)
[This is Lawson's comment. The rough book was his
notebook which he used to make the more polished
entries in the bound volumes.]

GIM, pp. 367-68

Sierra Leone
2 September 1876

Memo for Governor in Chief
relative to the Sumbuyah Country of which
Koota Modoo is King

The Sumbuyah Country comprises the North bank of
the Beri Eri River on the East and Moria or Sumbuyah
River on the North—it is approached by two main rivers viz the Moribiah and the Mania or Sumbuyah Rivers
both of which have several branches leading to other
trading stations—The Branches of the Moribah river
lead to Kokeh, Morifinyah—Madina Coromboyah and Moribiah—those of the Mania or Sumbuyah river lead to
Mania, Somaiah, Koryah, Doombuyah, Queyeyah, Fugumi
Gbokoroyah, Bomfeh, Yelmangia, Balaiah and Wonkafong
the Capital, all trading stations—A very large quantity of produce is taken from these rivers to Matacong
Is., Isles de Loss and to Factories at Mellicourie and
to Freetown for sale when cash is required—The prod-
cuts are Groundnuts Palm oil, Palm Kernels, Beniseeds,
Coffee, Gum Bees Wax, India Rubber, Hides, Oxen, Sheep,
Goats, horses, rice, honey, Gold from interior, Shea
butter, Calabashu, Baskets, Tanners, oranges, and
other articles.

I believe about Ь70 to Ь80,000 business is done
in the Sumbuyah Country during the season and perhaps
more—vessels can ascend the rivers to some distance
for cargo but generally anchor off Matacong Is, and at
the mouth of the river—The Chief of Moribiah under
Koota Modoo will expect to receive a handsome allowance
of Ь20—or 30 may be a proper one. The Chief of Kokeh
15 to Ь20 annually—they will distribute the amount to
other subordinate Chiefs—Koota Modoo the King who is
already receiving a stipend of Ь20 annually may have
an additional Ь40 annually in consideration of the cession. This amount with what is given to the Chiefs of
Moribiah and Kokeh will no doubt be considered a sufficient allowance. I simply express my views in the
matter Your Excellency can do what you shall see fit.

The Chiefs of the Northern Rivers are more intelligent more powerful and wealthier than those of
Sherbro and are much wealthier than the Timannee
Chiefs. I regret to state that Koota Modoo's men left
yesterday.

See Treaty No 58 page 406 Vol 2 being a treaty
of Friendship and Commerce on which Koota Modoo receives his present stipend.

T. G. Lawson
Govt. Interpreter

GILB, 1:53

Sierra Leone
February 3, 1877

No. 2b.
Memo in reference to the Arabic
letter from Alimami Bokharie

I have thought it my duty to give your Excellency
the following information respecting the statement
made by Alimami Bokharie with reference to the Great
Scarcies and the people in it—The King is in error in
stating that he owns the Country and is head over the
people of the same, this was what brought on the war
between him and the Timannees, the Country belongs
to the latter and they had only permitted the Soosoos
to reside there, they had never sold nor relinquish
their right and I fear if the King does not abandon
his idea and allow this Government to settle the dispute between him and the Timannees amicably but attempt to set one of his party as head it will result
in a renewal of the war.—The Timannees are determined
to maintain their rights as owners of the Country but
are willing to permit them to reside in their Country
if they would remain peacable—It is well to say that
he has no bad feeling against them but he should refrain from doing any thing that will create bad feelings in others against him.

(sd) Thos. Geo. Lawson
Govert. Interpreter

GILB, 1:149-50

July 14th 1877

The Messenger from the principal Chiefs of Mellicourie, Malaghia, Pharmoriah and other towns in the
Mellicourie River state as follows.

We are sent by our Chiefs of Mellicourie Yallam
Foday principal Chief of Pharmoriah, Fudiah Tomany
principal Chief of Malaghia Sipyarneh principal Chief
of Contah and other Chiefs of our Country on special
mession to the Governor of Sierra Leone.

We are requested to deliver to the Governor the
letter that we have brought addressed to him and to
inform His Excellency also that sometime last month
a circular letter or notice was conveyed and delivered
to each of the above named Chiefs by a Military Serjeant said to have been sent by the Commandant at
Benty in which they are informed that all the countries from Mellicourie to Sumbuyah including all the
rivers are French teritories—On reading the letter
all the Chiefs were annoyed and tore the letter in the
presence of the Serjeant and told him to tell the person who sent him that they have nothing to do with the
French and that they are in Treaty with the English
ever from the time of their ancestors and their country is under that Government and have never been informed otherwise the Serjeant then went away—six days
afterwards a Messenger came from Alimami Bokharri who
said that he was sent by the Alimami to request the
whole of the Chiefs and headmen to meet him at Benty
where the Commandant resides but the whole of them refused to go being of the opinion from the letter received from the Commandant that it was he who gave the
Commandant authority to make such a claim upon their
Country and they sent at once to protest against such
an act as no King in their country has power to cede
or transfer any portion of the country to any foreign
nation without the consent of all the principal Chiefs
and head men and also without the consent of the Governor of Sierra Leone to whom the country had been
ceded many years ago by their ancestors—Our Chiefs
sent us to know from the Governor whether he has any
knowledge of what we came for and if it is done with
his consent.

                         (sd in Arabic) Kaltigi Lahai
                    do [ditto] Alifa Ibrahima
                    do   Mangah Modoo.

                              Sorie $\overset{his}{\underset{mark}{X}}$ Bah

Witnesses to signature & mark
(sd) T. G. Lawson
     Govt. Interpreter

     G. M. Macaulay
     Protector of Strangers

GILB, 1:262-66

                              Freetown Sierra Leone
                              7th December 1877

Statement of Alikarlie Kardiata Modoo Chief of Calli
Modiah a principal Chief and a confidential friend of
Allimamy Bucharri King of Kissi Kissi or Moriah Country sent on a Mission to His Excellency the Governor
in Chief by that King.

     Myself as the head and 3 others are sent on a
special visit to the Governor in Chief by the King
with a letter written in Arabic as he could not get
a confidential person to write his mind in English to
the Governor, and as he could not state all he intended
to say to the Governor in that letter, he directs me
to state as follows

1. That he heartily thanked the Governor for the
short visit he made him in the latter part of last
month and that this visit has broken down a great barrier between him and the British Government and his
people and [territory] are [on the] eve of having the
whole dispute and threatening disturbance of civil war
in his country to an amicable settlement.

2. That he has always acknowledged the English Government who approved and recognise his Coronation as
King of the Moriah Country in 1868 to be the earliest

friend and protector of his Country since the formation of Sierra Leone by the English and that more than
60 years ago it was the Govt. of Sierra Leone under
Sir Charles M'Carthys Administrator which saved his
Country and the lives of many of the principal Chiefs
from being destroyed and the same Government more than
12 years ago saved the Country from a similar destruction by Civil war, in the person of Sir Arthur Kennedy.
The same Govert. again in last year June in Your
Excellency person brot amicable settlement of war that
had been raging between him and the Timnehs of the
Great Scarcies over two years which he hopes will be
finally and permanently settled in short.

3.   That he ever acknowledged his Country to be under
the protection of the English Government, as he told
your Excellency at his place last month.

4.   That from the rebellious state of several of his
Chiefs and people against him in the begining of this
year, and under the apprehension of fear of being
killed secretly as his late grand father Quiah Modoo
the first Allimamy of the Moriah country had been
killed his personal protection and that of his children he did put under the French Commandant at Binty,
but not the country, which he could not do by himself
alone, and that he never did at any time cede or transfer any portion of his country to the French Government but reckon them as friends.

5.   That on a visit to the French Commandant at Binty
about 5 or 6 months ago he sent for all the Chiefs of
his Country to meet him there, but they all refused
doing so under the impression that he has transfered
the Country to the French from a rumor and printed
notices that had been sent to them from the Commandant
at Binty to that effect, which in truth he had never
done, and that at that time I my brother Sattan Dawda
and others who are now here with several others were
present with him and heard him distinctly saying to
the French Commandant and other French Officials that
were then present that the Samo Country including
Karkootoolah island was not his Country nor has he any
jurisdiction there and that it belongs to the King and
Chiefs of that Country and that he has no power or
authority of giving or permitting any one to reside
in it.

6.   That at present his Country is in an unsettled

state and pray the Governor to do his best by adopting
a measures in having it settled, in order to have the
Great Scarcies matter permanently concluded.

7.   The King directs me further to state,
That a year before Governor Kennedy paid visit to his
Country to settle the Civil war between him and Maligy
Gbelly, a French Consul accompanied by Mr. Fred Reader
an English merchant Mr. Rosenbush of Conta a national-
ized Englishman and Merchant Mr. A. Valentine of Tam-
bayah and late Mr. Joseph Deliner both Mulattoes
French subjects but the latter employed at Binty by
Mr. Heddle an English Merchant paid a visit to Alimamy
at Fouricariah and that I and many others were present
at the time, the Consul said to the Allimamy that he
had come up there with these gentlemen as witnesses to
thank the Allimamy for the protection extended to the
French traders of his Country and that formerly they
the French were on the side of late Maligy Gbelly who
promised to protect them in the Country and as he is
now dead, being overcome by the Allimamy, he the French
Consul has come there to place all French traders under his protection; that no treaty existed between
them and Maligy Gbelly but bare friendship and that as
he is no more he therefore comes to be of the same
friendship with him, he being now the King, he then
brought out a paper which he read in English to us and
interpreted by myself in our language, purporting to
contain protection to the French Merchants and traders
in our Country; nothing was mentioned to us of transfer or Cession of any portion of the Country to the
French Government.   The Allimamy understanding it to
be so from the confidence he has in Mr. Reader an
Englishman, Mr. Rosenbush considered to be an Englishman, he signed the paper and it was arranged that Mr.
Reader, English Merchant, Mr. Rosenbush, English Merchant, Mr. Joseph Deliner agent of Mr. Charles Heddle,
English Merchant, and Mr. A. Valentine, French Merchant,
were each to pay 50 dollars a year for the protection
they are to receive as mentioned in the paper about 2½
years after this the Governor of Senegal with the Commandant at Binty went in a Steamer as far as Yainkissa
with a paper written requesting the Allimamy to sign
it he and the whole of us refused doing so, and he
threatened to fire on our towns, but went away without
doing so.

And that about 10 or 11 months ago the Governor
of Senegal came in a Steamer to Binty and invited the

Allimamy there, when he made some present to the Allimamy for protection of French Merchants in the Country, he said to the Allimamy that a little more delay
on the Allimamy present he would have gone away without seeing him, the Allimamy informed him that our
Canoes are not as swift as their boats are; the Governor promised to send him a fine boat on his return
to Senegal; at that time, he invited the Allimamy to
pay him a visit at Senegal, but he told him that he
would not go there even if he would send the biggest
steamer filled with dollars, but would send his son
to visit him & the place. On the following month he
sent the boat as he promised by a Steamer, and the
Allimamy also sent his son by the same Steamer on a
visit as he promised to do. The Allimamy sent me to
assure the Governor that in all this friendly trans-
action between him and the French, nothing is done to
his knowledge and understanding and that of his people
as to any portion of his Country being ceded or transfered to the French Government this I myself know of
my own knowledge to be the fact because in all the
interviews the Allimamy had with the French officials
I [was] always present.

8.   The Allimamy requests the Governor will be pleased
to allow me to receive whatever stipend may be due
him, and to repeat his thanks to the Governor for his
short visit.

(sd) in Arabic Alikarli Kardiata Mahomadoo
of Calli Modiah

Witness to signature in Arabic
(sd) M. Sanusi

GILB, 3:122-23

Freetown Sierra Leone
15th May 1880

Sir,

     I beg most respectfully to submit the following
statement for Your Excellency's information, That on
the visit of His Excellency the Governor-in-Chief to

the Moriah Country for the purpose of reconciling the
disaffected minded Chief Alikarlie Quiah Foday Dowoda
and others at Fourricariah to their right and lawful
King Alimamy Bokharie, King of that country in May
1878, at Karlai Modiah the King in the midst of all
his Chiefs distinctly stated to His Excellency the
Governor-in-Chief that he did sign a document with the
French Government for the protection of French Subjects in his country and their paying anchorage for
vessels belonging to them entering his waters and
nothing more and that upon the strength of which he
signed that paper, at the same time he asked the Governor to cause to be levied customs duties in his
country thereby His Excellency would be in position to
have his yearly stipend increased and would be able to
allow stipends to be paid to some of his Chiefs viz—
Alikarlie Kardiatta Modoo of Karla Modiah also Alikarlie Noah of Fourodugu and two others and that as the
Government of Sierra Leone always go into large expenses to keep their country in order it would in some
way go in help to that expense. He urged this to be
done as the merchants and captains trading in his rivers never fulfilled their promises. His application
had been repeatedly made since His Excellency returned
to Freetown. On the last interview His Excellency had
with the King here in the midst of his Chiefs on the
2nd and 3rd instants among other things in his conversation with His Excellency in your presence he made
use of a very important expression which he wished the
Governor to bear in mind that he had heard that several
of his subordinate Chiefs viz. Alikarlie Sorie Feekeh
Chief of Berrie Erie, Alikarlie Quiah Foday Dowoda
Chief of Fourricariah, Alikarlie Yellam Foday Chief of
Phamoriah, Alikarlie Foudia Toomany Chief of Mallaghea,
Alikarlie Sipianey Chief of Contah and 2 or 3 others
had lately signed some document with the French Commandant at Binty giving him [as a representative of]
the French Government the right of some portion of his
country and that he knows nothing of the matter nor
had they his authority to do so and wished the Governor to bear in mind that according to their country
laws whatever the Supreme King[,] termed in their expression Kandeh[,] decided or chose his Successor has
no power to reverse it and that he the present Kandeh
of the Moriah Country cannot undo or reverse what his
predecessors had done or decided but the Kandeh has
the power to undo or reverse the decision or act of
an Alikarlie, or other Chiefs in the country and this
was the reason he always considers the treaty entered

into by this Government with his ancestors for the
past 54 years to be good and valid and cannot be re-
versed by him or any other Kandeh. The King returned
home on the morning of the 13th. instant highly grat-
ified with his Chiefs and attendants for the kind of
reception and treatment they met with from your Excellency and was indeed thankful in having the opportunity of seeing the Governor-in-Chief before his embarkation for England.

I consider it part of my duty to submit the above
statement to you in writing for future reference if
need be.

I have etc.

Thos. Geo. Lawson
Govt. Interpreter

His Excellency
    The Administrators-
        in-Chiefs
    etc. etc. etc.

GILB, 3:174-78

Freetown Sierra Leone
2nd July 1880

Sir,

In obedience to your Excellency's instructions of
the 30th ultimo that I should to the best of my ability furnish for your information certain particulars
in reference to copies of documents written in Arabic
forwarded to your Excellency from the Right Honourable
the Secretary of State for the Colonies said to be a
protest sent from the Moriah country through the Secretary of Foreign Affairs protesting against certain
rights of the British as well as the French Governments [to take] possession of their territory or to
acquire rights or priveleges beyond those granted by
existing treaties.

I beg to state for Your Excellency's information

that from the present means I have in the Settlement
to acquire the particulars required[,] I have ascertained [them] from Alimamy Fenda Sanusi Modoo Chief
of Medina Bullom Shore and Bolbineh in the Bagga
Shores, an influential and powerful Chief, beloved
and respected by the whole of the various tribes bor-
dering this Settlement from Rio Nunez on the north to
the Gallinas on the South and on the east as far as
to Sago, and is also a brother-in-law of Alimamy
Bokharie King of the Kissi Kissi or Moriah Country
and has been connected with this Government in the
way of assisting the Government in peace making among
the various tribes when at war to my knowledge from
1841 to the present day.

1st. He knows the town and district of Berrie
Errie, there he was educated it is a portion of the
country known and called Kissi Kissi or Moriah Country and immediately under the King or Kandeh of the
same and not an independent country to it.

2nd. That the present Chief Sorie Feekeh is a
relative of his, and appointed Chief of that place by
an elderly regent Chief of Fourricariah when there was
no King reigning, Foday Wise being then dead. This
was after the death of the late Chief of that place
Alimamy Sarleah.

3rd. There being no King in the Moriah country
a younger cousin of Alimamy Bokharie named Maliggy
Gbailee usurped the crown and made himself King without the consent of Alimamy Bokharie who was the elder
and had the legal right to the crown, it being against
the custom of the country that a younger brother or
cousin should reign before the elder.

4th. That Maliggy Gbailee by making large presents to the Chiefs of Berrie Errie, Sorie Feekeh with
many of the Chiefs of that place sided with him which
brought a destructive civil war in that country from
1865 till it was amicably settled by Sir A. E. Kennedy
the then Governor of this place in 1869 and 1870. This
circumstance created great dread and fear in the minds
of the people of Berrie Errie, those of them who joined
late Malliggy Gbailee against Alimamy Bokharie[,] which
up to this day still working in the minds of great many
of them; this is why it appears as Berrie Errie is a
separate country from that of Kissi Kissi or Moriah,
whereas it is not the case.

5th. To the best of my endeavour to obtain information from people belonging to Berrie Errie I
failed to know as to the circumstances in which and
the places at which the memorials were signed, and
only gather from them that sometime in the early part
of 1878 the French Commandant and some French Officers
in a Steamer visited Fourricariah and went to Berrie,
what paper they signed then, they do not know the purport, but they have not heard the Chiefs of Berrie
Errie to say anything of protesting against the right
of the English or the French occupying any portion of
their country, but they all know and heard their Chief
(Sorie Feekeh) state that he wanted the French to occupy Matacong, in as much as they are not[,] as the
English [are,] preventing their keeping slaves and
this is the only ground they prefer the French to the
English. With respect to the document bearing the
signature of Alimamy Bokharie and some of his Chiefs
with him, what I gather from some of his principal
persons who are here agrees entirely with what himself
told me when he was here on a visit to the Governor in
May last, after our return from Government house to my
house in conversation he said to me in the following
words, Mr. Lawson I am glad indeed that I have come to
Sierra Leone to see the Governor before he leaves,
particularly on two points, first, to bid him goodbye
and accompany him down to the place of embarkation.
Secondly, if I had not come to see him I would not
have heard of a memorial being written in Arabic bearing my signature sent to England of which I know nothing, and would not have heard of it if I had not come,
I had never seen it nor heard of it or where it was
written nor by whom it was done. I will wait patiently
till I see the copy the Governor promised to send me
when he gets to England, and you may depend upon it
that the person who wrote my name on it whether it be
Foday Brimah my Chief Writer or Kardiattah Modoo the
best man I depend upon in the Moriah country, who is
also a relative and a friend of mine or if it be a
child of my own begotten[,] his life will be forfeited
or else all they possess will be confiscated and given
for the benefit of the poor in the country. The above
are his own words which he repeated over and over in
the presence of his Chiefs who were with him namely
Alikarlie Kardiatta Modoo Chief of Karley-Modiah,
Alikarlie Noah Chief of the Fourodugu, Foday Brimah
his principal priest and some others all of whom confirmed what the King said. The King was here from the
2nd to the 12th of May last and nothing galled his

mind as that memorial mentioned to him to have been
sent to England from his country. He told me also
that if it had not been for the leniency and kindness
of Governor Rowe who advised him not to take arms
against Berrie Errie and the refactory Chiefs in his
country the Chiefs of Berrie Errie and those at Fourricariah would have long before this know who is their
lawful King (whether I am or not) but the document
which he signed with the Governor at Karlay Modiah in
June 1878 is what tied him down and that Sorie Feekeh
has no authority or power from him to cede or give any
portion of the Moriah country to any one, nor has (he)
Sorie Feekeh the right or power to do so independent
of (him) Alimamy Bokharie.

I shall wait to obtain further information from
the Chiefs I heard will be soon sent here from him.

> I have the honour to be Sir
> Your most Obedient and
> humble Servant

> (sgd) Thos. Geo. Lawson
> Govt. Interpreter

His Excellency
The Administrator-in-Chief
etc. etc. etc.

GILB, 3:187-90

> Freetown Sierra Leone
> 14th July 1880

Sir,

I have the honour to report for the information
of His Excellency the Administrator-in-Chief that in
obedience to his orders of the 30th ultimo that I
should with Mr. Harding hold ourselves in readiness
to proceed on a mission to Alimamy Bokhari King of the
Kissi Kissi or Moriah Country who was at Kambia in the

Great Scarcies river, I accordingly on the 1st instant
waited on His Excellency when he handed to me his written instruction for my guidance; Boat being prepared
to take us, Mr. Harding and myself left Freetown at
11 am on the 2nd instant and arrived at Kikonkie about
6.30 same day. Captain Richmond the Commandant on
that station being absent we waited his return which
was not before the next morning at 9 am. Mr. Harding
having taken in his care money entrusted to him by the
Colonial Treasurer to be handed to him and also to
witness the payment of the Constables and other Government servants, we did not leave Kikonkie for Kambia
before 12.30 pm of the 3rd instant, and arrived at
Kambia the next day (4th instant) 4 pm. According to
the Custom of the Country we went direct to Santiggy
Brimeh Tooray who took us to Alimamy Sattan Lahai King
of Rowoolah we informed that King that it was right
that we should call on him first but that we were sent
directly by the Administrator in Chief with a letter
to Alimamy Bokhari King of the Kissi Kissi or Moriah
Country. He then directed the same man to accompany
us to Alimamy Bokharie, before this he took us to
Alimamy Amarrah the Governor of the town who directed
us to lodge with one J. T. Metzger a British subject
in whose house we accordingly lodged during our stay
at that place. Alimamy Bokharie was exceedingly glad
to see us and said that whenever he sees messengers
sent to him from the Governor of Sierra Leone his heart
is always filled with joy. I then handed to him the
letter addressed to him from the Governor-in-Chief sent
from England, also the documents written in Arabic
sent from England for his information, in receiving
the letter and those documents his expressions was God
is blessed and praise be to him, he then requested Mr
Harding to read the letter which he readily did interpreted by Alhoosiney the priest of Alimamy Sattan Lahai
in the presence of his own high priest, Ibrahima,
Alikarlie Noah Chief of Fourodungu and many other
Chiefs and principal people. He took the documents
written in Arabic from England with Foday Ibrahima and
minutely examined them over and over comparing them as
Mr. Harding was reading their translations in English,
after the reading of the letter and those documents,
he stated in the presence of all that he knows nothing
about those documents and that he thanked the Governor
for his kind letter and for his sending those documents
to show him, and that he blesses the Administrator
for not keeping them in Sierra Leone but forwarded
them to him for his explanation. I then in the

presence of all informed him that the Administrator-
in-Chief sent us to know from him and others for his
information the circumstance which led to the writing
of the memorials written in Arabic, the place where
they were written and signed, particularly whether his
signature which is attached on one of them is genuine
or not, and if it be so the reason for his not commu-
nicating with Her Majesty's Government through the
usual channel namely the Governor of Sierra Leone.
Also to enquire whether he authorized Chief Sorie
Feekeh and others to sign a separate memorial and if
so whether he therefore considers Beri Erie to be an
independent Kingdom from the Moriah Country. In reply
to this he said please tell the Administrator for me
that in speaking in the presence of my principal
Chiefs, also in the presence of the Kings, Chiefs and
people of this place and independent country to me
and to my Country that I know nothing nor heard anything of those memorials before my visit to Governor
Rowe in Sierra Leone nor was I aware of them before
therefore I do not know under what circumstance they
were written, nor the place they were signed, and that
I consider my name which appeared on one of them to be
a forgery and that Sorie Feekeh under me at Beri Erie
nor any other Chief or Chiefs have my authority to
sign a separate memorial touching any portion of my
country without my authority or independent of me and
that Beri Erie is not an independent Kingdom or Country from my Country the Kissi Kissi or Moriah Country.
Also tell the Administrator for me that if I have to
make any communication with our Good Friend the Queen
of England it is to be made through the Governor of
Sierra Leone who always conveys our minds to her Government in England. I am sorry that I will be obliged
to detain you here for a few days as I am determined
to come to the bottom of this matter. Alikarlie Noah
is here I shall ask him in your presence whether he
signed that document or not or knew anything about it,
he Alikarlie Noah being present at the time the King
asked him those question when he declared that he knew
nothing about it nor ever heard anything of it before
the day the King was informed of it by Governor Rowe
in Sierra Leone now little more than two months ago,
this he repeated to me himself very often during our
stay at Kambia. Alikarlie Yousufoo Chief of Mellicourie having been sent for as he did not come in time
and we being anxious to return we engaged Boat and
hands and left Kambia Sunday the 11th inst about 11 am
and arrived at Kikonkie 1.30 pm in the next morning

12 instant. We left Kikonkie the same day 10.50 am
and arrived in Freetown 10.30 pm. I beg further to
state for his Excellency's information that I made
earnest inquiry about the man Bocary of Killinkoh
whose name appeared on one of the memorials written
in Arabic, the King and his Chiefs informed me that
they knew no one of that name of any influence but
one residing in one of his slave villages and has no
influence whatever in the country.

I beg also to inform his Excellency that I was
obliged to pay (20/-) twenty shillings for the use of
the house occupied by us whilst at Kambia and (50/-)
shillings for the Boat and hands which brought us to
Freetown also (10/-) for the man who interpreted for
us it being preferable to have a proper interpreter
in the matter, also I was put to some incidental expenses to the amount of (10/-) ten shillings for which
no receipt was obtained. The various meetings held in
enquiring into the above matter were held public. The
country gives a very good prospect for good crops in
Ground nuts, rice, Beneseed etc. for next season.

I have the honour to be
Sir
Your most Obedient Servant

(sgd) M. Sanusi
Arabic Writer

T.G.Lawson Esq.

GILB, 3:341-42

Freetown Sierra Leone
11th February 1881

Statement of Simminee Foday and Cealah Tooray messengers
from Allimamy Bokharie King of the Moriah country [who]
arrived this morning with a letter from that King to
report his safe arrival at Mellicourie town 9 days ago.

The King sent us with a letter to report to his
good friend Governor Streeten of his safe arrival at
Mellicourie. He left Robearay a town opposite Kambia

in the Great Scarcies and halted at a village called
Modeah belonging to Alikarlie Yousufoo Chief of Melli-
courie town where he remained 13 days and on the fol-
lowing day we proceeded to Mellicourie town. From
Modeah to Mellicourie is fully about 5 or 6 miles in
distance. The Allimamy was accompanied by Allimamy
Sattan Lahai King of the Great Scarcies, Santiggy
Condomah Representative of Bey Faramah King of Kambia
and Magbaitee, Santiggy Korkonah Representative of
Bey Inga King of the Small Scarcies their respective
Chiefs and people.

While at Modeah messengers came from Mellicourie
said to be sent to the Allimamy from the Governor of
Goree to inform him that he is sent to Mellicourie by
the Governor of Senegal to receive him in an Official
manner on his return from the Scarcies to his country
and is there waiting to perform this service. The
Allimamy sent to inform him by the same messengers
that he thanked him for the compliment and that he
would go to Mellicourie at his convenience and that
if he wished to see him he sent horse by his own messengers to the Goree Governor to come and see him at
Modeah where he was and that the Governor of Sierra
Leone is the only friend that he has confidence to
meet with as a true friend. After the messengers
left he repeated the words in the hearing of the
Kings, Chiefs and the whole of us who were present
that he does not know the French more than strangers come to trade in this country and that the English are the ancient friends of his ancestors and
himself up to this day and that if it had been the
Governor of Sierra Leone who had sent to him he
would have hurried down to him. Five days after the
messengers returned the Allimamy the Kings and Chiefs
and the whole of us who accompanied him came down
to Mellicourie and found the Goree Governor had left.
The Commandant was there at Pharmoriah the opposite
town; 3 days after he went over to see the Allimamy.
The Allimamy was unwilling to see him but from the
persuasion of the Kings and Chiefs with him he did
so, after which the Commandant returned to Binty—
The Allimamy then sent us with a letter to report
to the Governor of his safe arrival to Mellicourie
and to give an outline of his travel from the
Scarcies to his country for his information. We
left Mellicourie last Monday and arrived here last
Thursday night.

                              (sgd) Simminee Foday
                               "   Cealeh Tooray

Witnesses to signatures)
in Arabic   )

Sgd. M Sanusi
     Arabic Writer
  " J. B. Prigg.

GILB, 7:136-37

                              Freetown Sierra Leone
                              19 November 1886

Sir,

        I beg to report for His Excellency's information
the arrival of 8 Chiefs from Bareira Northern River
formerly in connection with this Government under
Treaty No 44 ordinance book Vol II page 366; But since
1881 this Government has nothing to do with them as
that country is considered to be a French protectorate.
Governor Havelock never received them but refered them
generally to the French Consul and informed them that
[if] they have any thing to say to him [it] should pass
through that Consul. They brought a letter. I informed them that I cannot receive the letter nor themselves without receiving His Excellency's authority
and that I would report their arrival this morning and
wait for His Excellency's orders.

        It appears from conversation that they never enter
into treaty with the French Government nor desire to
have anything longer to do with them. I told them
that I have nothing to do with that, but whatever His
Excellency said will be attended to.

        These Chiefs gave much trouble to this Government
in 1878 or 1879 as they were the persons who went to
hand over to the French the Island of Matacong and
even attempted to hand over Yellowo Boyah and other
Islands in the entrance of the Great and Small Scarcies

Rivers which caused the Government without delay to hoist the English flag at Kikonkie to show that those places are British Teritory. The present Governor-in-Chief was at the time absent to Senegal while Administrator Streeten was acting during his absent.

Without instruction I cannot receive the letter nor themselves and I will with His Excellency's permission inform them to pass their letter through the French Consul.

Your Obedt Servant

(Sd) Thos Geo. Lawson
Govt. Interpreter

Mr J. C. E. Parkes
Govt. House

MILITARY MATTERS

Freetown
20th May 1879

Information for T. G. Lawson Esq.,)
Government Interpreter   )

It is rumoured here that the threatened war in
the Moriah Country is happily coming to a close. It
is said that a few days ago the French Commandant of
Binty who is said to have visited the Fourricariah
river made it his business to get Queah Foday Dowda
to ask King Bokharie's pardon at Yainkissa whither he
had taken him for that purpose. After he had succeeded
in doing this he took him to Binty and gave him a
present of some bags of rice and about ($200) two
hundred dollars to his uncle the King. Very little
however is said of Murry Cearay Daffae who is said to
maintain a strong Stockade abreast Fourricariah town
in direct opposition to the King. Having apparently
succeeded in separating him from his friend and ally
Queah Foday Dowda it is believed that he is thus rendered less able to prosecute his hostile intention.
The King of Sumbuyah is said to remark that Murry
Cearay Daffae being a stranger he shall see how easy
he can carry out his purpose without the aid of the
Turalakahs who are the owners of the Soil.

(Sgd.) M. Sanusi
Arabic Writer

GILB, 2:234-38

Freetown, Sierra Leone
18th July 1879

        Sattan Dowoda brother of Kardietta Modoo Chief of
Cala Modia and accredited messenger of Allimamy
Bokharie King of the Moriah Country states as follows,
for the information of His Excellency the Governor-in-
Chief.

        Eleven days ago Allimamy Bokharie our King re-
quested my brother Kardietta Modoo to come as a messenger from him to the Governor, my brother not being
very well and the weather being bad asked the King to
send me and his son Karrfala to come to the Governor
at Kambia as the whole of us have heard in our Country
that he was at that place and that the Timmanees of
that place had revolted against to him and intended to
make war on him and that they the Timmanees had collected 3700 fighting men for that purpose. On hearing
of this news the whole of us in our country were surprised and became enraged about it. The Allimamy directed that on our way to Kambia for to see the Governor, first to call at Mellicourie and see Alikarlie
Yousoofoo the Chief he being nearer Kambia to ascertain the correctness of the news which reached us.
Allimamy also gave me a letter addressed to the Governor and a present of a sheep. We left Yainkissah
the same day (Monday) and arrived at Mellicourie the
same day. I saw Alikarlie Yousoofoo and showed him
the letter the King sent and the present for the Governor and asked him about what we have heard at Yainkissah and Kalli Modia in reference to the Timmanees
intention of making war with the Governor, he said
that they have heard the same news but they don't believe it to be true and that he would send his son
Lusainy with a letter to accompany us to Kambia to
see the Governor or wherever he may be to know of this
matter.- We left Mellicourie the following day (Tuesday) and lodged in one of its villages called Kartam
I left Kartam the next day (Wednesday) and arrived at
Taweah where I was informed that the Governor had gone
down to Kaikonkie, I should have stated that my stay-
ing at the village of Kartam was done by the request
of Alikarlie Foodiah Toomany of Malaghea in order that
his messenger Murry Saidoo should come together with
us to see the Governor. The persons who informed me

at Taweah that the Governor had gone down to Kaikonkie
were Memmah Sorie, Fullah Yawreh, Yenna Modoo.   They
informed us that when the Governor came up he anchored
off his small Steamer, little abreast our town opposite Masammah, he said nothing to us but passed on to
Kambia and on his return he in like manner said nothing to us but went down and that many of them went
over to Kambia when he was there to listen to what was
going on and no more and the people of Kambia the
Timmanees said nothing to them about the matter, they
were talking and they too said nothing to them.   I was
there two days in order to obtain canoe to come down
but failed and left there by the land road (Friday)
and staid [at] a small village called (Kamp dee) Small
Sierra Leone I left there and arrived at Kitchum about
9 or 10 o'clock a.m.   I could not obtain any canoe to
take me to Kaikonkie to see the Commandant, what is
the reason I don't know.   On Monday two days after my
arrival at that place I got passage in some strangers
canoe who brought some palm kernels to sell at that
place they brought me to Kaikonkie.   I made them a
present of a shirt value ten shillings and was very
glad of it.   The Commandant received and treated myself and ten others with me kindly.   The next day
Tuesday morning he provided boat and hands which
brought us to Barloh Point [which] I passed on the
same morning and arrived at Medina Bullom Shore [where]
I found Allimamy Sanusi sick not well but he gave orders that care should be taken of us being weary and
tired with those that are with him[.]   We remained
there two days and then [he] sent us accross yesterday.
What the Allimamy and his Chiefs sent us particularly
to inform the Governor is that he and all his Chiefs
and people consider that from the Bagga Shores on the
north to the Gallinas Countries on the South are under
the rule and jurisdiction of the Government of Sierra
Leone and whenever they the native Chiefs are at war
with each other it was the Government of Sierra Leone
which always spend money and go into the trouble in
making peace between them, and for that Government to
go among any of them to be insulted and take arms
against it as he and his people have heard done by the
Kambia Kings and people they consider it a bad thing,
that all black people obtain powder, guns, flints,
swords and other implements of war from white men and
it is a folly for any black men to attempt making war
with white men and hope the Governor will not mind the
foolishness of the people of Kambia as it shows that
they are without sense and that people who are in the

custom of drinking liquor should not be relied [on],
they say one thing today and tomorrow they change it
and therefore hope the Governor should not look at
their conduct as that of a true people for no confidence can be placed in them, they being unlettered,
and that if it had not been the disordered state of
affairs in his country between him and some of his
subjects when the news reached him he would have
marched up with a large force to meet the Governor
at Kambia, now they seem to forget the timely interference of the Governor three years ago because peace
is between them and his country—All this was the Governor's doing but now they seem to forget the cause
which caused them to cede their country three years
ago to the Queen. He directed me also to inform the
Governor that up to this date the country is not properly settled in consequence of Foday Murry Cearay
Darfae's obstinacy to submit to his authority and that
he had heard that the Timmanees had stated at Kambia
that he Allimamy Bokharie has employed them to go over
to assist him in subjugating Murry Cearay Darfae, this
is not true, he did so before the Governor's going up
to Karli Modiah, last year and before signing a paper
with the Governor not to employ people to come into
the country after signing that paper, he sent presents
to inform them that he no longer required their service and that if they should go over it will be very
bad for them and this may also raise the question of
Gbelleh Foday Tarrawally's town mentioned to the Governor when at Kalli Modea last year which is still
strong in our minds.

In addition to the above statement Alikarlie
Yousoofoo Chief of the Mellicourie and Alikarlie
Foodia Toomany Chief of Mallaghea requested me in the
presence of their two relatives sent with me to inform
the Governor that they and their Chiefs very much regret to hear of the improper behaviour of the Kings &
Chiefs of Kambia towards him and that they have heard
that those warriors had intended to come to the Soosoo
Country in direct violation of the arrangement all had
come to and signed at Kambia with the Governor under
the pretext that our King invited them to do so, this
our King assured us is not true and that if they do so
it will be very serious to them therefore they send to
inform the Governor in time.

Signed in Arabic   Sattan Dowoda
                            Karifalli

Lusanny
Murry Saidoo

Witnesses to signatures)
written in Arabic in   )
our presence   )

(Sgd.) J. B. Prigg
(") M. Sanusi

The foregoing statement was taken by the request of
the Signatories read and explained to them in the
English and Soosoo languages who declared the same to
be what they were directed to state by their King and
Chiefs.

(Sgd.) Thomas Geo. Lawson, Govt. Interpreter
(") N. B. Harding

GILB, 2:240-41

Freetown Sierra Leone
18th July 1879

Statement of Sattan Dowoda the accredited messenger of
Allimamy Bokharie King of the Moriah Country and a sub
chief and brother of Cardiettah Modoo chief of Calla
Modiah.

In reference to the island of Matacong situated
at the entrance of the Bereira and Fourricariah Rivers,
It is a portion of the Kissi Kissi or Moriah Country
of which I am a native, it is well known in our Country and to myself being repeatedly told by our fathers
and elders as well as by our present King Allimamy
Bokharie and Chiefs that it and other portions of our
Country had been ceded to the British Government by a
former King in our Country named Allimamy Oomaroo many
years ago although the rent for the same is paid to
our King by whoever occupies it as a trading post or
factory. The former Kings of the Kissi Kissi or Moriah
Country acquired the Sovereignty of this Island as they
do other parts of that country including Mellicourie,
Malaghea, Fourricariah, Beriera etc. from the original

the Digsaing Timmanees and the Bulloms which countries
had been under the rules of our Kings and Chiefs for
more than two hundred years without any interruption
or question by anybody. More than twenty years ago
the agreement for the rent of Matacong was in the possession of Allimamy Ali Gbaricca late King of the
Moriah Country, when he died two of the rightful persons who had claims to the crown viz. the late Foday
Harfee and Foday Wise were contending for it. Harfee's
mother being a free woman the majority of the people
in the Country were in his favor. Foday Wise's mother
being a slave woman [he] had very few on his side[. He]
consequently appealed to the whole of the slaves in
the Moriah Country all of whom unanimously concluded
that unless the Crown be given to Foday Wise who was
the elder of the two and uncle of Foday Harfee and had
more right they will die with him if the crown is not
given to him and consider themselves no longer Slaves
to any one, this alarmed the country and many went on
his side, the foremost of whom was the town and district of Beriera which had more Slaves than any other
in the Kissi Kissi or Moriah Country. Foday Wise seeing this, to encourage and strengthen the hands of the
Bereira Chiefs and people who came on his side delivered the agreement for the payment of the rent of
Matacong (which was then occupied by the late Thomas
Reader Esq. a partner of the late Mr. Nathaniel Isaacs)
to Allimamy Sarleah the predecessor of the present
Chief Sorie Feekeh, that in future the Chiefs of
Bereira should receive the rent of the Island but the
Sovereignty was not given; thus did that Island fall
into the hands of the Beriera Chiefs. About three or
four months ago we heard rumoured in our country that
the Governor of Sierra Leone had gone to Matacong and
hoisted the English flag there, this we found after-
ward not to be true and that the French subsequently
went there pulled down that of the English and hoisted
theirs instead which about a month ago we heard was
pulled down and their Station houses taken away. Our
King and Chiefs heard of these things but say nothing
as no one has referred the matter to them but all in
the country knows that the Island was originally ceded
to the English by our ancestors and up to this moment
we consider it to be the English.

Signed in Arabic, Sattan Dowoda
Witnesses to Signatures
(Sgd.) Thos. Geo. Lawson
     Govt. Interpreter
(") M. Sanusi

GILB, 3:22-25

Settlement of Sierra Leone
Freetown. 10th December 1879

We the undersigned having been duly commissioned
and appointed by our King and Chiefs of our country on
this mission to His Excellency Governor Rowe the representative of our good friend the Queen of England
and the Governor-in-Chief of Her West Africa Settlement on their and our behalf to make the following
Statement for His information in the following words.

King Simminee Simbah the lawful King of our country Soombuyah comprising Maniah on the West, Fanjay on
the east, Berrie Erie Wooloongbongie on the north a
distance inland about 50 miles from Wonkaifong and
bounded on the South by the Ocean including the various towns in the boundary described above, namely -
Morobiah, Kokeh, Murrifingyah, Coromboyah, Medina,
Doombooyah Kabbae and other towns not herein named
including the Island of Matacong which Island more
than 50 years ago had been mutually agreed with the
King and [with the King] of the Moriah country ceded
and transferred to the British Government for to be
considered a neutral ground for the various countries
trading with the Settlement of Sierra Leone. The King
sent us on his particular subjects of great importance
to the Governor.

1st To inform the Governor that the Island of
Matacong and all lands afront to it are his being part
of his country Soombuyah and that the Island was with
the consent of his ancestors and predecessors with the
King Alimamy Oomaroo of the Moriah country ceded and
transferred to the British Government which cession
they their children still consider to be in full force
and effect, and that they have heard about 8 or 9
months ago that that Island had been given to the
French Government by Sorie Fekeh Chief of Berrie Erie
who is a Subchief under Alimamy Bokharie King of the
Moriah Country. We have actually seen the French flag
hoisted on that Island and that one of our brothers
Yeannah Toomany brother of Namina Dantoomah while coming to Sierra Leone to trade about 8 months ago landed
there and protested against the French authority for
so doing telling them that the Island Matacong belongs
to the English and that this was told him by his

Ancestors, for that saying he was flogged severely
near to death by the Jolloff Soldiers of the French
that were in the Island by the order of the Officer
in charge of them. Our King directs us to inform the
Governor that Sorie Fekeh has no authority whatever
as a King to give that Island to anybody. The agreement of the Island came into his possession through a
late Chief named Yimbay Lamina of Morecaniah who with
his family now residing at Morecaniah in the Samoo
country were originally residents of Morobiah whence
their father removed to Morecaniah he having some dispute with his relatives went to lay complaint to Bemba
Memmah Lahai late chief of Malaghea to whom he delivered the agreement for receiving the rent of Matacong.
From this Chief of Malaghea the agreement was taken to
Fourecariah, from that place it was taken to the Chief
of Berrie Erie simply for safe keeping till the family
dispute be settled, but up to this date it remained in
their possession. Sorie Fekeh has no power whatever
to transfer the Island to anybody, if he did so whoever received it from his received what is given him
on an unsound ground. The King wishes the Governor to
know that himself and all his country look to the English Government as their friend and that this [alli-
ance] was [made] before his birth in which friendship
he and his people determined to abide in as their
ancestors unless they should be cast away by the
English.

2ndly The King directs us to inform the Governor
as his friend that at present the Moriah country has
got into war with the people of Layah Bashia and has
now attacked one of the towns in his country called
Fendah Modia Bashia and that they have done everything
to provoke him and his people to war, and that he has
sent to Alimamy Bokharie who is the King of the Moriah
country who sent to inform him that the war is carried
on by his subjects who rebelled against his authority
namely Quiah Foday Dowooda his nephew, Foday Murry
Cearay Daffae formerly of the Fouricariah both of whom
are strongly supported by Sorie Fekeh Chief of Berrie
Erie and part of the people of that place and that he
sent us to ask the Governor to be pleased he being the
only European friend he has and depend upon to interfere so as to prevent his going to war and if possible
to put a stop to it altogether for if he and his country should take up the war it would be more serious
than those foolish young men imagine which will lead
Bokharie to interfere.

3.   That he and his country since last year had
been highly provoked to this war which he has endeavored to describe in his Arabic letter brought by us to
the Governor, he begs the Governor not to think light
of this application for if the war should come worse
it will effect the trade in the Bagga, Soombuyah and
the Moriah countries, Knowing this to be a fact caused
him to beg the Governor to interfere so as to get it
stopped.   The King further begs us to express his Sin-
cere thanks for the present sent him by Alimamy Barber
all of which he has received correctly.

The above statement is unanimously agreed by all
the Chiefs of the Sumbuyah country.

The King wishes us to return as soon as possible.

Witness our hands this tenth day of December 1879
in the presence of witnesses—

                    Mallay Modoo, grandson   )
                    of late Sanky Brimah one of)
                    the parties signing treaty   )
                    No. 17 page 305 Vol II.   )

                    Alimamy Musa, a principal   )
                    Chief of Morobiah.   )

                    Namina Dantoomah, son of   )
                    late Chief Yellie Simielah.)

                    Kallay Modoo, nephew of the)
                    King.   )

                    Mangah Woley, son of late   )
                    Chief Mallay Toomany.   )

                    Keah Musa, cousin of   )
                    Alimamy Musa of Morobiah.   )

                    their marks

Witnesses to marks   )
made in our presence)

(sgd)   J. B. Prigg
(")   M. Sanusi

We the undersigned do hereby solemnly and

conscientiously declare that the above statement has
been taking in writing by the request of the signatories, that it was read and explained to them in the
Soosoo language to the best of our skill and ability
and that each and every one of them declared to have
distinctly understood the same before affixing their
names to it.

Witnesses to signatures)   (Sg.) Thomas Geo. Lawson)
made in our presence   )   Govt. Interpreter)

(Sg.) M. Sanusi.   )   "   Thomas N. Grant   )
       Arabic Writer)   Interpreter of   )
                                       Supreme and Police)
   "   J. B. Prigg   Courts   )

GILB, 3:308-09
   and 313-14

                              Freetown Sierra Leone
                              6th January 1881

Sir,

        I beg respectfully to submit the following state-
ment as a report for the information of His Excellency
the Administrator-in-Chief on the present movements of
the Kings and Chiefs, of the Great and Small Scarcies
and the Moriah countries.

        Since receiving Allimamy Barakah's letter marked
A which I forwarded under covering letter marked B
dated the 4th instant and having read the letters sent
from the above Kings and Chiefs I have a firm belief
that the measure His Excellency has adopted will reconcile the Chiefs of those places to peace and good
will with each other more so [because] Allimamy Barakah
[is] being permitted by His Excellency to accompany
them in taking Allimamy Bokharie back to his country
in peace and assist in settling the dispute between
him and his Chiefs will prove to them the continued
friendly feeling and interest this Government has towards them and their countries.

        The present of ₤10 sent to Alikarlie Yousufoo of

Mellicourie and the £5 to each of the Kings of the
Great and Small Scarcies together with the kind treatment their messengers have received from his Excellency's hands since their arrival here with what the
Governor-in-Chief had shewn to them in 1879 entirely
proved to them the constant good will of this Government towards them. In a serious and truthful conversation I had with the messengers yesterday morning
they did not hesitate to say to me Mr. Lawson tell the
Governor for us not to mind our foolishness nor to
forsake us; our ignorance of European customs and manners as well as crediting false reports have always
been the cause of misunderstandings coming between us.
Our Kings and Chiefs have seen their folly in what had
taken place in May 1879 at Kambia. All what had been
told us and our Kings both by white and black traders
we found to be false and all have regretted very much
for the conduct of some of their warboys when the
Governor-in-Chief was at Kambia at that time, and hope
soon to come down in order to be of one mind with the
Government. Upon the strength and proof of which they
all have agreed to take Allimamy Bokharie King of the
Moriah Country back to his country in peace as they
are sure this will please the Governor when he hears
of it instead of hearing that we went there with war.

    In reply I stated to them that I am very glad to
see that they have seen their folly and wish them to
understand that I am one of themselves, that is, an
African in the true sense and meaning of that appella-
tion and that providentially I was brought here grown
up and reside with whitemen now 56 years and have a
little knowledge of their feelings towards us and that
I am certain and sure that the English Government
never want an inch of our country nor desire to take
it by force but should they take any portion at all it
would be for to benefit us. They all seem quite to
understand this and appear satisfied.

    Allimamy Barakah's going up as I stated in my
covering letter marked B will serve also to give free
passage to the numerous caravans or native traders who
are on their way from the Interior with trade but are
compelled to stop at a country lying between Futah
Jallow and the Moriah Country from fear of the warmen
congregated on the roads in consequence of the dispute
between Allimamy Bokharie and some of his Chiefs which
will be able then to come down freely with safety.

Having known this to be the fact I deem it necessary to submit the same in writing for His Excellency's information and will confidently say that the expense he has undergone in this affair will not be a waste of money to this Government, if only the Northern question between the British Government and that of the French be decided in our favour. (A)

Lieut. Thackeray
Aid-de-Camp
Government House

(A - Concluding part of Report dated 6th January)

In conclusion as I consider it would not be out of the way to state for His Excellency's information the cause of the present disturbed state of the Moriah Country which the Chiefs mentioned above are going to settle.

I beg further to state that shortly after the Governor-in-Chief returned from Fourricariah in June 1878, about the early part of the following year (1879) Allimamy Bokharie reported to the Governor-in-Chief the improper conduct of his nephew Alikarlie Quiah Foday Dowda, Foday Mori Cearay Darfae, Wondai Simmila of Darry in the Moriah Country near Fourricariah and some others, who contrary to his orders and against his authority carried war and attacked Bashea an inland town some distance from Fourricariah.

The Bashea people in retaliation brought war down, destroyed Darry, killed great number of people and made prisoners of great many. The Allimamy being annoyed of the conduct of these his rebellious or refractory Chiefs reported the matter to the Governor-in-Chief I believe in March or April 1879 at which time His Excellency wrote to the King, his nephew Quiah Foday Dowda and others pointing out to them their evil conduct in disobeying and slighting the authority of their King.

The Berrie Errie Chiefs joined these rebellious Chiefs against their King so as to fight the Bashea people.

The Soombuyah King interfered in the way of peace

making but he was slighted and many of his people ill used, one of his sons badly wounded and some of his people made prisoners, all of which he patiently forebore and it appears that his patience is worn out, and about the latter part of last year he determined to take war against the Moriah people which he intimated to His Excellency in his last letter brought by Mr. Douglas in November last, but the various Kings and Chiefs who had been upholding Allimamy Bokharie are now determined to carry him home in peace and not in a hostile manner, this is in compliance with the requests of the various Chiefs in the Moriah Country who have seen their folly in rebelling against the authority of their King, they have also sued to Balla Demba King of the Karloom Bagga Country to come to their aid in the way of peace making between them and their King (Allimamy Bokharie) this was intimated to His Excellency in that King's letter brought by Mr. Douglas to His Excellency in November last and I am told he is now on his way to join the other Chiefs at Mellicourie, in fact it appears that the whole of the Chiefs have seen their folly and are tired of the war and I have a firm belief that the peace makers will succeed as I have in that [success] of Bey Mauro far up the Sierra Leone River in the dispute arising out of the late war brought by Miseerie against Mormoh Racca for which the shaking hands now only remains.

                          I have the honor to be
                                   Sir
                          Your Obedient Servant

                          (sgd) Thos. Geo. Lawson
                          Government Interpreter.

Lieut. Thackeray
Aid-de-Camp
Govt. House.

GILB, 3:476-77

Freetown Sierra Leone
17th June 1881

Sir,

I beg to state through you for His Excellency's information that yesterday I received a letter dated the 10th instant from Mr. N. B. Harding late in the Service reporting the death of the good old King Bey Farimah King of Kambia and Magbaitee in the Great Scarcies which took place on the 9th instant and from what he had gathered about the peace making undertaken by Allimamy Sattan Lahai King of Rowoolah and Bey Inga King of the Small Scarcies between Allimamy Bokharie King of the Moriah country and some of his refractory Chiefs against him they will be obliged to return home without success; this then will surely break out into war again in that country and might likely bring some disturbance in the Scarcies River.

If this will be the case those Kings will be obliged to bring back Allimamy Bokharie to Scarcies.

The whole of this matter would be easily settled by this Government if the Northern Question between it and the French had been decided which I hope and pray will terminate favourably on our Side.

Very little faith is to be placed on Bey Inga from his treacherous behaviour to this Government when Sir Samuel Rowe went up to Kambia in June 1879.

I am glad to report that trade from the Interior viz. Sago, Boreh, Futah, etc. had not ceased coming almost every day, not in great number but by 10, 20, 30 to 50 at a time.

I have the honor to be
Sir
Your Most Obedient Servant

(Sgd) Thos. Geo. Lawson
Govt. Interpreter

The Honble.
T. Risely Griffith
Col. Secretary and
Treasurer.
etc. etc. etc.

GILB, 4:108-19

Freetown Sierra Leone
22nd March 1882

Sir,

The enclosed letters had been handed to me by the Traders in the Great Scarcies and Bey Inga King of the Small Scarcies. I forgot to take them this morning to the Acting Governor, I therefore forward them to you for that purpose as soon as my report is fairly copied. I shall forward the same.

I have etc.

(sgd) Thos. Geo. Lawson
Govt. Interpreter

I. M. Lewis Esq.,
Governor's Clerk.

Freetown Sierra Leone
22nd March 1882

Sir,

I beg respectfully to state for His Excellency's information that in obedience to his orders I left Freetown in the morning of Friday the 10th instant at 10 a.m. having a strong head wind against us I arrived at Medina Allimamy Sanusi's place Bullom Shore at 2:30 p.m. Saw Allimamy Sanusi and warned the witnesses to attend the Supreme Court to give evidence in a case of slave dealing on Monday the 13th instant, the wind being still ahead I passed the night at that place, next morning the 11th I left the place at 5 a.m. the wind still being ahead till we passed Barloh Point when it became favourable we passed on and arrived at Kaikonkie at 2 p.m. I left that place at 2.30 p.m. and arrived at Mambolo 5.30 p.m. the tide being against us we passed the night there and after seeing the Chiefs, delivered His Excellency's message that they should not interfere or meddle with the war going on in the Moriah country—I found at that place everything quiet and peaceable, and in the neighbouring places; they assured me for His Excellency's information that they

have nothing whatever to do with that war and that
they are only anxious to have a new King crowned in
the stead of their late King Bey Sherbro; next day
the 12th I left Mambolo at 6.30 a.m. and landed at
RoCooproo 10 a.m. Saw Chief Sinneh Womgbo and others;
they also assured me of their not interfering in the
war. I left that place at 10.30 a.m. and arrived at
Kambia 1 p.m., Several of the Chiefs received me kindly
and found lodgings for us, a messenger was sent immediately to apprise Allimamy Sattan Lahai King of
Rowoolah of my arrival. On the 13th the messenger
returned late in the evening while waiting the return
of the messenger I learnt from information that on
Friday 10th there had been a battle which took place
on that day between the Soosoos and the Timmanees, the
former having brought a large army and erected three
large stockades within three or four hours walk to
Kambia and were defeated and driven back with heavy
losses. I saw several warmen at that place, likewise
Allimamy Bokharie, he called to see me, and informed
me that through the treachery of his subjects and
their rebellion against his authority he was obliged
to take war to Fouricariah and that the Government of
Sierra Leone as well as the French Commandant before
the present one, as well as the Timmanee Kings and
Chiefs have done all they could for the past two years
to reconcile matters between him and his Chiefs but
failed, which compelled him to adopt the measure which
he has now done; I told him distinctly that His Excellency the Governor-in-Chief had nothing to do with
him and that he should not have come over to Kambia to
induce the Timmanees into his war, and that the Governor is much displeased of his conduct and that he
should remove himself to some other locality, and that
the French are also displeased of his conduct. Early
next morning the 14th I left Kambia 6.55 for RoTinta
an inland town where Allimamy Sattan Lahai resides. I
went in hammock carried by the men provided me by His
Excellency the Governor-in-Chief after three hours
walk we arrived at that place 9.45 a.m.. Saw Allimamy
Sattan Lahai, his Chiefs and about 250 persons, also
Allimamy Loonsenay of Digsaing, the two Kings received
me kindly and about half an hour afterwards I read to
them His Excellency's letter no. 22 of the 8th instant,
they were much pleased and said the Governor has done
them one of the greatest favour by sending me, after
which, I delivered His Excellency's message to them in
the following words, You all know that the Government
of Sierra Leone is the truest friend you have on this

part of the Coast who always assist and protect you in
all your difficulties and troubles and always befriend
you. On the arrival of His Excellency from England he
expressed a strong friendly desire to see you all but
up to date none of you have seen him personally. When
he heard that there would likely be a broken-out in
the Moriah country he wrote you letters warning you as
friends not in any way to meddle with it, when he heard
also that Allimamy Bokharie had taken shelter in your
country he sent letter with messenger Momodoo Wakka
repeating his warnings to you and not to allow Allimamy Bokharie to stay in your country but to his regret you allow him to remain, and further than that
he has a letter of complaint written to him by the
French Consul and the Commandant at Binty informing
him that the warmen that attacked Fouricariah and
places near it are your people Timmanees and that the
bodies of those killed in the war had been recognized;
in this you have left yourself open to be attacked by
the French Government who now owns the Moriah country
if they see it necessary to do so, and which they will
surely do, and that whatever takes place between you
and them you must not blame the British Government for
not interfering, more so that it is reported for his
information that you Allimamy Sattan Lahai and Bey
Inga of the Small Scarcies have added two slaves each
to three of Allimamy Bokharie's making in all seven to
engage the Moricaniah and Samos Chiefs to join this
war, all of which show that you have hands in it.

Allimamy Sattan Lahai after hearing all what I
have stated rose up and stated that he thanks the Governor for sending me, for what I have stated to them
are grave and important; that he Sattan Lahai can declare positively that he has not hands in the war and
that he cannot say that the warmen that went to the
Moriah country great many of them were not mixed with
Timmanees and that the Timmanee nation is large and of
many tribes, that when he received the Governor's letter he warned the whole of his people not to mix themselves with the war and passed a law at Kambia not to
allow any warrior to pass through that town or any
part of that country over to the Moriah country, and
that if any of them should touch anything belonging to
the traders or anybody in that town he is to be killed,
he said that Kaiblie the war Chief is a Timmanee but
not of the Scarcies line, he belongs to Bey Bureh of
Casseh near Port Lokkoh and was employed by Allimamy
Bokharie in the last war he had with his late cousin

in 1865; at that time the whole of them joined Allimamy Bokharie in that war; after peace was made he
went and resided in the country of Bey Inga, some
years after, a falling out took place between him and
Bey Inga when he removed to his own King Bey Bureh,
until about two or three years ago Allimamy Bokharie
got him again.

Another warrior called Carrimoo Gbambalie is also
not of his country but of the Gbambalie country, a
country high above Port Lokkoh, he also was employed
by Allimamy Bokharie in that same last war and about
two years ago employed by Quiah Foday Dowodah of Fouricariah to fight some war little above that town.
Allimamy Bokharie succeeded in getting him on his side.

Cearay Amarah is a native of Sierra Leone, his
father being a liberated African; his mother Cearay is
native of Allimamy Colleh's country, he was taken to
that country by his mother when a child and brought up
in it and became a warrior and had always been fighting for Allimamy Bokharie, they heard that he is killed
at Mellicourie.

Another warrior named Gbomgbotoe who also is said
to be killed at Mellicourie is a Lokkoh man under
Sorie Kehsehbeh of Rotifunk in Bompeh; he came with
Bey Mauro six years ago and when Bey Mauro returned he
remained with Allimamy Bokharie.

Santiggy Kookoonah belongs to the Interior part
and resides with Bey Inga but had left Bey Inga three
or four years ago, he is not killed he is alive, and
that he Allimamy Sattan Lahai would be very glad to
see any of the persons caught at Mellicourie to testify that they belong to his country or [were] sent by
him to the war. He said with respect to the two slaves
which they alleged that he gave to assist Allimamy
Bokharie in getting warmen from Moricaniah and Samoo
he can positively declare that he never did and if
those slaves are not disposed of he would be very glad
if they could be produced to testify against him, and
that with regard to the French going to assist the
Moriahs against them he is certain he never injured
the French and that if they the French had assisted
them when they were at Mellicourie to settle the matter between Allimamy Bokharie and his people this war
would not have taken place, but as they [have] power
they can do as they please; they cannot prevent them.

He said that no doubt you have seen some warmen walk-
ing about at Kambia town and that was few days ago.
The Moriah people erected three warfences in which
they had large armies about four hours' walk to Kambia,
and to save their country in self defence they were
obliged to go and drive them out of it, which they did
in a very short time and that this was three days before I arrived at Kambia this is the reason why they
are there. With regard to Allimamy Bokharie taking
shelter in their country he said [it] is not their
wish and since his arrival there not one of the principal Kings and Chiefs have seen him, but he must go
from there to some other place, and that according to
their country customs he said that if the Soosoos knew
that Allimamy Bokharie was in their country, and they
had no intention to war against them[,] the Scarcies
Timmanees[,] it was their place to send messengers to
apprise them and demand him, and if they refused giving him up or drive him out of their country then it
will be just to bring war on their country but to
attempt to come there by force to take him is also a
cause of war between them.

     The Timmanee warmen that Allimamy Bokharie hired
are not of this country Scarcies, nor do they pass
through the boundary of the Scarcies, they passed on
the upper part and congregated at a place called
Bashia a Soosoo town from whence they went and fell
upon Fouricariah, on their being driven out of it they
came and stopped at Digsaing near Mellicourie where
they are now. After some more conversation with him,
I told the whole of them distinctly that they have to
abide to whatever comes upon them; I then left RoTinta
4.5 p.m. and arrived at Kambia 6.40 p.m. same day.
15th Wednesday, I had a meeting of the British traders,
Mr. Thomas, J. Johnson, Mr. James Metzger, Mr. Reader
Son of late Mr. Edwan Reader, one Mr. Richards, Mr.
Coker, Mr. Moses Bentine, Mr. Harleston, Mr. Cole,
Mrs. Brown, Mrs. Wilhelm and about twelve others when
I delivered His Excellency's letter to them. The letter was read to all in my presence by Mr. James Metzger
who had previously read it in Freetown before I left
for Kambia. I gave them all the friendly advice I
could and on the following day 5.20 in the morning I
left Kambia, I arrived at RoCooproo 8.30 a.m. saw the
Chiefs and repeated His Excellency's warning to them

as I did when going up and left that place 9.30 a.m. and arrived at Mamnolo 11.40 a.m. the tide being against us we passed the night at that place the following day 17th being out of provision I procured some and then left that place 8.5 a.m. and arrived at Tombo 9.40 a.m. and their waited for the flood tide. We left Tombo 3.55 p.m. and at Kartongu 6.55 p.m. where we were kindly received and housed by the Chiefs. Next morning 18th we left Kartongu 6.55 a.m. and landed at Ro Mangay Bey Inga's residence 9.10 a.m. a few minutes afterwards I had an interview with him, he received and treated me very kindly, he sent a sheep as a present to me and a basket of rice, the sheep was killed and distributed; he then sent for his principal chiefs and headmen and at 2.30 p.m. a meeting was convened when I brought out His Excellency's letter no. 22 of the 8th instant which was handed to one Mr. Reffel a British trader there who read it to the hearing of all present about 150 persons. The King and Chiefs were exceedingly glad to see one, the King said that all doubts and false reports are now ended, Mr. Lawson say to the Governor that I have no hands whatever in this war, nor do I desire to have hands in it, there are people here who can testify to this fact. People are here, Soosoos, belonging to Mellicourie, Fouricariah, Moricaniah and other Soosoos towns and even at Mellicourie there are people there to testify that I have no hands in this war, nor do I send anybody there.

Santiggy Kookoonah mentioned to have been killed and said to be a subject of mine is not killed nor is he my subject he had been living here some time in my country but from some falling out I drove him away.

Kaiblie belongs to Bey Bureh in the Casseh country not very far from Port Lokkoh and he had been employed by Allimamy Bokharie to war since 1865, nor is he residing in my country; I know nothing of him of late; I desire no war what troubles my mind just now is that I heard Allimamy Bokharie is at Kambia Bey Farima's jurisdiction and I do not wish him to be there; I have no quarrel with the Soosoos, myself and Alimamy Sattan Lahai and others went to make peace in their country between them and their King, as we did not succeed I returned home to my country and made myself quiet and advised all my people to attend to their

farm work; the only thing which troubles my mind much
is about crowning a new King at Mambolo and another
in the stead of late Bey Farima and then we all can go
in person to see the Governor. I would have long before this done so, but [was] prevented by the circumstance I stated.

     With regard to my giving two slaves to assist
Allimamy Bokharie to procure warmen at Moricaniah and
Samoo, there is no truth in it. We thank the Governor
very much for sending you to enquire and know about
these things; we cannot hide anything from you. I
speak positively for myself that I have no hands whatever in the war. The meeting then broke up; when I
returned to my residence several of the Soosoos of
Mellicourie and other towns in the Moriah country residing with Bey Inga called to see me and assured me
that really and truly Bey Inga has no hands in the
war. Next morning the 19th Sunday I left Mangay 8.25
and arrived at Tombo 4.5 p.m. The tide being against
us I passed the night at this place under showers [of]
mosquittoes. Next morning the 20th. I left Tombo 8.30
and arrived at Medina, Bullom Shore 4 p.m. While at
Tombo I learnt before leaving that place that the
Soosoos came in a large body with some French Soldiers
and attacked a town in the Digsaing country, they succeeded in destroying it with rockets but were defeated
and driven back to Mellicourie with many killed and
others wounded. 21st I left Medina 8.40 a.m. and arrived here 12 noon I did not see Allimamy Colleh when
going up to Kambia on the 12th I landed there but he
was not at home and on my returning I did not land
there being anxious to get down in order to meet His
Excellency before his leaving for Monrovia. From all
that I gathered through Allimamy Lahai [he] seemed to
speak fair, but my impression is that he must have
some hands secretly in this war, more especially what
betrays him more is his allowing Allimamy Bokharie to
remain at Kambia till this day. Bey Inga from all I
could gather and see of him he seems to be truly de-
sirous not to have anything to do with that war; what
enboldened me so to speak is his allowing many of the
people belonging to Mellicourie and other towns of the
Moriah country to reside in his country free from molestation whereas the Soosoos from all what I heard
are killing every Timmanee person they see in their
country innocently simply because they are Timmanees.
At Ro Cooproo down to Mambolo, this is the same case,
no Soosoo man is molested.

Strangers from the Interior are coming down in great numbers to Kambia with produce hides, oxen and gold etc.

While at RoTinta great number of them met us there from Futah, they had with them 100 oxen and other articles to trade.

The British subjects at that place gave me a letter in reply to His Excellency, likewise Bey Inga gave me one.

I may here add that while at Kambia and at RoTinta several of the Chiefs as well as Allimamy Sattan Lahai spoke to me about the rum seized at Kaikonkie whether it would not be restored to them. I told them plainly that the Government had been very lenient with them in that matter in allowing their canoes to be restored and that they can have the rum restored in like manner when the duty is paid on it and that the Governor has no intention to injure any of them as long as they employ with the laws of the Queen. I asked them if they think it right that whilst other people are paying duties on articles taken to their country as well as up to the Sierra Leone river and the Sherbro to allow them to take goods of the same sort into their country without paying the duties and that on the other hand they taking all their produce to other foreign ports for sale which give no advantage to the Government which protects them, they said no, it is not right. I also told them that whatever they buy at Sierra Leone and at Iseles de Los would give them no trouble when going up their rivers as they have simply to show the Collector's permit. Many of the chiefs and principal men see the reasonableness of this, but the Allimamy seemed to be against it. When at Mangay Bey Inga and his chiefs brought the same question to me, I explained to them as I did at Kambia and they at once see the propriety of it, and said that it is better for them to come direct to Sierra Leone to buy things than going about to Mellicourie and other places to trade and that if merchants trading in their rivers would give them goods as reasonable as they would get them in Sierra Leone they see no necessity of coming to Sierra Leone to buy things except what cannot be obtained from the factories in their rivers.

I conclude this by stating for His Excellency's information that the two policemen who accompanied me behaved themselves very well.

I have the honor to be
Sir
Your Most Obedient Servant

(sgd) Thos. Geo. Lawson
Govt. Interpreter

Capt. H. M. Jackson R.A.
Private Secretary and
   A.D.C.
I.M. Lewis Esq., in his absence.

GILB, 4:338-41

Freetown Sierra Leone
17th August 1882

Memo for His Excellency's information.

Sir,

    The war Chief Kibalie who is reported to be the
Leader of Allimamy Bokharie's warmen in the war now
going on in the Moriah Country is truly a Timmanee man,
not under Allimamy Sattan Lahai nor Bey Inga King of
the Small Scarcies but is immediately under Bey Borreh
King of the Kasseh Country (see treaty No. 6. Vol. V
page 330) a Country lying in the Interior or East between Port Lokkoh and the Small Scarcies. He was employed by Allimamy Bokharie in 1865 when all the Timmanees of Port Lokkoh, Small and Great Scarcies aided
him in his late war with his cousin Malliggy Bailee,
Kibalie then came from his country and became the
leader of the warmen belonging to the present Bey Inga
and a former Sattan Lahai. The success they had at
that time led Kibalie to reside at RoManga Bey Inga's
town, until few years ago it was reported they fell
out when Bey Inga drove him from his country altogether.
This Bey Inga stated when he was here last. However
Allimamy Bokharie always keeping [Kibalie] with him as
his war Chief wherever he is. Before he [Bokharie]
commenced this fresh outbreak, about the beginning of

this year, I heard he sent for him [Kibalie] while he was at Mellicourie, there he [Bokarie] made all his arrangements with him, and he [Kibalie] went up in the Interior where he employed many of the different Timmanee tribes to come to this war, furnished with large presents for that purpose by Allimamy Bokharie to obtain warmen for him [Bokharie]. They are those Timmanees who are now heard of engaged with him in the war and another is called Carrimoo Gbambalie. Every assurance has been had both from Allimamy Sattan Lahie and Bey Inga of their having no hands in the war; what led me to believe this more is that no information has been had from the numerous British traders at the Great and Small Scarcies especially from Kambia that the Kings of those places have hands in the war or seeing warmen going from Kambia to the Moriah Country to fight.

On the other hand the Chiefs of the Moriah Country through whose conduct all these troubles broke out[,] namely Alikarlie Quiah Foday Dowda of Fouricaria, Alikarlie Yellam Foday of Pharmoriah, Alikarlie Fudiah Toomany of Malaghea, Alikarlie Yousufu of Mellicourie (Tye Gbai). Alikarlie Sippiana of Contah and others[,] will not hesitate to affirm that the Timmanee warmen who drove them from their towns are Allimamy Sattan Lahai and Bey Inga's people which they cannot prove but because[,] as they believe[,] they [the Timmanee warmen] are Bokharie's friends. Momodoo Wakka who lately came from there when sent there by His Excellency positively stated that the Allimamy declared that he has no hands in the war nor did he see any signs of his having any hands in the war.

With respect to the other war Chief Boatemane as one of the Timmanee war leaders I do not know who he is, perhaps the name is not properly spelt; I shall however make enquiry. Very often native warriors make use of the names of Chiefs who never sent them, stating I am sent by such Chiefs, this was proved some years ago by some warmen from the Mendi Country to the Masimerah country stating that they were sent there by the Governor of Sierra Leone.

It would be well if the Soosoo would show a little courage to fight and succeed to make prisoners of one or two of the persons they know belonging to Allimamy Sattan Lahai and Bey Inga, this will be a sure proof on their part and not to be stating things

under suspicion because they believe Allimamy Sattan
Lahai and Bey Inga are friends to Bokharie. Timmanees
wherever they may be when a war is led by one of their
war Chiefs and meet with success in way of plundering
and making captives require nobody to ask them to join
it, but this the Soosoos have no courage to prevent,
instead of which they are running away from their towns
desiring others to fight for them.

I have since ascertained the proper name of the
warrior Boatemane to be Boatmonneh a Timmanee belonging to the Sandah Country not Brimah Sandah's country
but another Sandah in the Interior near Tambacca, but
Timmanee. Momodoo Wakka heard of him when he was at
Kambia last and that man is in no way connected with
Allimamy Sattan Lahai or Bey Inga. I am told that
there is a highway road which leads from the Interior
where all these warmen pass to meet Bokharie.

I know the Soosoos and the present state of affairs with them will not make them hesitate to state
or say anything to their Commandant that will be in-
jurious to Allimamy Sattan Lahai or Bey Inga, all
under suspicion.

The meaning of the name Boatmonneh signifies to
place trouble or impose trouble, and that of Kibalie
signifies the basket.

I have etc.

(sgd) Thos. Geo. Lawson

Lieut. V. M. Garland
Acting Private Secretary &
A.D.C.

GILB, 5:23-24

19th December 1882

Memo for His Excellency's information.

Statement of Alimamy Damoh Sorie of Kambia sent by Ali-
mamy Sattan Lahai King of Rowoolah Great Scarcies and
Alimamy Lusaney of Digsaing on a special mission to
His Excellency the Governor-in-Chief arrived yesterday.

. . . .

I am sent by Alimamy Sattan Lahai and Alimamy Lusaney particularly to see the Governor and to report what is now going on in our country; to say that from the day they promised the Governor to have no hands in the war, they are of that mind to this day. Alimamy Bokharie is not in our Country but he is at Bolo Bashea Karliloo's place; nor do we allow any of his warmen to stop in any part of our Country; by our orders two of his warboys are now in stocks, they came to Kambia as we do not prevent anybody to come there being a large trading place, but do not allow any one to show any motion of war. These two men went and forcibly took some oranges from some people in the market, we have them apprehended and they are now in stocks as a warning to others.

The Alimamies send me to inform the Governor that they have no hands in the war though people say so, yet they have no hands in it, and they would say so plainly if they have hands in it.

They send one to complain to the Governor that about 3 or 4 weeks ago the Soosoo people in the Moriah country brought war and attacked a town in Alimamy Lusainy's country called Tarnah destroyed it, killed some of the people, made captives of others and took them away under the supposition that we at Kambia and Digsaing Countries are aiding Alimamy Bokharie in his war against them; this the Alimamies and all the Chiefs in the country positively declared is not the case; this matter pains the whole of us in the country and we are considering what steps to adopt to avenge ourselves of this matter, but cannot do anything before reporting it to the Governor in order to get his advice.

As for the French Government at Binty, nothing can persuade them to believe that we have no hands in the war, but we are sure ourselves that we have no hands in it, and consider ourselves to be friends with them. Their Factories are in our country and we do not disturb them, but they believe the statement of the Moriah Chiefs as we believe in the Koran; they beg also that the Governor should send to the French Government to direct their people (the Soosoos) to return their people to them quietly, this is the matter the Alimamies with the other Chiefs send me to report to the Governor.

                                                his
                              (sgd) Alimamy X Sorie
                                                mark

Witnesses to Signature in Arabic

(sgd) M. Sanusi

   "   J. B. Prigg

                                   Freetown Sierra Leone
                                   19th December 1882

Sir,

     I forward the enclosed for His Excellency's in-
formation it being the statement of Alimamy Damoh Sorie
of Kambia. Alimamy Lousaney also sends one of his
sons to come with him.

                              I have etc.

                              (sgd.) Thos. Geo. Lawson
                              Govt. Interpreter.
Lieut. A. H. Butler
Private Secretary & A.D.C.

GILB, 5:54-57

                                   Freetown Sierra Leone
                                   12th January 1883

Sir,

     I would have long before this forwarded for His
Excellency's information the informations required in
your Memo Local No. 29 of the 9th instant relative to
the persons mentioned below it said to be the subjects
of the Alimamy Lahai who was said to be recognized
fighting for Alimamy Bokharie against the Soosoos, but
did not do so before today in as much as I wished to
to have a clearer information of it.

1.   Carimoo Lahai said to be killed at Mamfourona,
this man is a Limba by nation residing at Kambia and
is a great friend of Alimamy Bokharie since 1865 when
there was war between that Chief and his cousin
Malliggy Gbailee when the whole of the Chiefs of the
Great and Small Scarcies as well as the Limbas were
employed by Alimamy Bokharie to fight him. After that
war, he resides at Kambia but generally visits his own
country and has a town of his own some distance inland
from Kambia. I am informed that when Alimamy Bokharie
was ordered out of Kambia last year by Alimamy Sattan
Lahai, he of his own will secretly went with him as
his friend with whom he had continued until he received
a wound sometime last year and when he came back
wounded Alimamy Lahai ordered that he should not return to Kambia but go where he came; so he died of the
wound at his village and Alimamy Sattan Lahai did not
permit his remains to be interred in his country. I
am told also that he joined Bokharie's war to revenge
the death of his great friend the high priest Foday
Ibrahima who was murdered in cold blood by order of
Yallam Foday of Pharmoriah with many other Sarrakulaes
and Mandingo residents at that place.

2.   Barri, which means dog said to be a Servant of
Sorie Cannikoh said to be killed at Pharmoriah, I am
told that this man is a Mendi or Kossoh, but a man of
the same name Servant of Sorie Cannikoh is now with
him at Kambia and was here a few days ago in one of
his canoes he never went to the war at all.

3.   Kamba Koureh is not known, there is no one of that
name at Kambia as I am informed.

4.   Konko Yama [was] said to be wounded at Romagalli
[but this] is not true as I have heard, and [he] does
not belong [to] Kambia. He is a native of the Gbamg-
balie country wrongly spelt Bambaly.

5.   Bambaly said to be killed at Fouricaria is not
known; he might be a man from the country of that
name; many of whom are employed by Alimamy Bokharie
in his war. They are all Timmanees but not of Great
Scarcies.

6.   Mahmadou Condoma[,] said to be from Kambia and to
be a father-in-law of Yellam Foday, no doubt meaning
Yallang Foday one of the principal Chiefs in the Moriah
against Bokharie[, is] said to have been wounded by a
bullet on the thigh at Contah and is still suffering

from the wound; from all I could gather, he is not a
native of Kambia but has been residing with Alimamy
Lahai for a long time. I learnt this morning that his
being wounded is true; he is a Mahommedan and I am
told he joined that war in revenge of Mahommedan
friends who had been murdered at Pharmoriah by order
of his son-in-law Yellam Foday but had not been sent
to the war by Alimamy Lahai, so far I have been able
to gather for His Excellency's information. Perhaps
it may be well to inform Alimamy Lahai of these circumstances. I learnt that the war which attacked
Tannah in the Digsaing country and the town Soombieyah
in Alimamy Sattan Lahai's country are the Bennar Soosoos employed by the Moriah Chiefs to their assistance
as Bokharie employed the Timmanees to his assistance.

7.   That Alimamy Lahai to have heavily fined two powerful Timmanee Chiefs living in the neighbourhood of
the Scarcies, Bey Faroma no doubt meaning Bey Farima[,]
and Morrehcanou Colleh of Taweah for refusing to join
him in his friendship with Bokharie; there is no truth
in that statement. Bey Farima had never been fined by
Alimamy Lahai. He and Sattan Lahai I am told are now
at Mambolo to have a new Bey Sherbro crowned, he is
the King of Kambia as His Excellency would see by
Treaty No. 3, Page 272 Ordinance Book Volume III which
supersedes Treaty No. 54 Page 396 Ordinance Book Volume II[;]both Alimamy Sattan Lahai and Bey Farima are
not in good terms with Alimamy Colleh for his conniv-
ing some way or the other in the war. He appears to
manifest a friendly feeling towards Bokharie and the
Mellicourie Chiefs who are his immediate relatives.
Bokharie's relatives and many of the Soosoos from the
Moriah country are taking refuge in the portion of the
country under him which is the Digsaing country, also
his attempting of assuming the right of that portion
as his own country is what brought the unfriendly
feeling between him and the Great Scarcies Kings and
Chiefs. It is true that he is ready (not Bey Farima)
to join the Soosoos (which he himself is) should any
attack be made on Kambia by the Soosoos, at this the
Timmanee Kings and Chiefs seem to be aware of and consequently closely watching his movements, for the Soosoos from all information are determined to destroy
Kambia and to stop the trade in retaliation to what
had been done to them in Mellicourie and Pharmoriah,
there might have been some of the people who secretly
went to the war from the localities of Kambia but the
Alimamy positively declared that no one went by his

orders, not that he and his Chiefs are afraid, but because they have been advised by the Government not to interfere in the war and they found that it will be for their good.

I have etc.

(sgd) Thos. Geo. Lawson

Capt. H. M. Jackson R.A.
Private Secretary & A.D.C.

GILB, 5:197-198

Freetown Sierra Leone
2nd July 1883

Memo for His Excellency's information.

. . . . . .

Learnt on the 29th ultimo that the Soosoos from Mellicourie on a night during last week made an attack on Almamy Bokharie at Rogbairay a town on the north bank of the Great Scarcies river almost opposite Kambia when several of his principal people have been killed, others made prisoners and taken away. Among those who were killed was Boye Bouyah a Chief of that town and among those made prisoners and taken away was Kardiatta Modoo, Almamy Bokharie's right handed Chief, relative and adviser, a worthy man indeed and a true hearted friend of the Almamy. It appears that some of the Timmanees have been bribed to join the Soosoos. Some stated that the Soosoos have succeeded in sending to the Yonnie country and obtained lots of the Yonnie warriors to the Mellicourie by water course, and that Almamy Bokharie himself narrowly escaped. One does not know how to show any sympathy if the news be true of the killing of the chief of that place (Boye Bouyah) for if he and his people had taken the Governor-in-Chief's advice as not to allow Almamy Bokharie to stop at his place, he would not have lost his life. It is reported that the Timmanees and the people of that part of the country are determined to follow them up to Mellicourie to avenge the death of their chief.

The confirmation of the above report will in a day or two be obtained.

It is reported also that Almamy Sattan Lahai of the RoWoolah has caught two of the Timmanee warriors belonging to Almamy Bokharie for infringing his laws by forcibly taking away some property belonging to strangers coming from the Interior to Kambia for the purpose of bringing their trade here and determined to put them to death by cutting their throats in order to deter others from doing the like. Further information when obtained will be forwarded.

Nothing is heard of Momodoo Wakka as yet. He left here on the 15th ultimo.

(sgd.) Thos. Geo. Lawson
Govt. Interpreter

Capt. H. M. Jackson R.A.
Private Secretary and A.D.C.
etc. etc. etc.

GILB, 5:203-04

Freetown Sierra Leone
5th July 1883

Sir,

I believe it would be well to do as stated in your minutes. The Governor-in-Chief sent me up to Kambia with a letter to all the traders I believe in March last year to warn all of them trading up the Kambia to remove to safe localities and if they should remain there it was under their own risk; that letter I think can be seen in the Native Chiefs' book under local. At the same time perhaps it would be well to wait the receipt of the Chief's letter said to be on the way coming.

Referring to my Memorandum book I found noted that I left here on that mission on the 9th of March last year. The Governor's letter was read and explained to all the traders there then on the afternoon of 15th March last year.

I have etc.

(sgd.) Thos. Geo. Lawson
Govt. Interpreter

Capt. H. M. Jackson R.A.
Private Secretary
and A.D.C.

Freetown Sierra Leone
5th July 1883

Further information of affairs received from Kambia
Great Scarcies.

1. It is reported that the Soosoos by the Timmanees
warriors whom they employed to their assistance have
succeeded in taking another town in the Digsaing
country.

2. Kardiatta Modoo Almamy Bokharie's principal chief
who was reported to have been captured a few days ago
at Rogbairay, is taken down to the Commandant at Binty,
this might save his life. This I can swear would have
been the case if it had been British Government.

3. It is also reported that his relatives and friends
especially the principal leader of the war (Alikarlie
Yallam Foday) in the Moriah country seeing the condition [in which] he was brought to Mellicourie wept;
this grieved the Timmanee warriors whom the Soosoos
were obliged to pay two slaves to appease them.

4. Almamy Sattan Lahai has given a general notice to
all the traders to remove all their property down the
river, as Kambia may be attacked at any moment, they
are now determined to defend themselves and country
to the utmost and that they cannot bear any longer,
but will not take war to the Moriah Country unless
when they are attacked by them.

5. The Almamy's messengers are said to be on their
way with letter to the Government and may be here in a
day or two.

6.   The attack made on Rogbairay and the present one
reported to have taken place at Digsaing were done by
the Timmanee warriors employed by the Moriah Soosoos.

7.   Almamy Sattan Lahai and the other Timmanee Kings
and Chiefs stated that they firmly believe that these
disturbances are backed by the French at Binty.

                         (sgd.) Thos. Geo. Lawson
                         Govt. Interpreter

Capt. H. M. Jackson R.A.
Private Secretary and
A.D.C.

GILB, 5:279-85

                         Freetown Sierra Leone
                         27th September 1883

Sir,

     The following is the report of Momodoo Wakka on
his being sent with letter to the Kings and Chiefs
of the Great and Small Scarcies to ascertain the present state of affairs in those places.

                         (sgd.) Thos. Geo. Lawson
                         Govt. Interpreter

     Momodoo Wakka states:- In obedience to His
Excellency's direction I left here on the morning of
the 7th instant in the Government hired boat and arrived at Kaikonkie on the afternoon of that day. Early
next morning the 8th I left Kaikonkie and arrived on
the evening at Kartonghu in the Small Scarcies River
about 7 p.m. I left there next morning the 9th and
arrived at Mahfalla about 6 p.m. Left that place early
next morning the 10th and arrived at RoMangay Bey
Inga's town about 3 p.m. This loss of time was occasioned by the strong current which runs rapidly down
at this time of the season. I found the place quiet
and no warmen were seen there. The King was absent to
an inner town of his called RoGbonkoh to see that his
men attended to their work and to prevent any warmen

coming through his territory. I met Almamy Borroh the
Chief whom he left in charge of the place. I requested
him to allow me to pass on, he said no, but he would
send to apprise the King of my arrival. In the evening the messager returned with a message and informed
me that he has received the letter with much thanks to
the Governor and that I should lose no time to come to
him but pass on at once, and that he would send his
reply either to me at Kambia or send one of his principal Chiefs with it direct to Freetown. He requested
me to say to the Governor that on his part all is well,
and that he has nothing to do with the war up to now.
Next morning 11th, having known the road myself from
Small Scarcies to Kambia I left RoMangay in the morning and went direct to Bey Farama King of Magbaitee
and Kambia who was in one of his towns called Cammar-
rankah and arrived there about 3 p.m. On the same
evening I proceeded with His Excellency's letter
jointly addressed to him, Almamies Sattan Lahai and
Lunsenny. He was much pleased to see me, hear the
letter read and said that the Governor's advice to
them from the beginning was for their own good. Early
next morning 12th I proceeded on to Kambia. Almamy
Sattan Lahai was absent at Rotintah. Next morning 13th
Santiggy Binneh who was left in charge of the place
sent two men to accompany me. We left Kambia about
9 a.m. and arrived at Rotintah about 2 p.m. and saw
the King in the midst of great number of his principal
persons and people. Almamy Lunsenny was absent but
left a Representative with Almamy Lahai named Allie.
I read his Excellency's letter to him in the presence
of those who were present. I was able to read it flu-
ently because it was written in Arabic. He in the
presence of his people said that he was very glad to
receive the Governor's letter and as he has promised
the Governor from the beginning he is of the same mind,
but the behaviour of the French to him which led to
the destruction made on Rogbairay caused all his people not to take my word from him and he does not know
in what way to restrain them and that the Commandant
at Binty had written him 3 letters calling upon him to
get the peace made but he informed him the Commandant
that he cannot do so without obtaining permission from
the Governor of Sierra Leone. He told him further
that no war would go from the Moriah to his country
any more. About 6 days after this promise the war
attacked Rogbairay, killed Boye Bouyah and many re-
spectable persons, this is what caused him to lose all
confidence in the French Commandant at Binty. He

further stated that the only point in which they sym-
pathize with Almamy Bokharie is, that he is a King
crowned in their presence and in the presence of the
Officers of the Sierra Leone Government and that the
way he has been dealt with by his people, their own
people might do the same to them, therefore they do
not know in what way to drive him out of their country
to the place he ran away from, where nothing awaits
him but death and that the French are only seeking
quarrel with them without a cause and they do not consider themselves to be enemies to the French and that
it is not a new thing for a King to run away for protection to another country when his subjects rebel
against him and they have been told that some of the
French Kings and Emperors did so for safety and why
should the French think hard of them because Almamy
Bokharie takes shelter in their country and that they
thought when Bokharie takes refuge in their country
the French authorities at Binty would adopt a measure
by calling the assistance of the English who are their
friends to have this matter settled, but this they
have not done only blaming them for keeping Bokharie
in their country and that they know the Governor has
done his best to prevent this war and if the French
authorities had done what the Governor of Sierra Leone
did, it would have come to an end long ago, and up to
this moment they consider them as friends but have no
confidence in them. He gave me a letter written in
Arabic. Next day the 14th I returned to Kambia, for
want of conveyance I remained there 10 days. Trade
is still going on there. The Traders seem to be under
no apprehension of danger. The country is full of
warmen, all of whom have crossed over to the Soosoo
side and are highly engaged in destroying the Bennah
country; they being the persons who destroyed several
of their towns over whom the French authorities declared to the Governor of Sierra they have no control.
Several great men of that country were caught and
killed; they intend as soon as finishing with that
part of the country to turn their attention to the
parts (Mellicourie, and other places) and if Yallam
Foday and others who take refuge near Binty are not
turned out of that place, they would visit Binty too,
running all hazard; this is a common talk among the
warriors whom I saw at Kambia.

Having obtained conveyance I left Kambia on the
23rd together with the carrier who went with me and
landed at Kissy Wharf last night. I paid for myself

and the carrier (2/6) two shillings and sixpence for conveyance. While at Kambia I learnt that there were messengers coming from the King of Foulah on a visit to the Governor, sent by Almamy Amadoo whose time of office is expired this year and Almamy Sorie now resumes the Kingship.

(sgd) M. Wakka.

Witness to Signature

(sgd.) W. L. King

Freetown Sierra Leone
28th September 1883

Sir,

I shall do my best to be able to give you some account of the present war in the Kissi Kissi or Moriah country as well as that in the Sherbro as requested in the following order now looked upon as French territory.

Almamy Bokharie King of the Kissi Kissi or Moriah country is the lawful crowned King of that country. In his strict adherence to the laws of the Koran [he] created bad feelings and disatisfaction in the minds of his principal Chiefs and some of his subjects; namely Alikarlie Queah Foday Dowoda his nephew, Alikarlie Yellam Foday his step son, Alikarlie Yousufoo Chief of Mellicourie, Alikarlie Foudiah Toomany Chief of Malaghea, Alikarlie Sippeanah Chief of Contah and Foday Murry Searai Daffae, these with many others combined in conspiracy against him because he determined to punish Foday Murry Serai Daffae by death for gross offence against the laws of the Koran. The King found that his authority [was] slighted [and] left the country in 1880 to implore the assistance of the Timmanee Kings and Chiefs of the Great and Small Scarcies; these went with a view of reconciling matters together as friends but failed after spending eight months to do so; and instead of receiving thanks they were abused[. He stated] to them that [where] horses [were] fighting together instead of bringing another horse to make peace between them he brought asses. The Timmanee

Kings and Chiefs returned to their country. Not very
long about the year 1882 Mellicourie was attacked with
several other substantial towns in the Moriah Country
by Timmanees, Lokkohs and other people from the interior country employed by Almamy Bokharie. Almamy
Bokharie then took shelter in the Timmanee country
where he still resides. The Moriahs also employed
great number of the Bennah Soosoos to their assistance
and succeeded in destroying several towns belonging to
the Timmanees because Almamy Bokharie took shelter
among them; this is the war which is still going on in
the Moriah Country. The Moriah Soosoos since peace
had been made up the Sierra Leone river succeeded in
getting many of the Timmanees to their assistance.

    With respect to the war in Sherbro one would say
that that country is the constant seat of war although
much moderated for the past 15 years. The present war
originated from 2 Chiefs, Seppeh of Yengehmah in the
Bompeh Mendi country and Gberry of Gbongay in the Big
Boom River, from jealousy and false reports are the
causes which set these two at variance each having
friends below the river and up in the country, got
their friends to side with them, thus Seppeh got the
aid of Gpowe of Talliah, the Kings and Chiefs of the
Imperreh country and in the Small Boom as well as some
of the Chiefs residing at the river borders who are
secretly aiding him. Gberry also in like manner obtained the aid of the Looboos and Big Boom Kings and
Chiefs to aid him. Gbowe because [he is] so stubborn
and obstinate and fancied that his town Talliah is so
fortified against any attack [was] emboldened enough
to send his warmen on British territory, plundering
canoes on all sides, not respecting even the Government's although seeing Police Constables in them, refusing to make any redress when called upon to do so;
this is what caused the two last expeditions to visit
the Big and Small Boom and led to the destroying of
the impregnable town, Talliah belonging to Gpowe
which in few hours was reduced to ashes by few men of
the 2nd West India Regiment and some Police Constables
under the gallant management of Colonel Talbot and
Captain H. M. Jackson R.A. in the presence of Administrator F. F. Pinkett during the absence of the Governor-
in-Chief in England.

    I would have added more on both of these trans-
actions but no time to do so.

I have etc.

(sgd.) Thos. Geo. Lawson
Govt. Interpreter

The Honble.
T. Risely Griffith
Colonial Secretary & Treasurer
etc.   etc.   etc.

P.S.

Almamy Bokharie was crowned King of the Kissi
Kissi or Moriah Country in July 1865 in the presence
of the 1st Lieutenant Mr. Ferkinson and other officers
of H.M.S.S. "Zebra" acknowledged and recognized by
this Government (Colonel Chamberlayne) as much by
Commissioner Horatio James Huggins late Chief Justice
of this settlement.

I was with him.

(Intl) T. G. L.

GILB, 6:418-19

Freetown Sierra Leone
20th May 1885

For the information of   )
The Honourable the Colonial   )
Secretary and Treasurer   )

Sir,

A little while ago, I was informed by MR THOMAS
J. JOHNSON one of the principal Traders of the GREAT
SCARCIES river that the SOOSOO warmen who had attacked
and destroyed KAMBIA nearly two weeks ago, have come
down as far as to ROBAT and destroyed it also, and
that it is their determination to attack MAMBOLO and
KYTCHUM.

Knowing that those places are looked upon as

BRITISH territory, I consider that it is my duty to
report it for information that necessary steps may be
taken, should you consider it advisable to do so, as
I suggested in my memo of the 11th instant.

I have heard nothing fresh from other quarters.

I have etc.

(Sgd.) Thos. Geo. Lawson
Govt. Interpreter

Freetown Sierra Leone
21st May 1885

Memo for His Excellency)
the Governor-in-Chief)

1. Larger vessels than the "COUNTESS OF DERBY" had on
several occasions anchored [off] ROBAT in the GREAT
SCARCIES, a distance of about two hours rowing to
KAMBIA. In 1858 and 1859, Her Majesty's Ships "PLUTO"
"SPITFIRE" and "TEAZER" anchored off there. In 1868
or 1869, Colonial Steamship "CAROLINE" anchored off
there. In 1871, Colonial Steamship "SHERBRO" anchored
there and I think the "COUNTESS of DERBY" could go
there easily by the use of HARRY as he is well acquainted with the channels of that river.

2. I learnt that the head warrior of the SOOSOO war
now at KAMBIA is called YANSANNEH LAMINA of FOURRI-
CARIAH; he is a brother-in-law to M. SANUSI the Government Arabic Writer and can listen to him [better]
than great many other people. They consider myself to
be a great friend to ALMAMY BOKHARIE and have very
little confidence in me in that respect, perhaps he
may be met up with at ROBAT. From all what I learnt,
it was reported of him and his warmen that in many respects they have behaved very well to many of the
BRITISH Traders found at KAMBIA when it was attacked
on the 8th instant. He is a daring young man but I
believe Your Excellency finds him to be submissive for
he behaved so to MR. VOHSEN when he went up there on
the 11th or 12th instant.

I enclose herewith the memo I wrote to the Colonial Secretary on the 20th instant.

3. It might not be well to give any present to the warmen, as they might term it that it pleases you for their destroying that place. There will be time enough to give presents when Your Excellency shall observe that your caution to them is adhered to.

4. Mr SANUSI, M. WAKKA and SANNOKKOH MADDI have been warned to hold themselves in readiness to accompany Your Excellency this evening.

(Sgd.) Thos. Geo. Lawson
Govt. Interpreter.

GIM, p. 29

T. G. LAWSON'S ROLES AND ATTITUDES

Sierra Leone
1st March 1873

Memo for the Information of
His Excellency the Governor in Chief

Sir,

It is gratifying to learn from the letter of Fode
Tarawallie hereto attached that he has succeeded in
reopening the road for trade, and effecting a permanent peace between the Chiefs of Moreah and Benna
Countries. But the difficulty that Governor Pope
Hennessy was anxious to have settled is the war long
existing between the Kukuna Soosoos and Bilali which
is not.

As Allimamy Sannasee, Bey Mauro and other Chiefs
are requested to call upon the Chiefs of the contending parties to settle the same, it would be advisable
to wait the result of the Mission and until Professor
Blyden return from Timbo.

The men can be sent back with a present of Ƀ5 to
the Chief who sent them.

T. G. Lawson
Govt. Interpreter.

GIM, pp. 89-90

Sierra Leone
20th September 1873

Memo for the information of
His Excellency the Governor in Chief

Sir,

I have carefully read the petition and other papers of British Traders in the Great Scarcies—

The war alluded to in the petition is the same which Governor I. Pope Hennessy C.M.G. foresaw when he went to stop the threatened disturbance in the Scarcies last year that His Excellency deputed Alimami Sanusi and Bey Mauro, Bey Inka, Bey Farima, Worokia Silimani and other principal Kings and Chiefs in that district to settle it, but the wet season prevented them attending to it before this—

Alimami AlHay has always been found to be a good King and why he has now acted to the contrary I cannot explain but I think he will readily obey the request of the Government—I would respectfully suggest that as the Agent to the Interior is here and is well acquainted with the Chiefs and the whole matter, he might be requested to proceed to Kambia and RoWoolah to ascertain the cause of the disturbance and if necessary to see the contesting parties and have matters amicably settled.

To accomplish which it would no doubt take him 3 or 4 weeks.

He should carry a letter from Your Excellency to the Chiefs to show that he is sent by Your Excellency.

As soon as Your Excellency has dispensed with the numerous matters now on hand, and time permits, Your Excellency may visit that country or send some one to do so in your behalf.

Since writing I have had conversation with a young Chief named Binneh Sankong from the Moriah Country on his way to Port Locco from whom I have

learnt that the war reported of in the petition was
occasioned by the Chief and people of Kukuna in the
Moriah district, they wantonly destroyed a town named
Bashea on the Timneh side under Chief Kaliloo a friend
and ally of Alimami AlHay King of RoWoolah which seems
to show why he has interfered in the war.

                              (sd) T. G. Lawson
                              Govt. Interpreter

P.S. I think Bey Inka King of the Small Scarcies will
be of some service to the one that will be sent.

GIM, pp. 308-10

                              Sierra Leone
                              21st June 1876

Memo for the information of
Excellency the Lieut. Governor

Sir,

        The Boat sent with a letter to Allimamy Bokary
King of the Moriah Country return this morning with
favourable report which I direct the Police Constable
that went to commit in writing without delay for your
and the Governor in Chief information in as much as he
brought no letter, he told me the King was joyful of
your letter and making preparation at once to resort
to Calli Modiah in order to be there to received Your
Excellency.

        I regret to say that it had escape my mind to
suggest to Your Excellency that it would be adviseable
to write to the Chief of Bereira and Cokeh of your
Excellency's intended visit to Allimamy Bokary and
will visit them too at Bereira as any Treaty with
Bokary with whom they [are] at present at variance
would not affect that Branch of the river as far as
to the Eastern Bank of the Morribiah River—Sir Arthur

when he made peace between them and Bokary in 1869,
Strove hard to reconcile them together, which they
promise to do but have not yet been done, and Your
Excellency may take advantage of the opportunity in
order to get them to be parties to the Treaty to got
them reconcile, therefore it would be adviseable that
Letter be sent at once to them to inform them that
Your Excellency will be at Calle Modiah as soon as
convenient and will pay them a visit at Berierra at
which place the Cokeh Chiefs are to meet your Excellency in order to secure the peace of their Country
and its welfare for the future. The Chief of Berreirra
is in Treaty with this Government and received Stipend
on Treaty No 40 and 44 page 356 and 366 Ordinance Book
Vol 2. The latter is in force, Cokeh has no Treaty
with this Government, but properly speaking they are
all under the King of Fouricaria, but since the war
between them in 1865, although Sir Arthur made peace
between them, yet they refuse allegience to him,
Berrierra is a large and popular native Town and full
of Trade, It and Fouricaria has one intrance, but di-
vide as the Port Lokkoh and the Rokelle up the Sierra
Leone River does, the people there very strong and
powerful, the Chief of that place sent Messenger to
visit Your Excellency in October last and went away
please and I am sure they will be very glad to see and
Treat with Your Excellency in anything good;

From yesterday I began to feel the effect of my
old Bowels Complaint began to trouble me I would respectfully beg, at your and the Governor in Chief
hands two or three days leave so to get myself in a
fit state, to accompany Your Excellency whereever my
service would be required, I fear this Bowel complaint
would be the cause of my death, but I hope not before
these important business to the future benefit of the
Colony now under contemplation by Your Excellencies be
accomplited.

The Honble Wm Grant will be of great help in the
Berierra affair he having much influence with those
Chiefs.

I have etc.

(sd) Thos. Geo. Lawson
Govert. Interpreter

GIM, pp. 329-30

July 6, 1876

My dear Friend,

It is now a long time since I wrote you, you must not think that I forgot you, I hope your messenger Malay Modoo whom you sent here to the Governor some time last year inform you that I have not, I write this particular to inform you by some of your people who came here with Oxen and other things to trade from Moribiah that the Governor who has the welfare of your country at hand and wishes to secure it from all trouble, wishes very much to see you, and may likely pay you a visit at Wonkafong and if himself do not go you will surely see the Lieut. Governor who treat with your messengers when you last sent them here, he as well as the Governor in Chief who return from England some time last month on behalf of the Queen has the welfare of our country at heart, no doubt when he is going he will take me with him[,] your nephew Alimamy Babbah and if possible Alimamy Sanusi if he is well enough to accompany him—You know I am an African like yourselves I have been little more than 50 years under the training and care of the English nation and knows how deeply they have the interest of our country at heart and never decive any one that they deal with, Therefore I strongly advice you that should the Governor come to you you may be ready to comply with what he may request you to do. I cannot write every thing in the letter, as you cannot read English yourself but when you see Alimamy Babbah and myself that is, if the Governor will take me with him I will then explain every thing to you—I think it will be more convenient for the Governor to meet you at Moribiah than going up to Wonkafong, which is more further up, I will then advice you if you wish to see him to come down to Moribiah with all your Chiefs.

The Governor in Chief or the Lieut. Governor will be going to the Fouricariah on a visit to Alimamy Bokcary in a few days to endeavour to settle the war palaver with him and the Great Scarcies Chiefs and if he should be inform that you are at Moribiah he might go there at once to see you and get matters settled. My respect to Alimamy Yollah Baywoolie, your principal Chiefs with due regards.

                                    I remain
                                    My dear friend
                                    Your Obedient Servant

                                    (sd) T. H. Lawson
                                    Govt. Interpreter

Kutah Modoo
King of Wonkafong
Soombuyah

GILB, 2:323-26

                                    Freetown
                                    3rd November 1879

For the information of His)
Excellency the Governor-)
in Chief   )

        The town in which late Maliggy Gbailee was caught
and killed is called Fangucigar by the brook near that
town he was put to death by the instigation of one of
the Tooray tribe named Yimbah Dembah against the wish
of Alimamy Bokharry, this took place about the year
1866 or 1867. It was after the coronation of Alimamy
Bokharry to be King over the Moriah country. The crown
was placed on him by a Chief called Bambah Sinneh
Tooray of Tannah contrary to the ancient custom of
that country which was that all Kings who are to be
crowned King lawfully over the country must be [crowned
by] the Ulah tribe [which consists of] the house[s] of
Malaghea, Kalla Modiah, Berr and other Ulah, Yansanneh
and Doonbuyah[,] which are one tribe. Alimamy Sanusi
of Medina Bullom Shore is of the same tribe. In consequence of this the old man Bambah Sinneh when caught
in war was cut in pieces.

                                    (sgd) Thos. Geo. Lawson
                                    Government Interpreter

Freetown Sierra Leone
5th November 1879

Sir,

I beg to bring to your Excellency's notice a circumstance which I did not before state nor would I at
this moment remember saying anything about it, if I
had not seen a Treaty said to be signed by late Maliggy
Gbailee with the French Government. His Excellency
Colonel Chamberlayne when administering the Government
of the Settlement in the absence of His Excellency
Governor Blackall on leave in England sent me on a
mission to Alimamy Bokharry King of the Moriah Country
to recover from Slavery a daughter of a British Subject named Sally Bailey now in the Settlement, on my
way going I stopped at Medina Bullom Shore[,] Alimamy
Sanusi['s] place at which place I met the late Maliggy
Gbailee with his principal Chiefs and attendants then
about to return to Beriera from his visit to this Government and the Chiefs of Port Lokkoh. I passed the
night at that place, [and] next morning before leaving
for Mellicourie he called me to a house [in] which he
had been lodging in the presence of Alimamy Sanusi and
his two principal Chiefs Yellang Foday of Pharmoriah
and Dalloo Seckoo who were his strongest adherents and
supporters in all his actions against Alimamy Bokharry
and [he] sent a message by me to be delivered to Alimamy Bokharry in the following words[:] Mr. Lawson I
am glad you are going to Mellicourie to my elder
brother Alimamy Bokharry, I know he is elder than I
and has the right to the Kingship of the country, tell
him for me that although war is between him and myself
yet I beg him as he is now the King of the country not
to give a hand breadth of it to any white man or others
as [I] would not do so if even I were to be killed, I
knew if Bokharry were to catch hold of me he would put
me to death and if I were to catch hold of him [I]
would do the same but I hope we both would leave the
country as our forefathers left it to us. I then told
him that I would deliver his message and would advise
him to remain at Bullom and not return to Berieara
till the Governor could see in what way to get matters
settled between them he said that he must go as he is
urgently sent for by the Chiefs who are helping him
and that the French had promised to give him assistance against Bokharry. I told him I would advise him
not to go and that if he do so his presence would only
revive the war afresh he said he must go lest his

friends would attribute it to cowardice I passed on that day to Mellicourie and he went on with his people to Berieara, shortly after his arrival there the war began afresh until he was caught and through the instigation of one of their cousins named Yimbay Dembah against the wish of Bokharry was killed. At the time he sent the message by me to Bokharry the Government letter which I took to Bokharry written from the Colonial Secretary's Office and signed by Colonial Secretary Nicol can show the proper date and year, at present I think it was in August 1865 as in looking over my old memo book I found my report sent on this mission dated August 1865 the Secretary's letter must be written some time in that month. If it is required and report cannot be found at the Secretary's quarters, correct copy can be made from the memorandum book I kept. What I have above stated can be testified to by Alimamy Sanusi of Medina Bullom Shore and Alikarlie Yellang Foday of Phamoriah Mellicourie. I delivered the message to Alimamy Bokharie in the presence of his cousin Yimbay Dembah, Kolleh Tanguyah his principal advisers and other Chiefs he was pleased to receive it and said his brother (meaning Maliggy Gbailee) was deceived by taking wrong advice from people. He also at time pointed out to be his cousin Yimbay Dembah who he said would succeed him if he dies. This man is the one alluded to above [as] being the instigator of Maliggy Gbailee being put to death,

> I have the honour to be
> Sir
> Your Excellency's
> Most Obedient Servant
>
> (Sgd.) Thos. Geo. Lawson
> Government Interpreter

P.S. In looking over my report I found that the letter which I took up was addressed to Foday Yimbay Laminah of Morricaniah then at Mellicourie.

> T. G. L.

His Excellency
    The Governor-in-Chief

GILB, 1:356-57

Freetown Sierra Leone
6th April 1878

My dear Friend,

    The Governor will be at Kambia at the full moon,
as you will see in his letter to you, for the purpose
of making a final settlement of the peace making between the Timmanee and the Soosoo, You know Allimamy
is the King of the Moriah Country and the Governor
hope you will do your best that he should be present,
that he and all the Timmanee Chiefs should shook hands
together and become friends in his present and then he
(the Governor) and all the Timmanee Chiefs will proceed to your Country to settle the dispute between the
Allimamy and your people, so the whole of the Country
may be at peace with each other, the Governor send
Allimamy Barber to explain this to you, and the Governor hope to see yourself and the Allimamy, so to
have all these things settled, he had been very ill
during the past two months, it was what prevented his
going up before this; and he hope you will do your
best in assisting him to get these matter settled
first at Kambia and then in your Country - With kind
regard

I remain
Your obedt. Servant

(sd) Thos. Geo. Lawson
Govert. Interpreter

Allikarlie Kardiatta Modoo
Chief of Callee Modiah

GILB, 1:402-15

Freetown Sierra Leone
24th June 1878

Memorandum for His   )
Excellency the Governor)
in Chief   )

Sir,

Although it is needless of my furnishing any memorandum on your Excellency's expedition to the Kissi Kissi or Moriah Country in the present month being aware that your Excellency had with you on the mission qualified and intelligent Officers who accompanied your Excellency in the persons of Mssrs. L. H. Edwards assistant Colonial Secretary and W. I. H. Bond Lieutenant of the 2nd W.I. Regt. your aide camp both of whom I am sure were on the alert to supply better and [more] correct information than anything I could ever attempt to do, yet I think it would not be out of the way to send in to you this memorandum as there may be something in your Excellency's proceedings with the Kings and the Chiefs of that Country which might not come to their knowledge, I therefore humbly and respectfully beg to submit the following statements.

Your Excellency embarked on board the "Prince of Wales" on the morning of the 8th inst. Mssrs. Edwards, Bond myself and others were previously on board; We left the harbour on board the "Prince" about half past 8 that morning and anchored off GBarika 6.30 p.m. that day. Your Excellency kindly give permission to the Clerks on board who might have desire to go on shore to see any of their friends in the place, almost the whole went on shore that evening, and returned on board early next morning the 9th instant, on which morning we left that place 6 a.m. and anchored off Callamodiah about 7 a.m. Your Excellency sent me on shore to inform the Chief of that place Alikarlie Kadiatta Modoo and Alimamy Fenda Sanusi Modoo Chief of the Medina Bullom Shore, of your Excellency's arrival— I did so and came off to the vessel with those Chiefs and some of their principal headmen, when your Excellency received them kindly and informed them among other things that you are gone up there as promised in October last, and that you had sent Alimamy Sanusi before hand as a pledge of your going up there. They returned ashore and despatched messengers to inform the King and the various principal Chiefs of your Excellency's arrival and of their meeting together without loss of time. Salute was fired in honor of your Excellency's arrival and this was previously arranged to be a notice to the Chief of the fact. On the afternoon of the same day your Excellency accompanied by Messrs. Edward and Bond myself and others went on shore to pay visit to the Alikarlie and the Chiefs of that place, after some conversation with them [we] took a little walk viewing different parts of the town

and the road leading to Yainkissah the King's residence, Fouricariah, Mellacouri, and other important
towns and returned on board 7 p.m. that evening—Next
morning the 10th instant Your Excellency left Fouricariah by the barge accompanied by Mssrs. Edwards,
Bond, myself and others where we arrived about 10:30
a.m. The Alikarlie Quiah Foday Dowodu was absent.
Your Excellency went direct from the landing place and
took seat in the town Hall (Barray) finding the Alikarlie being absent paid visit to Foday Tarrawally the
high priest of the Country who formerly resided at
Gbilleh near Kambia in the Great Scarcies, he immediately sent for the principal men of Fouricariah and
advised them without delay to send messenger to inform
the Alikarlie of the Governor's arrival and to come
without delay. Your Excellency finding the delay in
the Alikarlie's coming left the Barry quietly as it
were for a walk and in about an hour's time returned
with the Alikarlie his Chiefs and attendants. This
was the first noble step taken by Your Excellency in
breaking down the barrier that was in Your Excellency's
way of getting the serious matter settled. After an
interview with the Alikilie and the Chiefs Your Excellency left Fouricariah 6 p.m. and arrived alongside
the "Prince of Wales" little before 8 p.m. When your
Excellency was informed that the King had arrived at
Callamodiah that afternoon, I was sent on shore by
your Excellency to pay respect to the King and inform
the Chiefs of your return which I did and returned on
board about 8 next morning the 11th instant. Your
Excellency accompanied by Mr. Bond A.D.C. with myself
and others went on shore to see the King; the King and
Chiefs were very glad of seeing your Excellency and
stated among other things that he was glad of your
coming up for the purpose of settling the dispute existing between him, his Chiefs and people and that
from the confidence he entertained in your Excellency
and in the British Government[,] the old friends of
his ancestors and himself[,] has prepared himself to
abide by whatever Your Excellency's decision would be,
therefore left himself and the whole matter entirely
into your Excellency's hands, the King spoke in the
presence of more than 400 of his Chiefs and people.
After some important conversation we returned on board.
On the 12th Your Excellency left for Fourricariah
about 12:30 a.m. accompanied by Mr. Edwards, the Engineer of the yacht, myself and others and arrived there
about 2.30 p.m. Your Excellency was received by the
Alikarlie his principal Chiefs and headmen[,] all

about 2 or 300 persons[,] when long conversation in the Town Hall (Barray) [about] their grievances against the King [were carried on] through the Alikarlie.

The Alikarlie and the Chiefs promised to inform Your Excellency as soon as the Chiefs that are sent for arrived at Fourricariah, as he would not like to see the Alimamy the King in their absence, Your Excellency then left Fourricariah and returned to the Yacht lying off Calla Modiah. Your Excellency sent me to report to the Kings and Chiefs of Your Excellency's return which I did—On the morning of the 13th went on shore, took the land road on horse back and I [traveled] in your Excellency's hammock [and set out at] about 8 a.m. for Fourricariah where we arrived about 10.30 a.m. taken the Chiefs as it were by surprise, many of them not believing that a personage as you are the representative of the Great Queen of England, and the dread Europeans generally have of the African climate would cause Your Excellency to attempt taking such a route through such bad road full of bushes, water mud of bad stench and rotten scaffold made in lieu of bridges; this special act of Your Excellency is what convinced the whole of the Fourricariah Chiefs and people of the earnest desire and wish Your Excellency had in going to their Country for the purpose of doing their Country good, and to save the country from bloodshedding. About 1 p.m. the Barge arrived at Fourricariah having on board Mr Edwards and Mr. Hutchinson the Chief Engineer of the "Prince of Wales." After some long private conversation with Alikarlie in his private residence, Your Excellency left Fourricariah and returned to the vessel. Next day Friday the 14th about 12.30 p.m. the Alikarlie and many of the principal Chiefs and headmen came down to the Steamer to pay respect to Your Excellency, this day is an unusual day for Mahommedan Chiefs of rank to travel but Your Excellency's visit to them overland seemed to overpower all their ideas and wrought in them the thought of considering it highly necessary to lay aside all ceremony. When the hour of prayer came while on board they were permitted by Your Excellency to do so on board, permitting M. Sanusi the Arabic Writer who they considered more qualified and of higher rank in their faith to officiate to them on that occasion— after some refreshment in tea and bread they returned to Fourricariah. On the evening of the same day Your Excellency went on shore for a walk and had conversation with some of the Chiefs and then returned on board.

On the morning of the 15th Saturday Your Excellency
left in the Barge for Fourricariah I went with Your
Excellency when all the Chiefs that were needed to be
present were assembled with the exception of the Chiefs
of Berrie Erie, Mellacourie, Pharmoriah, and Contah.
After some long conversation Your Excellency succeeded
in getting them all to agree to lay down arms and not
to fight, and to have the dispute between them and the
King settled amicably without war, they requested that
this their sentiment be committed into writing which
they will sign as their promise to Your Excellency,
this Your Excellency agreed to and a document or a
memorandum to that effect was written out to which
Alikarlie Quiah Foday Dowoda and the principal or main
Chiefs attached their signatures in Arabic to which
Foday Tarrawally the high priest of the Moriah Country,
his son Foday Lusainy and step-son Foday Sanusi who
are next in rank to him attached their names as witnesses. This being done it was arranged that the Alikarlie his principal Chiefs of Fourricariah and of
those of other important towns as well as the high
priest Foday Tarrawally and his two sons, his sub-
priests, should accompany Your Excellency down to
Calla Modiah for the purpose of shaking hands with the
King. Those of them well enough and able to walk were
enumerated to do so, two large canoes were then got in
addition to Your Excellency's Barge to bring them down.
The Alikarlie two of his immediate relatives of some
influence in the country, the high priest and his two
sons came in the barge with Your Excellency, the rest
came by two canoes. On your Excellency's arrival on
board with these Chiefs and people, Mr Prigg was sent
on shore to bring off to the ship Alikarlie Kadiatta
Modoo and Allimamy Sanusi; on their arrival on board,
Your Excellency had interview with these two Chiefs
from shore on the bridge of the vessel informing them
what your Excellency did at Fourricariah and also requesting them to inform the King and the Chiefs on
shore that Your Excellency had brought the Alikarlie
and the Chiefs from Fourricariah for the purpose of
shaking hands with the King and that they should inform the King and Chiefs on shore of this and to have
a proper place prepared for a general meeting that
evening. About little before 6 p.m. that evening Your
Excellency accompanied by Messrs Edwards, Bond,
Mohammed Sanusi the Arabic Writer, Mr Prigg, myself
and others with all the Chiefs and people from Fourricariah about 250 including their Yellimen and Women
went on shore, and went from the landing place direct

to the place that had been prepared for the meeting
and it was between the Mosque and the gateway leading
to the place where the King resides.   The Fourricariah
Chiefs, people and the high priest took sittings on
the north side of the table near the Mosque, the King,
his sons, Chiefs and people sat on the south side near
to his gateway in which side Your Excellency and followers also sat, the King sat on your Excellency's
right to you.   On the approach of the King taking his
seat near the table by Your Excellency and seeing his
nephew (the Alikarlie) and other relatives one could
decipher from his countenance that joy and rejoicing
of his heart which was plainly afterwarded manifested
by the shaking of hands, greetings, salutations and
other marks of love and respects to each other.   The
document that was written and signed at Fourricariah
was then read to the hearing of the King and his Chiefs
to which all agreed.   Similar document of same purport
as the one written and signed at Fourricariah was
drawn up and signed by the King and the principal
Chiefs that were with him after which the memorandum
signed at Kambia on the 27th April last was read and
ratified by the King which he signed as being a party
to that memorandum.   This being done to the satisfaction of all present Your Excellency called upon Alikarlie Dowoda to come forward and in your presence and
that of all to shake hands with his Uncle the King, on
which occasion Your Excellency took the hand of the
Alikarlie placing it into that of his Uncle the King
with the following expression, King I bring your son
home to you, Alikarlie I return you to your Father,
hold to each other.   I am sorry I have not time to
stay any longer to see the whole matter settled as I
have many important business to do at Sierra Leone
from your promise I have no more apprehension of your
going to war with each other, I leave the matter in
the hands of your high priest Foday Tarrawally with
the assistance of Alikarlie Kadiatta Modoo to have it
settled amicably.   After invoking the blessing of God
in what had been done by the Priest, he gave us a lec-
ture on the evil of subjects rebelling against their
Rulers because they may be harsh in their dealings
with them—The meeting was dispersed about 10 p.m.
under great joy and excitement—Some of the Fourricariah Chiefs with the high priest returned to Fourricariah that night—Alikarlie Quiah Foday Dowoda and many
others remained at Calla Modiah that night which had
not been the case for the past 18 months—After the
dismissing of the meeting Your Excellency had a private

interview with the King in his house in the presence
of Alikarlie Kadietta Modoo and myself when Your Excellency gave him a wholesome and friendly advice for
the good governing of his people, how Rulers should
strictly uphold the laws of their country, and how
they should in a great measure, bear the weakness of
ignorant subjects, The King thanked Your Excellency
for all what you had done and for the friendly advice
given him and then bade Your Excellency goodbye. The
whole of the tedious and the hardest native matters to
be settled could not be settled so amicably without
some heavy unavoidable expenses in the way of presents
more especially by the unwearied personal exertion and
effort of Your Excellency which are rare to be seen in
Governors on the Coast.

In conclusion I beg respectfully to state for
Your Excellency's favourable consideration some of the
important and necessary requests of the King and Chiefs
for the future good of themselves and Your Excellency's
Government. 1st. The King requested that duties
should be levied on goods and articles going to his
Country for trading purposes, and that he is led to
request this from the unfair manner in which the merchants and traders are in the habit of dealing with
him, by not paying to him proper anchorage and other
dues [to] which he [is] entitled, and that this will
enable Your Excellency's Government to allow him ample
and proper remuneration as King of his Country, and
that stipends will be allowed to some of his Principal
Chiefs who are assisting him in taking care of the
country who hitherto received none, as the Chief of
Calla Modiah, Fourodugu, Fourricariah, Pharmoriah and
Contah, and also increasing that of those who are already allowed stipend.

The next important request was about the restora-
tion of the Town Gbilleh near Kambia on the Great
Scarcies which had been an ancient residence of the
high Priest Foday Tarrawally, but taken in the last
war by the Timmanees of Digsaing the original Owners
of that land—begging your Excellency's interference
that it should be restored to them without war, and
that is the only sore remained to be healed between
them and the Timmanees in the Great and Small Scarcies,
Digsaing and the Moriah Country. All other grievances
and disputes from 1875 to the present time have been
settled by Your Excellency—Your Excellency left Calla
Modiah on the morning of the 16th about 6.30 a.m. and

arrived in Freetown 4 p.m.

Covering letter to the above forwarding it to His Excellency.

> Freetown Sierra Leone
> 25th June 1878

Sir,

I herewith beg respectfully to submit the enclosed for His Excellency's information, it being a memorandum of some of the proceedings on His Excellency mission to the Moriah Country.

I desire particularly to bring to His Excellency's special notice . . . the King's request in the clause next to the conclusion viz. The King's request that duties should be levied on Goods etc. as can be seen in that clause throughout.

> I have the honor to be
> Sir
> Your Obedient Servant
>
> (sgd) Thos. Geo. Lawson
> Govt. Interpreter

W. I. H. Bond Esq.,
A.D.C.
Government House

GILB, 3:28-29

> Freetown Sierra Leone
> 31st December 1879

Memorandum for His Excellency's
information in reference to
the messengers sent from
the Moriah Country

Your Excellency has before you principal messengers from Alimamy Bokharie King of the Moriah Country, Quiah Foday Dowoda Chief of Fouricariah and Fudiah

Toomany Chief of Malaghea this gives Your Excellency
ample opportunity of speaking at length to them about
the war now going on in their country between them and
the Bashia people brought about by Quiah Foday Dowoda
nephew of the King and Foday Murry Cearay Daffae both
of Fouricariah who are strongly supported by Sorie
Feekeh of Berrie Erie contrary to the wish of their
King. Your Excellency whilst thinking well of Quiah
Foday Dowoda and thanking him for rescuing one of the
Queen's Subjects out of Slavery and will send him a
small present for so doing, on the other hand Your
Excellency is much grieved in seeing how he violated
his promise by making war in the country and that if
it had not been Your Excellency's timely interference
last year by this time the Alimamy would have overran
the whole of the Moriah country with warmen [that] he
had prepared for that purpose and as Your Excellency
has now seen them in Your Excellency's house Your Excellency will take the opportunity of sending message
to Quiah Foday Dowoda in the following language.

1st. That your Excellency is surprised to hear
how he has violated his promise in June 1878 at Fouricariah and Kallae Modiah and that it is now left to
Your Excellency to see what steps to take.

2nd. That if Foday Murray Caeray Daffae is the
crowned King of the Moriah country instead of his
uncle Alimamy Bokharie let him as well as the whole of
the Moriah Country go on in supporting him but it would
be better for him and the rest of them to give up supporting and adhere to their own lawful King.

3rd. The King of the Country is always of the
Tooray family backed and supported by the Yansanneh
and the Youlah family but that does not make all
Toorays to be King and Commanders of the Country whilst
the lawful King exists or to do contrary to the wish
of that King etc. etc.

As for your Excellency's part you will back the
King as long as he acts in consistence to the terms
stipulated in the Treaty between this Government and
their country.

Tho. Geo. Lawson
Government Interpreter

GILB, 3:118

Freetown Sierra Leone
4th May 1880

My Dear Friend,

The Governor has seen your messenger Murry Gbai whom you sent to Mr. Grant, he directed me to inform you that although you have not sent to him yet he takes the opportunity to send you by him three bags of rice and requests to tell you that he has not forgotten you nor the morning he breakfasted at your house at Fouricariah and that the letter he sent to you last with a present of £6. by Sarcorbah must have been improperly translated to you as you informed Mr. Grant that it was a bad one. His Excellency thinks that you have not acted up to the promise you made with him at Fourricariah and Karlai Modiah by your carrying on war in the country without first informing him the cause of your so doing and that it is what grieves him very much as war is distruction to lives and property and debars trade. He left here on leave to England and will return in a few months.

I am
Dear Friend
Sincerely Yours

Tho. Geo. Lawson
Govt. Interpreter

Alikarlie Quiah Foday Dowoda
Chief of Fourricariah

GILB, 3:170-71

Freetown Sierra Leone
1st July 1880

My dear Friend,

I am glad to inform you that your friend Governor Rowe K.C.M.G. our Governor-in-Chief arrived safely in England and does not forget you. I am happy also to say that according to his promise to you on the evening of the 2nd and 3rd May last to send you a copy of

an Arabic petition sent to England and to France protesting against the right of either nation to the
Moriah Country he has now fulfilled the same which
the Administrator now sends by Alpha Sanusi and Mr.
Harding to be handed to you. You told the Governor
at the time that you know nothing of that document being written signed or sent and that you had not even
heard of it before that evening, and that you wished
the Governor to understand distinctly that what a
former Kandeh that is a lawfully crowned King of the
Kissi Kissi or Moriah Country decided and settled his
successor or successors cannot undo or revert and that
you had no power to undo what had been decided by Alimamy Oomaroo. The Administrator wants you honestly
and truthfully to inform him the fact of this matter
whether it was your doing or by your authority or not,
if so where and who it was that brought the document
for your signature. You know that I am an African as
you are and have been placed under the care of the
English now 55 years and know a little of their manners; there is nothing in the world they hate more
than a liar and two faced person as well as a thief.
I know you now nearly 20 years during which time I
have proved you to be a truthful and honest King. I
hope therefore you will prove yourself to the Administrator in that respect. You may rely on him as your
entire and true friend who will do you good and not
harm, and one upon whom you can depend. He wants
those informations from you for the purpose of forwarding them to the Government of your friend the Great
Queen of England and Governor Rowe.

With kind wishes.

                              I remain
                              My dear Friend
                              Ever Sincerely Yours

                              (sgd) Thos. Geo. Lawson
                              Govt. Interpreter.

Alimamy Bokhary   )
King of the Kissi Kissi)
as Moriah Country.   )

GILB, 3:302-03

Freetown Sierra Leone
28th December 1880

Sir,

   The enclosed is a private letter written in Arabic said to be sent from Allimamy Bokharie King of the Moriah country addressed to me which I had translated purposely to be submitted for His Excellency's information. I heard of this before that all the Kings and Chiefs of the Great and small Scarcies have agreed to take Allimamy Bokharie home to his country without war.

   Of myself I would rather advise him to wait until the question of the Northern rivers between the French and our Government [is] settled as he is no friend to that Government and I think they would not hesitate if they get him in their power to molest him.

I have the honour to be
Sir,
Your Most Obdt. Servant

(sgd) Thos. Geo. Lawson
Govt. Interpreter   ·

Lieut. Thackeray
Aid-de-Camp
Govt. House.

Freetown Sierra Leone
1st January 1881

No. 1

Sir,

   I respectfully beg to forward the enclosed for His Excellency's information being the letters written in Arabic with their translation brought yesterday by the messengers sent from the Kings of the Great and Small Scarcies rivers and the Chief of Mellicourie Alikarlie Yousufoo. They are to inform His Excellency of their intention to accompany Allimamy Bokharie King

of the Moriah Country back to his Country for the purpose of settling the existing dispute between himself
and his people in an amicable way [rather] than fighting. The letter of the Kings of the Great and Small
Scarcies show some friendly feeling towards this Government since the last disturbance between us and them
in 1879, this appears to be much brought about by the
kind treatment the first messengers from those Chiefs
received from this Government shortly after the
Governor-in-Chief returned from there.

    With His Excellency's authority I shall not fail
in doing my best to make them satisfy before they
leave. Alikarlie Yousufoo the Chief of Mellicourie,
who is a good man and in treaty with this Government
(vide treaty no. 36 Ordinance Book Vol. II page 346)
in his letter asked for some assistance in the way of
money to assist him in the good work of peacemaking.
I don't think his stipend is due, . . . the Colonial
Secretary and Treasurer can furnish His Excellency
that information and if nothing due it would not be
out of the way in sending him small present likewise
small presents to the 4 principal messengers that come.

                        I have the honor to be
                                Sir
                        Your most Obdt. Servant,

                        (sgd) Thos. Geo. Lawson
                        Govt. Interpreter

Lieut. Thackeray
Aid-de-Camp
Govt. House

    P.S. I would respectfully recommend that a pres-
ent of £10 be sent to Alikarlie Yousufoo Chief of
Mellicourie.

GILB, 3:305

                        Freetown Sierra Leone
                        4th January 1881
Sir,

    I herewith beg respectfully to submit the enclosed
letter handed to me this morning by Allimamy Baraka in

person for the information of His Excellency the Administrator-in-Chief; What he stated in the letter is true and I am sure it will be good for the interest of the Settlement if he be assisted with some money to go up in order to give some assistance to the Chiefs that are going up with Allimamy Bokharie to get the matter in the Moriah country settled. It will also show that this Government has interest in Allimamy Bokharie's affairs.

The roads from the Interior through that part of the country will be free. The only thing presents any doubt in my mind is the Northern question between this Government and the French; if the question decides in the favor of this Government it will not be a waste of money and in expectation of such favorable decision, I don't think (₤20) Twenty pounds is too much to assist in this matter.

I have the honor to be
Sir,
Your Most Obedient Servant

(sgd) Thos. Geo. Lawson
Government Interpreter.

Lieut. Thackeray
Aid de Camp
Govt. House.

GILB, 3:681

24th November 1881

Memo for His Excellency the Governor-in-Chief in reference to Chief Allimamy Colleh in the Great Scarcies who arrived here with a great retinue of about 109 persons.

I know [of] no existing treaty between this Chief's Predecessor and this Government, only the name of one of his predecessors is mentioned in Treaty No. 2 and 3 page 269 etc. Vol. III signed Allimamy Sambah amongst other signatories. Another predecessor of his named Worookia Silimany entered into an agreement with

Governor Hennessy in 1872 or 1873, when 400 bars stipend was promised him, but I do not know what became
of that agreement, however presents are usually given
the Chiefs when they visit this Government or the Governor visits the Great Scarcies. Properly speaking
the Country which they possess is the Digsaing country
under its proper King Allimamy Lusainy but they had
been residing there as I have been told for the past
80 or 90 years.

    After Your Excellency's hearing what they have
[to say] and the cause of their visit Your Excellency
in reply might say to them, I am glad to see you and
your Chiefs and would have been more pleased to have
seen you come together with Allimamy Sattan Lahai and
Allimamy Lusainy and other principal Chiefs in the
country as I wish to be made acquainted with you all,
and as I am expecting Allimamy Sattan Lahai and
Lusainy. I need not say much to you in hopes that on
their coming you will come too and the persons who are
to be crowned as Bey Farima of Magbaitee and Bey
Sherbro of Mambolo.

                          (sgd) Thos. Geo. Lawson
                          Govt. Interpreter.

GILB, 4:256

                          Freetown Sierra Leone
                          7th July 1882

My dear Friend,

    I hope yourself and family are all well. When
the Governor was at Kitchum in May last at the time he
brought up your messenger Lamina Capinderh or Carpenter,
he was pleased to hear that you, Bey Inga and other
Chiefs were engaged in crowning a new Bey Farima at
Carneah and hope you have by this time finished with
that service, and turned your attention to have a
proper person crowned at Mambolo also; reports have
since reached him that Pharmoriah and other towns in
the Mellicourie River have been attacked and destroyed
by Allimamy Bokharie's warmen; he hopes that you and
all your people will have no hands in it, as his

anxious desire is to keep you and your Country free from other people's troubles and disturbance, and that you will not allow yourself and people to mix with other people's quarrels.

He directs me particularly to inform you that the promise made to you and other Chiefs by Governor Hennessy in January 1873 for the increase of your stipends he is in position to have it confirmed and pay to you as soon as you all can make it convenient to meet with him; and in the meantime that you and the rest of the Chiefs will keep your Country in a peaceable state as it is now.

I remain
My dear Friend,
Your Obedient Servant,

(sgd) Thos. Geo. Lawson
Govt. Interpreter

Allimamy Sattan Lahai,
King of RoWoolah,
Great Scarcies

GILB, 5:240-42

Freetown Sierra Leone
1st August 1883

Sir,

The enclosed letter was handed to me today 2 p.m. by messengers sent from Bey Inga King of the Small Scarcies. It appears that he wrote this letter in concurrence with the other Kings and Chiefs, namely Almamy Sattan Lahai King of RoWoolah, Bey Farrimah King of Kambia and Magbaitee, Great Scarcies and Almamy Loonseeny King of Digsaing all of whom have met at Romangay to consult what steps they are to take about the last attack made on Rogbairay by the Moriah Soosoos sometime last month, and it appears that the others have come to the conclusion, except himself at present, to pursue those who attacked them but he (Bey Inga) [is] not willing to join them in so doing before reporting the matter to the Administrator and receiving his advice. He seems plainly to blame them for keeping Almamy Bokharie in their country which brings all this trouble on them and which appears at present to leave them no alternative but to fight.

I know myself that every precaution and friendly advice have been afforded them by the Governor-in-Chief under heavy expenses and have warned them on no account to allow Almamy Bokharie to remain in any part of their country and when the Lieutenant Governor of the French was here before His Excellency left for England, the Governor wrote to them not to allow Almamy Bokharie to remain at Rogbairay or any part of their country as it would bring trouble on them as it is now seen. On the face of all these plain truths, it appears that they are ashamed to report this attack made on Rogbairay because they find that they themselves are to be blamed.

I would respectfully suggest that a friendly letter be sent in reply to the one now sent from Bey Inga that the Governor thanks him for the report he has given of affairs in the Great Scarcies and that the Government will still advise him to keep aloof from the war and still to refrain from mixing with it and that he should inform the Great Scarcies Kings and Chiefs that the Government regrets very much to hear of all the evils reported in his letter and that they had been brought on by their not acting upon the friendly advice of the Governor, that they should not blame the Soosoos who attacked their country but Almamy Bokharie whom they obstinately keep in their country against all friendly advices, and that they should not pursue these who attacked them but remain and defend their countries, and if the Soosoos hear that Almamy Bokharie is not residing in any part of their country they will not take any war to their country, and should His Excellency consider it necessary Momodoo Wakka might be sent with the letter and the messengers to Bey Inga and might see Almamy Sattan Lahai and the others.

The Great Scarcies King and Chiefs would succeed in destroying the whole of the Moriah Country but this might be considered by the French as infringing on their territory and would cause them to take the war up, while on the other hand it does not appear that they in any way are doing anything to prevent the

Soosoos attacking Timneh territory in search of Almamy Bokharie.

The messengers express a desire to return as soon as possible. I learnt this morning that since the Soosoos have heard that the Timnehs have congregated to attack them, the town of Mellicourie is deserted.

I have etc.

(sgd) Thos. Geo. Lawson
Govt. Interpreter.

Capt. H. M. Jackson R.A.
Private Secretary
and A.D.C.

P.S. The messengers are seven in number the Chief-one is a nephew of Bey Inga. I provide for them.

(Intl.) T. G. L.

GILB, 5:242

Freetown Sierra Leone
6th August 1883

Sir,

I lost no time yesterday when I left you to send to the alien Mohammedan headmen who appear to misbehave yesterday when churches were engaged at worship. Their principal ones called on me this morning requesting me to beg and apologise for them and to say that it was done from pure ignorance and that such practice will not occur again. I told them that while the authorities have no desire to interfere in their mode of worship . . . at the same time they would not be allowed to act in anyway to disturb that of others and which might have led to a serious riot, and that they should put their words in writing which I would submit for your information; this they have done which I herewith forward with its translation. I further told them that they might have been summoned every one of them before the Police Magistrate for provoking

riot, but you do not wish to do so but warn them.
They appear to be much alarmed about it, and all appear to be really sorry and regret for what had taken
place and promise never to repeat it, they further say
that it was their intention to pay their respects to
His Excellency today but now this their conduct pre-
vents their doing so on this occasion and beg that
yourself and the Administrator would forgive them this
time.

                    I have etc.

                    (sgd) Thos. Geo. Lawson
                    Govt. Interpreter.

Capt. H. M. Jackson R.A.
Private Secry and
A.D.C.

GILB, 5:247-48

                    Freetown Sierra Leone
                    14th August 1883

Sir,

     The alien Mohammedans who have misbehaved them-
selves on Sunday before the last (5th instant) on account of which conduct few of their principal ones
wrote a letter in Arabic to ask His Excellency the Administrator to forgive them, daily call upon me to
know whether their letter has been accepted by His Excellency to forgive them and promise in future to be-
have better.

     I told them that you have been ill and that I have
all reason to believe that the illness was brought on
you from the bad conduct which irritated your mind
fearing that their behaviour would produce a riot on
that day and that as soon as you are better, I shall
be in a position to inform them His Excellency's mind.
They say they shall pray through Mahomed for your re-
covery. Early this morning they sent a messenger to
know from me whether you are better as some of their
people had seen you going up to Government house a day
before yesterday. I have sent to inform them that you
are much better but still weak; they are much anxious
about this matter and therefore pray you will please

let me know His Excellency's mind that I may inform
them.

I have etc.

(sgd.) Thos. Geo. Lawson
Govt. Interpreter

Capt. H. M. Jackson R.A.
Private Secretary and
A.D.C.

TRADE INFORMATION

27th October 1881

Sir,

    I forward the enclosed for His Excellency's infor-
mation. It was handed me this morning, sent from
Kambia in the Great Scarcies by one Mr. Johnson an old
resident trader of that place who has a very good knowledge of that country. What he stated I believe to be
correct, and some immediate steps should be taken to
put a stop to what he reports in his letter; as it is
the only safe road now which all the Interior strangers
depend upon through which to come down with their produce for trade. I shall draft out letters for His
Excellency's corrections to be sent to Allimamy Sattan
Lahai King of the RoWoolah and other chiefs to do their
best in removing those warmen from the road; these war
people are not directly his own, but people residing
beyond his jurisdiction and might be the same warmen
His Excellency heard of few days ago. I believe if
Mr. Johnson and Mr. Metzger elder brother of Mr. I. M.
Metzger in His Excellency's office are requested to
see those Chiefs with letters from His Excellency they
will be able to do some good. The letter may be sent
to Kaikonkie and from thence to Kambia by Police
Constables.

                    I have the honor to be
                         Sir
                  Your Obdt. Servant

                  Thos. Geo. Lawson
                  Govt. Interpreter

Lieut. A. S. Roberts
Private Secretary and
Aide-de-Camp.

GILB, 4:459-61

Freetown Sierra Leone
2nd November 1882

Information gathered from Mr. Thomas J.
Johnson a principal trader and an old
Resident at Kambia, Great Scarcies, states,
    Kambia is a quiet state.

Trade flourishing, strangers flocking down from the
Interior with trade. The only road which gives some
trouble to strangers coming down, is the Limbah road,
but the Alimamy is doing his best to put a stop to it.

    The plunder and capture made in the Moriah Coun-
try by the people employed by Alimamy Bokharie in his
war is of great temptation to the Timmanees of the
Great and Small Scarcies, as well as those in the
Mambolo Districts, but the Kings and Chiefs are very
particular in watching over their people so as to prevent any having hands in the war. They threatened
their people with death should any be found mixing in
the war.

    Alimamy Damoh Sorie who has charge of the town
Kambia is now here on trading purposes, and is vigi-
lant to see that the King's laws are complied with, he
is the best and truthful man in Kambia.

    Sometime last week suddenly Kibalie the head-war-
Chief employed by Alimamy Bokharie made appearance at
Kambia in a very plain manner with two or three men,
and two of his wives. He was enquired the reason of
his coming there, he stated, "simply to pass on to a
village beyond Kambia to make sacrifice for a dead
friend of his who died few months ago in his absence,
and to return". He was told to pass on and not to
stay at Kambia. He did so, 2 days after finishing
what he went for, he returned to the Moriah Country.

    He did not see any of the Kings and principal
Chiefs of that place. The Moriah Country is now des-
olate, the only part remaining is the Beri Erie
Districts which they intend as rumoured when the
brooks on the roads are dried a little will also be
attacked. The order to the war-men is, disturb no
English or French Factories, except they show fight
or resistance.

The above is gathered in conversation with Mr. Johnson which I herewith forward for His Excellency's information.

He further states that from all what he had seen, he observed nothing to lead him to believe that Alimamy Sattan Lahai, Bey Inga, and the other Chiefs have hands in the war, but one can observe in them secret rejoicing of the destruction of the Moriah people, on the following grounds:—

1st. That when they went to intercede between them and their King they refused and abused them, calling them "Jackasses", and now they can see how the Jackasses can kick.

2nd. That the whole of the trade is now coming to their Country instead of going to the Moriah Country.

Another thing is rumoured about the Timmanees' intention to keep Tah-gba (Mellicourie Town) which is part of the Timmanee-land (Digsange Country) which the Soosoos were allowed to reside on and have ever since took possession of, refused to pay rent to them, or even acknowledging them to be the rightful owners.

GILB, 5:287

Freetown Sierra Leone
2nd October 1883

Return showing the number of Caravans arrived in Freetown from 1st January to 31st December 1882.

1882	Man-dingoes	Foul-ahs	Sarra-coulaes	Bun-dookahs	Fala-bahs	Soo-soos	Sanga-rahs
From 1st January to 31st March	785	3	133	20			40
1st April to 30th June	720	13	65				
1st July to 30th September	305	20		8			
1st October to 31st December	482						15
	2,292	36	198	28			55

These strangers do not include those who daily resort to the settlement from below Falaba viz, Limbahs, Lokkohs, Timmanees, Soosoos, Sherbros, etc.

GILB, 5:287-89

                                   Freetown Sierra Leone
                                   4th October 1883

Memo for the information of His Excellency the
Governor-in-Chief.

        Information received from the Great Scarcies.

        At present no warboys to be seen at Kambia nor in
any part of that locality, all having crossed to the
Moriah side. It is reported that the Timmanees and
others employed by Almamy Bokharie are wreaking ven-
geance on the Bennah Soosoos for the death of late
Boye Bouyah Chief of Rogbairay and others who had been
killed by them at that and other towns, killing every
grown person they come across and now have in their
hands over a thousand prisoners and apparently destroyed every town in that part of the Soosoo country.
All the roads by which trade finds its ways to the
Moriah country are blockaded, consequently trade is
flocking to Kambia and other parts in the Great Scarcies. Great number of the Interior strangers found
their way to Kambia and over thousand of them are now
there. Some are trading there, others waiting till
the weather is favourable to come to Freetown.

        It is stated that Almamy Sattan Lahai and Lunsenny
have prepared letters to explain themselves and show
the condition of the country to Governor, long before
Momodoo Wakka was sent up, but from one thing to another prevented it being sent before this, but they
still intend to send them; they contain the communication of the Commandant at Binty and all what took place
between them and the French Authorities before the attack was made on Rogbairay. Their reason for so to-
tally destroying the Bennah country as stated by them
was that the French Authorities reported to the Governor when their towns were attacked sometime ago that
they (the French) have no control over the Bennah Soosoos. Whereas they are the persons whom the Moriah
Soosoos employed to their assistance. At present free
communication is passing between the warmen of Almamy
Bokharie and the Soombuyah country, the King of which
country sent 40 oxen sometime last year to present
Almamy Bokharie and still aiding him in the way of
money (that is in merchandize). The traders at Kambia
are still there, but keep most of their produce and

goods at Mambolo and towns below it. It is also stated
that Bokharie's warmen as soon as completed with the
Bennah Soosoos will turn their attention to Berrie
Erie one of the principal parts in the Moriah Country,
vide Treaty no. 44 page 366 Ordinance Book Vol. II,
and if succeeded in destroying it then they will come
down to Mellicourie which place they will request the
French authorities either to give up to them or drive
out of the same country the originators of the whole
disturbances viz. Quiah Foday Dowoda, Almamy Bokharie's
nephew Yellam Foday his step son, Alikarlie Fudeah
Toomany Chief of Malaghea, Alikarlie Yousufoo Chief
of Mellicourie and Alikarlie Sippeanah Chief of Contah
who are taking shelter in towns near Binty and that
they have no war with the French only they (the French)
are forcing themselves into it because they have power.

I have heard this information more than 8 or 9
days ago but waiting to know the truth of it before
reporting the same, but as it has been confirmed to me
yesterday by Mr. Thomas J. Johnson one of the principal
and oldest traders at Kambia who knows great deal of
what is going on in that country and can be relied
upon, I am therefore emboldened to report the same for
His Excellency's information.

                              I have etc.

                              (sgd.) Thos. Geo. Lawson
                              Govt. Interpreter

Capt. H. M. Jackson R.A.
Private Secretary and
Aide de Camp.

GILB, 8:138-39

                              Freetown Sierra Leone
                              23 November 1886

Memo for His Excellency's information

Several more of the Interior Strangers arrived
here yesterday, nothing is heard of Momodoo Wakka and
Police Constable Weeks; Trade finds its way here very
well from the various rivers, more especially Port

Lokkoh, Rokelle, Small Scarcies and the Northern rivers, as far as the Rio Nunez very little trade is doing now at Kambia in the Great Scarcies, all trade find their way to the Northern rivers, overland on account of the cheapness of Rum, Gin, Tobacco, Muskets and powder as the French receives no duty on these articles imported to those places. This is the great reason why all the trade finds its way to the Northern rivers overland, consequently many of our Merchants have formed Establishments there but many of them bring their produce in crafts and boats here to be shipped to Europe.

Yesterday the firm of Messrs Paterson & Co brought here from Domingia, Rio Pongas 11 Puncheons and 2 barrels of India Rubber besides others—The Firm of C. A. Verminck brought and shipped from here all the produce they brought up the Sierra Leone river but shipped all they brought in the Northern rivers in their own vessels from the Great Scarcies to the Nunez.

It is reported that the Alikarlie of Port Lokkoh is very ill, such expression of Native Kings denotes their death but I do not think this amounts to that as yet but further enquiry will be made about it.

(Sd) Thos. Geo. Lawson
Govt. Interpreter

Mr. J. C. E. Parkes
Govt. House

ALIMAMI SAMORI TURE

Freetown Sierra Leone
3rd October 1884

Sir,

His Excellency the Governor-in-Chief desired a
few days before leaving for England that I should furnish him with some account of the great Mohammedan war
termed "Jehadee" (meaning holy war) which is now rol-
ling from the interior downwards and has now reached
Fallaba under the command of Alpha Sahmadoo Chief of
Koneah and Alpha Daramy a native of Futah Chief of
Behrehburainyah, countries in the interior about 300
or 400 miles from this place. This war commenced
about 1870 First between Sarmado and the people of the
Wahsohlong country a large district in the Mandingo
country which he conquered. After which he conquered
another Mandingo country called Torron, thence to
Kolong Karlang next to a country called Hammannah from
there to Kang Kang . . . because [he was] a friend to
the King of that country but afterwards they fought
and he conquered them too. He next went to Barleyah
and conquered there, also another country near there
called Byloh in the Futah district. The following
year, he went on to an interior country called Semee
Korroh which he conquered, all of which are very large
Mohammedan countries in the interior. The inhabitants
are pagans but are now subjugated to the Mohammedan
religion. While at this place, his friendship was
sought for by another great Mohammedan priest named
Alpha Daramy a native of Futah now Chief of Behrehburainyah, inviting him to co-operate against Abal a native of Futah who rebelled against his government with
great many others and settled themselves at a country
lying between Fulah and Falaba Sulimah country to
which he gave the name "Hamdahlie" meaning praise be

to God and rest from oppression. Accordingly they
became one and have with them numerous host of warriors, destroying all the countries before them till
they came to Abal's place. This Abal, is a native of
Futah Jallow, but from being dissatisfied with the act
of the authorities of Futah, he rebelled against the
King and located himself in a forest lying between
Falaba and Futah as before stated.

Great number of his countrymen (Fulahs and others)
removed and resided with him in that locality. About
10 years ago, Alimamy Sorie the King of Futah Jallow
of the present reigning King Almamy Ahmadoo[,] brought a
large army to attack him for not only rebelling against
his King and country, but [for being] a molester to
all travellers passing through that way. The Futah
army was defeated and the King caught, but he chose
death rather than to be made a captive and abused. He
refused to go quietly and consequently was killed.
This made Abal and his people to be lifted up in pride
and became worse. He was a molester to all travellers
going up or coming down the roads, killing and plundering all he came across, thus he made himself an enemy,
and obnoxious to all the interior tribes. About the
beginning of this year, Daramy, with the united force
of Sahmadoo attacked him, succeeded in destroying his
place and putting him to death. His head was sent as
a trophy to assure Alpha Sahmadoo of the success,
they made his right hand and one leg to show the King
of Futah, one leg sent as far as Kambia in the Great
Scarcies to show all the Chiefs on the roads to that
place. This place Hamdahlie is about 200 miles from
Freetown. It is now reported that Sahmadoo and
Daramy's war is encamped around Falaba. If Falaba
will not agree to embrace Mohammedanism it will be destroyed. The motto or plea of this heavy army march-
ing down is, that all places where travellers are molested will be destroyed and made safe that a single
woman can travel from the waterside to the interior
and from the interior to the waterside. Falaba is now
surrounded with 19 war Stockades and is on the eve of
being destroyed, threats have been sent to the Chiefs
of Bombabah and Bombadee in the Limba country, countries about 4 or 5 days walk from Port Lokkoh. Should
they succeed in destroying that country, Port Lokkoh
and other countries below this place will be in great
jeopardy and might give occasion to this Government to
interfere as the Government of Senegal did about more
than 20 years ago, for there had been a similar

Mohammedan Chief called Alhajie Oomaroo, father of the
present King of Sego and Argiboo, King of Dingarreway
who brought a large army to the countries lying to the
east of Senegal destroying them till they came to the
territory of the Senegal Government. The French did
not wait any longer but sent out an army to meet them
which miserably destroyed and scattered his army.
Since then, they never attempt to go that way. On his
retreat, he went to a country lying on the way to Sego,
there in November 1862 to my knowledge, he sent messengers to the Kings and Chiefs of Port Lokkoh, Rokelle, Massimerah and Marampa, calling upon all Mohammedans to prepare themselves to receive him in subjugating all heathens around them to Mohammedanism. I
saw some of his messengers at a town called Rogbairay
up the Sierra Leone river opposite Forodugu in the
Rokelle river, being sent up that place by His Excellency late Governor Blackall, when a large Timmanee
war came down and destroyed all the places in British
Quiah as far as Rogbairay, this was in December 1862.
I told the messengers at the time to tell their chiefs
to be careful in what they were doing and that the
British Government is the best friend to Africa and
the Africans and that it wishes nothing but their
prosperity, peace and welfare.

The motto of the war coming down is very good in
itself but the proceedings should be closely watched
by the Government. As these weak Chiefs near the Settlement have not as yet sent to report this great war
coming on them and ask the aid of the Government it
would be well to wait till such be done, and in the
meantime to watch the proceedings.

I saw some of Daramy's warmen from Falaba in
Freetown on the 30th ultimo, they brought some oxen
and other things to trade. In conversation with them
they informed me that they were sent as messengers to
Almamy Bokarie King of the Moriah country to inform
him to rest assured that in the coming dry season,
they will come to his assistance and know what to do
with the Chiefs who are constantly disturbing the roads
from the waterside to the interior. So far I would
state at present for the information of the Government.

I have etc.

(Sgd.) Thos. Geo. Lawson
Govt. Interpreter

Lieut H. C. B. Dann 2nd W. I. R.
Private Secretary and
A.D.C.   etc.   etc.   etc.

P.S.

    I should here mentioned above that Governor-in-
Chief has written to the head Chief Alpha Sahmadoo
sometime in April last, Vide Governor's letter Aborigines No. 22 dated 9th April 1884 enclosing with it a
copy of a former letter No. 47 dated 14th October 1880,
when a present of Ь35 was sent him and Ь15 to his messengers.   The letter was taken by some of his Yellie
men who happened to be here.

(Intld.) T. G. L.

GILB, 6:327-29

Freetown Sierra Leone
26th January 1885

Sir,

    I beg to report for His Honor's information that
from Saturday to Sunday the town is covered with interior Strangers from Falaba and other interior countries also from countries below Falaba and downwards.
Those from the interior not less than 1149 and about
2000 remained at Kambia and other towns near it.   On
the arrival of the Chief messenger who is sent from
the great Mohammedan War Chief Alpha Mahomadoo Sahmadoo
at Kambia, he sent for all the Kings and Chiefs in the
Great Scarcies when he found that all the Stores of
the traders were closed in consequence of the warmen
about the town.   He asked Almamy Sattan Lahai and the
rest of the King and Chiefs why it is so and that he
does not blame the warmen but them (the Chiefs) and
that the Sierra Leone traders do not go up there to
lock up their stores, but to trade, for the Government of Sierra Leone pay money to them every year, to
keep the roads free and that their great Chief Sahmadoo
has heard too much of what is going on at Kambia in
disturbing strangers who are going on to Sierra Leone,
and that it is his determination to remove every obsta-
cle in the way which would prevent their doing so, and
that the warmen who are invited there by Almamy Bokharie

should pass on to the country where he called them
for, and the stores must be opened at once for trade
and that the Almamy should make a law to prevent any
of the warriors from disturbing the trade. Brisk
trade is now going on at place. Twenty four canoes
were ordered to convey those who desired to come to
Freetown to trade, the whole of those canoes will return this morning to bring others down. Small Scarcies (Bey Inga's territory) is also filled with them,
on their way coming here. The head messenger has not
as yet arrived. He told them distinctly that they
will go to Sierra Leone to trade in spite of all opposition. They brought ivory, gold, hides, Shea butter
and great number of cattle, among which 503 oxen and
a beautiful grey horse.

Trade also is coming down well from the Port
Lokkoh and Sierra Leone rivers.

I have etc.

(Sgd.) Thos. Geo. Lawson
Govt. Interpreter

Lieut. H. C. B. Dann 2nd W. I. R.
Private Secretary
and A.D.C.
etc. etc. etc.

Freetown Sierra Leone
26th January 1885

Sir,

The enclosed are the letters brought by the messengers who came down from the interior, One is written in Arabic which I had translated, herewith forwarded.

This chief should be kindly treated and made to
see the movements of British Soldiers. They seem to
be a little tired and wish to have one or two days'
rest. They brought a horse as present to the Government which I still allow to be in their care. I am
told that the Chief he sends and is now here, is his
principal messenger and that they are doing immense
good from the Interior downwards and their influence

has now reached Kambia, Great Scarcies. When his messengers were here in 1880, they had a grand reception and handsome presents sent the chief. Sir Samuel Rowe wrote this Chief in 1879 letter dated 12th April of that year, another letter was sent him dated 27th April 1880, No. 25, In that year October 12th, a present of ₤35 was sent him and ₤15 given to his messengers. In 1884 a letter was sent him dated 9th April of that year No. 22. Communication commenced with this Chief in the time of Sir Arthur Kennedy when late Mr Winwood Reade was sent to visit that locality by the late Governor, I believe in 1869 and 1870, vide Mr Reade's large map at Government House.

I have etc.

(Sgd.) Thos. Geo. Lawson
Govt. Interpreter

Lieut. H. C. B. Dann 2nd W.I.R.
Private Secretary
and A.D.C.
etc. etc. etc.

P.S. 27th instant. Yesterday 321 of the interior Strangers arrived with trade; oxen, hides, gold etc. Those who came yesterday expressly to the Government as stated in the fore part of this letter, appear to be very weary and wish to have one or two days rest before seeing his Excellency. I have no safe place at present to keep the horse which they brought, perhaps His Excellency will permit me to send it up Government House to be kept in one of the Stables where care can be taken of it until it can be disposed of.

(Intld.) T. G. L.

GILB, 7:9-12

Freetown Sierra Leone
19 June 1885

Memo for His Excellency's information relative
to the mission to be sent up to the Interior

The SOFAS that have arrived at present at SARMAYAH came down as I am told by the invitation of ALMAMY BOKHARIE against his subjects in the MORIAH country.

1. Against the breach of the KORAN regulation that no
subject is to rise against his King and that such a
person is doomed to be destroyed, unless atonement be
made by him.

2. That their determination is to take ALMAMY BOKHARIE
back to his country under all hazard.

3. To put an end to the plundering, killing and disturbing of travellers from the Interior to SIERRA
LEONE and back.

4. If possible to subjugate all infidels to
MOHAMMEDANISM.

        In the latter they have succeeded from the Inte-
rior including FALABA as far as down to SARMAYAH.
SULUKU the King of BOMBABAH in the BEREWAH LIMBAH
country has yielded under oath to them; it remains
now a portion of the LIMBAHS, those of TUNKOH, LOKKOH
and the various TIMMANEE tribes as they put in plea
that they are doing this for the whitemen at the water-
sides whose merchandise they require in their country
and who have spent large amount of money to obtain
this advantage and failed, they will now obtain it by
their swords.

        As the principal trade of the Settlement is more
from those adjacent countries from FALABA down to the
waterside and from the interior countries of the MENDIS
down to the SHERBRO and GALLINAS, it would be well
that a proper and suitable European be sent up who is
qualified at the same time to take the bearings, routes
and position of the countries although this season of
the year appears to be against Europeans being sent
but there are some Europeans who have the zeal of
their country and Queen [and] would rather work in the
rains than in the dries, as it is cooler to their con-
stitions. With hopes Your Excellency will succeed in
obtaining such an one.

        I believe Your Excellency will find such an one
in the person of MAJOR FESTING whose appearance is not
watery. I think if such an one reaches SARMAYAH from
PORT LOKKOH and see ALPHA ALLIEU the present General
of ALPHA SARMADOO's army since the death of ALPHA
DARAAMY he might be able to do great good in preventing their destroying the countries below that place.

The route from PORT LOKKOH to SARMAYAH can easily be obtained from Chiefs BOCARY SAILEY and ABDUL LAHAI KALLOKKOH.

When the mission arrives at PORT LOKKOH, the Alikarlie should have your Excellency's instruction to render all assistance to further it on, in like manner the stipendiary Chiefs through whose countries it will pass especially when they all will hear that it will in some measure prevent the SOPHAS from invading their territories in an hostile manner and all should agree not in any way to molest caravans and others passing through their various countries.

ALPHA ALLIEU will be informed that Your Excellency has great respect and regard for their Chief SAMADOO and had written him a letter 6 years ago to that effect dated 12th April 1879, a copy of which if necessary should be written in ARABIC and taken by the Officer when going, a subsequent letter No. 25, dated 27th April 1880 was sent him with a large amount of presents which never reached him. The first letter is what roused the mind of ALPHA SAMADOO with the wish and thirst that his country and other interior countries should have free intercourse with the Settlement without molestation on the way.

As far as I have ascertained DOWDAH with the assistance of ALPHA ALLIEU is turning the attention of the caravans to the PORT LOKKOH route.

ALPHA ALLIEU and those with him will be informed that your Excellency is still a great friend to them and the whole of the interior tribes, and that they should remember that the Kings, Chiefs and people of those lower countries had been their ancient friends, and that it is the wish of Your Excellency that matters should be amicably arranged between them without war, and that if they find any of those Kings and Chiefs who refuse to give free passage to caravans and others to the Settlement and back, they should report it for Your Excellency's information and that Your Excellency is glad to hear that amicable arrangements have been made between them and SULUKU and desires to know who is the present Chief of FALABA and is now left in ABAL'S place Chief of HAMDALAH to whom Your Excellency had written a letter, dated 12th April 1879.

                              (Sgd.) Thos. Geo. Lawson
                              Govt. Interpreter

To the Private Secretary
etc.   etc.   etc.

Arrival of QUIAH MODOO son of ALMAMY BOKHARIE

                              Freetown, Sierra Leone
                              20th June 1885

Sir,

     I beg to report for His Excellency's information,
the arrival of QUIAH MODOO son of ALMAMY BOKHARIE,
King of the MORIAH Country and 19 others on a special
and friendly visit to His Excellency. He brought a
letter written in ENGLISH which I enclose herewith.
He states that his father has heard with pleasure the
arrival of His Excellency the Governor-in-Chief his
best of friends and would have long before this sent
to welcome him once more to the Settlement but the
great annoyance and trouble which he had lately, prevented his doing so before this.

     With His Excellency's authority, I can receive
them and provide lodgings and maintenance for them.
They arrived yesterday 5 p.m.

                              I have etc.

                              (Sgd.) Thos. Geo. Lawson
                              Govt. Interpreter

Capt. J. J. Crooks
Private Secretary
etc.   etc.   etc.

Appendix

SELECTED LIST OF RULING FAMILIES IN THE NORTHERN RIVERS

The Ture Kings of Moriah During the Eighteenth and Nineteenth Centuries

Name	Years in Office	Town
Fode Mamudu Katibi	Before 1720-?	Furikaria
Manga Abu Bakari b. Fode Mamudu	1750s-1760s	Yankissa
Fode Mori Imran (Morani) b. Manga Abu Bakari	1770s	Yankissa
Quia (Koya) Modu[a]	1780s	Yankissa
Mustafa b. Fode Mamudu	1790s-1802	Gberika
Amara (Omaru) b. Fode Imran	1803-1826	Yankissa
Ali Gberika	1827-1849	Gberika
Quia Fode[b] (Regent)	1850-1852	Yankissa
Fode Wise	1855-1862	Furikaria
Maligi (Mange) Gbaily[c]	1862-1866	Furikaria
Bukhari[d]	1865(8)-1883(5)	Yankissa
Quia Fode Dawda[e]	1883-	Furikaria

---

[a] The sources disagree about Quia Modu. He was a son of either Fode Mamudu Katibi or Fode Mori Imran, and his relative position in the list of kings is not definite. He was killed by mustafa.

[b] Fode Wise claimed to be alimami beginning in 1852, but he had a rival—Ali Fore Ture, from Furikaria—and it was not until 1855 that Fode Wise could definitely claim to hold that position.

[c] Maligi Gbaily was named alimami by his uncle, Lahai Sware, who was next in line for the position but too old to assume it. Maligi Gbaily was assassinated by forces of Bukhari in 1866-1867.

[d] Bukhari took the position of alimamy from Maligi Gbaily by force. He was deposed by force with the assistance of the French.

[e] Although Quia Fode Dawda claimed to be alimami, he was only recognized by the French colonial government as alkali of Furikaria. By the late 1880s, however, he was being referred to as alimami in the French government sources.

Dumbuya Alimami or Kandeh at Kukuna,
from about 1750 through 1978

Name	Years in Office	House
Wule Brahima	1750- ?	Bramaia
Wule Maligi	?	Maligia
Mori Fasinneh	Before 1820- ?	Bramaia
Namina Sheka[a]	Died ca. 1837	Maligia
Terena	?	Bramaia
Arafan Mumini	ca. 1850-1874	Maligia
Fode Silla	1874-1889	Bramaia
[Suri I[b]	?	Maligia]
Basi I	Died in 1905	Bramaia
Suri II	1905-1913	Maligia
Gbinti Terena	1913-1922	Bramaia
Sattan Modu (Ahmadu)	1922-1925	Maligia
Kole (Kolleh)	1926-1939	Bramaia
Sadu I	1940-1953	Maligia
Basi II	1955-1965	Bramaia
Sadu II	1966-	Maligia

[a]Given as the father of Lamina Bilali in Sierra Leone archival sources.

[b]Suri I is mentioned by only one of the sources as alimami
of Kukuna. He may have been added to provide consistency in the
system of alternation between the two houses. This particular
oral source, however, gives other names not found on lists, and
it is possible that Commissioner Sayers's list (Sierra Leone,
Kambia District Archives: Susu-Limba File [Kukuna], Report by
E. F. Sayers, June 29, 1926) may have become the official list.
It is also not unlikely that names of regents were omitted from
other lists but retained by the oral source.

Sankoh Alimami or Kandeh at Tawiya,
from about 1750 through 1978

Name	Years in Office
Fode Mamudu[a]	Mid-eighteenth century
Ibrahim[b]	Late eighteenth century
Fori Sineh[c]	Early nineteenth century
Dura Tumani	1830s and 1840s
Fode Tumani[d]	?
Samba Umwoli	1850s and 1860s
Worikia Sulimani	Died in 1874
Alkali Ansumana (Regent)	1875- ?
Mori Kanu Kolleh[e]	1880s and 1890s
Siri Kolleh[f]	(Deposed ?)
Noah I	Died in 1915
Bokari	1916-1934
Noah II	1934-1937
Suri	1937-1970
Kandeh Bokari "Terrner"[g]	1975-

---

[a] In two Sankoh family traditions and in a Fofana tradition, Fode Mamudu is given as the founder of the Sankoh section in Magbema kingdom and possibly the founder of Tawiya.

[b] Ibrahim was a grandson of Fode Mamudu.

[c] Fori Sineh was a younger brother of Ibrahim's, and Dura Tumani was Fori Sineh's youngest son.

[d] Although he is listed separately in one source, Fode Tumani may be the same as Dura Tumani.

[e] Mori Kanu Kolleh is the first paramount chief of Tawiya officially recognized by the Sierra Leone government, in 1896.

[f] There seem to have been two Kollehs; the second was deposed for antigovernment activity.

[g] According to Sankoh sources, Kandeh Bokari is a maternal relative.

Notes

PREFACE

1. M. Crowder, *West Africa Under Colonial Rule* (London, 1968); C. Fyfe, *A History of Sierra Leone* (London, 1962); J. Hargreaves, *West Africa Partitioned*, vol. 1: *The Loaded Pause, 1885-89* (London, 1974); B. Harrell-Bond, A. Howard, and D. Skinner, *Community Leadership and the Transformation of Freetown (1801-1976)*, (The Hague, 1978); and J. Peterson, *Province of Freedom: A History of Sierra Leone 1787-1870* (London, 1969).

2. Fyfe, *A History of Sierra Leone*, pp. 125-26, 185-86, 242, 256, 286, 297, 329, 609.

INTRODUCTION

1. Ibid.; Peterson, *Province of Freedom*, J. Walker, *Black Loyalists: The Search for a Promised Land in Nova Scotia and Sierra Leone, 1783-1870* (New York, 1976).

2. United Kingdom, Public Record Office (hereafter referred to as PRO): CO 267/91, Commissioners Rowan and Wellington, pp. 59-70; CO 267/172, Commissioner Dr. Madden, Report and Appendices. Church Missionary Society (CMS): C A1/07, Annual Reports; C A1/033, Attarra.

3. PRO: CO 267/90, Commissioners Rowan and Wellington; CO 267/91, Commissioners Rowan and Wellington; CO 267/172, Commissioner Dr. Madden, Report and Appendices; CO 267/298, Mr. Laurie's Report and Enclosures.

4. In 1800 there had been serious trouble between the government and dissident Nova Scotians who were allied with a local ruler, King Tom. In November 1801 a Nova Scotian led a force comprised largely of Koya Temne against Fort Thornton, but the British troops with the aid of the Maroons put down the rebellion. A Susu force, instigated by Temne leaders, attacked in April 1802, but with no success. Although Alimami Dala Modu, a leading representative of the powerful Dumbuya clan from the

Northern Rivers and a resident of the colony, helped to negoti-
ate a settlement, he was suspected of supporting the attack.
Fyfe, *History of Sierra Leone*, pp. 81-91. PRO: CO 268/8, 1810,
Three Arabic Letters.

5. CMS: C Al/El-E7. D. Skinner, "Islam and Education in the
the Colony and Hinterland of Sierra Leone (1750-1914)," *Canadian
Journal of African Studies* 10, no. 3, 1977.

6. Skinner, "Islam and Education." CMS: C Al/0108, Haensel;
C Al/0192, Schlenker; C Al/0193, Schmid; C Al/0231, Wiltshire.

7. Peterson, *Province of Freedom*. A. B. C. Sibthorpe, *The
History of Sierra Leone* (London, 1970). The Fourah Bay Institution gradually evolved into a college with a general academic
curriculum. After 1864 it was called Fourah Bay College, and in
1876 the college became a secular institution affiliated with
Durham University. Fourah Bay College is today one of the two
campuses of the University of Sierra Leone.

8. PRO: CO 267/231, desp. 48, March 13, 1853. Frequently
the cases against accused liberated Africans failed because their
peers refused to convict them.

9. A. Howard, "Big Men, Traders, and Chiefs: Power, Commerce, and Spatial Change in the Sierra Leone-Guinea Plain,
1865-1895" (Ph.D. diss., University of Wisconsin, 1972); Harrell-
Bond, Howard, and Skinner, *Community Leadership*, chapters 1-4.

10. Howard, "Big Men, Traders, and Chiefs"; Harrell-Bond,
Howard, and Skinner, *Community Leadership*, chapters 1-4.

CHAPTER ONE

1. J. Duncan, *Travels in Western Africa in 1845 and 1846*,
(London, 1847), 1: 98-102, 144, and 172-73; and F. Forbes,
Dahomey and the Dahomans (London, 1851), 1: 98-102.

2. United Kingdom, Public Record Office (PRO): 30/29,
Granville Papers 269/72, enclosures 24 and 25, letters from
Ashongbor Kragey and others to King G. A. Lawson III and mer-
chants at Little Popo, Jan. 12, 1884.

3. PRO: Granville Papers 269/Confidential 4955, no. 28,
W. T. G. Lawson to Gov. Rowe, Sept. 13, 1883; no. 11, statement
by the Lawson (Jogbe Aworku) family. The identification of the
Lawsons with Aworku (Aokoo) gives credence to the explanation
that Thomas George Lawson was born at Little Popo of Ga
parentage. (There is some indication that the first Lawson to
settle at Anecho may have returned to Africa from Brazil.)

4. Several of the names associated with the Lawson family—
for example, Acquatay (Akwete), Lattey (Latei), and Tetteh
(Tete)—are Ga in origin; others are Ewe/Dahomey. Little Popo
was one of the places on the coast where Ga settled during the
late seventeenth century. It was a crossroads that attracted
people of different origin. For Ga history and organization see
M. Field, *Social Organization of the Ga people* (London, 1940);
and M. Manoukian, *Akan and Ga-Adangme Peoples of the Gold Coast*
(London, 1950). I am very much obliged to Mrs. Marion Johnson
of the Centre of West African Studies at the University of
Birmingham for providing me with important information and references about the Little Popo area.

5. Duncan, *Travels in Western Africa*; Forbes, *Dahomey and
Dahomans*; the Commissioners for Trade and Plantations, *Journal*,
January 1759 to December 1763, pp. 73-74.

6. The Lords of the Committee of Council appointed for the
Consideration of all Matters relating to Trade and Foreign Plantations, *Report*, Part 1: Special Information, no. 4, J. Mathews,
et al. to J. Tarleton, Esq., April 16, 1788 (London, 1789).

7. PRO: Granville Papers. Duncan, *Travels in Western
Africa*; Forbes, *Dahomey and Dahomans*. Sierra Leone Archives (SLA):
Local Letters to the Governor, T. G. Lawson's Report on mission
to king of Ahwoonah, Dec. 7, 1868. PRO: CO 267/270, Desp. 74,
Gov. Hill to Secretary of State for the Colonies (SS), April 20,
1861, enclosing letter from T. G. Lawson to SS, April 18, 1861.
In 1868 T. G. Lawson was sent on a mission to his uncle, the
king of Ahwoonah (Awuna), east of the Volta River near the coast,
because he was familiar with customs and language of the people.

8. PRO: Granville Papers 269/Confidential 4955, no. 28,
W. T. G. Lawson to Gov. Rowe, Sept. 13, 1883.

9. Duncan, *Travels in West Africa*; Forbes, *Dahomey and
Dahomans*.

10. PRO: CO 267/270, Desp. 74, Gov. Hill to SS, April 20,
1861; Granville Papers 269/72, Meade to Lister, June 18, 1884.

11. PRO: Granville Papers 269/72, encl. 8.

12. PRO: Granville Papers 269/Confidential 4955, encl. 23;
Granville Papers 269/Confidential 4994, encl. 2.

13. PRO: FO 84/1466, p. 81.

14. PRO: Granville Papers 269/48, Meade to Lister, Oct. 29,
1884.

15. PRO: Granville Papers 269/10, encl. 11.

16. PRO: FO 881/Confidential 4962/6, Rear Adm. Salmon to the secretary of the Admiralty, Jan. 9, 1884.

17. PRO: Granville Papers 269/17, Gov. Rowe to SS, pp. 24-25.

18. PRO: CO 267/270, Desp. 74, Gov. Hill to SS, April 20, 1861. SLA: Local Letters to Gov., T. G. Lawson's Report on mission to king of Ahwoonah, Dec. 7, 1868.

19. PRO: CO 267/270, Desp. 74, Gov. Hill to SS, April 20, 1861; CO 267/363, Desp. 160, Gov. Rowe to SS, May 18, 1886.

20. PRO: CO 267/193, Desp. 119, McDonald to SS, July 13, 1846. SLA: Governor's Letter Book, Local Letters, 1846-1848, Letter to Alkali Namina Modu, Port Loko, May 29, 1847; Letter to Bora Lahie, Melikuri, Aug. 3, 1847; Letter to Moribah, Contah, Sept. 10, 1847.

21. PRO: CO 267/222, Desp. 126, Macdonald to SS, July 6, 1851.

22. PRO: CO 267/363, Desp. 160, Gov. Rowe to SS, May 18, 1886. J. Hargreaves, "The Evolution of the Native Affairs Department," *Sierra Leone Studies*, new series, no. 3, 1954; D. Skinner, "Thomas George Lawson: Government Interpreter and Historical Resource," *Africana Research Bulletin* 4, 1974; *Sierra Leone Weekly News*, Sept. 13, 1884, p. 2.

23. Skinner, "Thomas George Lawson"; Hargreaves, "Evolution of Native Affairs Department." SLA: Government Interpreter's Memoranda, 1873-1876; Government Interpreter's Letter Books, 1876-1889.

24. PRO: CO 272/50, Sierra Leone Blue Book, 1873, p. 102.

25. PRO: CO 267/363, Desp. 153, Gov. Rowe to SS, May 14, 1886, enclosing letter from W. T. G. Lawson, Feb. 19, 1886.

26. SLA: Aborigines Minute Papers 159, Bai Kompa to Gov. Hay, March 31, 1890; AB MP 158, W. T. G. Lawson to Parkes, March 29, 1890.

27. *Sierra Leone Weekly News*, Oct. 27, 1906, and April 4, 1908.

28. *Sierra Leone Weekly News*, May 29, 1886.

29. *Sierra Leone Weekly News*, May 9, 1896.

30. *Sierra Leone Weekly News*, June 18, 1903.

31. *Sierra Leone Weekly News*, May 9, 1896, and Dec. 9, 1899.

32. *Sierra Leone Weekly News*, July 9, 1887.

33. *Sierra Leone Weekly News*, March 13, 1897; SLA: Government Interpreter's Letter Books, October 28, 1878.

34. C. Fyfe, *A History of Sierra Leone* (London, 1962), pp. 418-19.

CHAPTER TWO

1. PRO: CO 879/35/411, Collection of Treaties with Native Chiefs, etc. on the West Coast of Africa, Colonial Office, 1892, pp. 65-66.

2. Sierra Leone Company, *Substance of Report* (London, 1791). Sierra Leone Company, *An Account of the Colony of Sierra Leone from its First Establishment in 1793* (London, 1795). "Journal of Mr. James Watt in his Expedition to and from Teembo in the Year 1794," Rhodes House Manuscript Collection, Oxford (hereafter called Watt's Journal).

3. Watt's Journal.

4. Sierra Leone Company, *Substance of the Report Delivered by the Court of Directors* (London, 1804), pp. 8-9.

5. PRO: CO 267/51, Desp. 237, Gov. MacCarthy to SS, March 12, 1820; CO 267/56, Gov. MacCarthy to SS, Sept. 24, 1822. In 1817, seventeen ships with a total tonnage of 2,990 served the port of Freetown, while in 1821 the number of ships rose to twenty-six with a total tonnage of 6,804.

6. PRO: CO 267/60, Desp. 6, Gov. Hamilton to SS, April 21, 1824.

7. A. Howard, "Big Men, Traders, and Chiefs: Power, Commerce and Spatial Change in the Sierra Leone-Guinea Plain, 1865-1895." (Ph.D. diss., University of Wisconsin, 1972); B. Harrell-Bond, A. Howard, and D. Skinner, *Community Leadership and the Transformation of Freetown (1801-1976)* (The Hague, 1978), chapters 2 and 3; D. Skinner, "Mande Settlement and the Development of Islamic Institutions in Sierra Leone," *International Journal*

of African Historical Studies 11, no. 1, 1978. PRO: CO 267/49, Gov. MacCarthy to SS, Nov. 18, 1819.

8. C. Fyfe, *A History of Sierra Leone* (London, 1962), pp. 18, 94. CMS: C Al/El-E7, Reports, Letters, and Diaries of the Susu Mission.

9. PRO: CO 267/90 and 91, Report and Appendices of Commissioners Rowan and Wellington, 1827; CO 267/172, Report of Commissioner Dr. Madden, 1841; CO 267/298, Mr. Laurie's Report on the Schools of Sierra Leone. In this study I am using Northern Rivers to refer to the region between the Kaba River and the Baga territory north of Sumbuya (see Map 3).

10. PRO: CO 267/29, Mr. Dawes, Nov. 11, 1811.

11. PRO: CO 268/8, Translation of three Arabic letters; CO 267/27, Testimony of Dalu Mohammed, p. 43.

12. PRO: CO 267/29, Mr. Dawes, Nov. 11, 1811.

13. PRO: CO 267/38, Desp. 52, Gov. Maxwell to SS, May 1, 1814.

14. CMS: C Al/El/116a, Rev. Hartwig's Journal, 1805; C Al/El/89, Gov. Ludlam to Rev. Pratt, Dec. 20, 1806.

15. CMS: C Al/El/81, Rev. Hartwig, Oct. 16, 1806; C Al/El, Reports by Rev. Butscher, Rev. Renner, and Rev. Passe, 1806-1807.

16. CMS: C Al/El/115c, Rev. Renner's Journal, 1807. The influence of Islam in, and other characteristics of, the Mandingo and Susu territories north of the colony are analyzed in Chapter three.

17. J. Corry, *Observations upon the Windward Coast of Africa* (London, 1807). PRO: CO 270/8, Mr. Bright's Journal, Sept.-Oct., 1802; CO 270/8, Mr. Smith's Journal, Dec. 1802; CO 267/10, Arabic manuscript; CO 268/8, Translation of three Arabic letters.

18. PRO: CO 879/35/411, Collection of Treaties, nos. 4, 10, and 13, July 1807, p. 69. A bar equaled 3 shillings, 4 pence sterling.

19. PRO: CO 267/27, Colony Budget, Feb. 26, 1810. The government had been making payments to insure peaceful trade routes. SLA: Governor's Letter Book, 1808-1811, Ludlam to Mauri Bramah Concurri (Alimami Mori Brima Konkori of Port Loko), April 9, 1808.

20. PRO: CO 267/45, Desp. 113, Gov. MacCarthy to SS, Aug. 5, 1817; CO 267/49, encl. in MacCarthy to SS, Nov. 18, 1819; CO 267/53, Desp. 14, Gov. Grant to SS, Sept. 24, 1821, encl. A. Laing, *Travels in Timannee, Kooranko, and Soolimania Countries in Western Africa* (London, 1825).

21. SLA: Governor's Letter Books, 1808- and Colonial Secretary's Letter Books, 1820- . The government letter books for the nineteenth century, kept in the Sierra Leone Archives at Fourah Bay College, contain a great deal of important data on African-British contacts.

22. PRO: CO 879/35/411, Collection of Treaties, pp. 70-71; CO 267/47, Desp. 156, Gov. MacCarthy to SS, July 20, 1818.

23. PRO: CO 879/35/411, Collection of Treaties, pp. 72-82. The Spanish dollar equaled five shillings.

24. PRO: CO 267/60, Desp. 29, Gov. Hamilton to SS, Nov. 11, 1824.

25. PRO: CO 267/65, Desp. 26, Gov. Turner to SS, June 25, 1825.

26. PRO: CO 267/66, Turner to SS, Oct. 28, 1825. Turner allocated ₤500 for gifts to African rulers.

27. PRO: CO 267/66, Desp. 86, Turner to SS, Nov. 1, 1825.

28. Howard, "Big Men, Traders, and Chiefs"; D. Skinner, "The Development of Islam in Sierra Leone during the Nineteenth Century" (Ph.D. diss., University of California, Berkeley, 1971); E. Ijagbemi, "A History of the Temne" (Ph.D. diss., Edinburgh University, 1968).

29. PRO: CO 267/66, Desp. 91, Turner to SS, Dec. 20, 1825.

30. Ibid. PRO: CO 879/25/332, "Sierra Leone: Despatch from the Administrator-in-chief, enclosing information regarding the different districts and tribes of Sierra Leone and its vicinity," London, 1887, p. 24.

31. PRO: CO 879/35/411, Collection of Treaties, p. 82. CO 879/25/332, "Sierra Leone: Desp. from Administrator-in-chief," p. 24.

32. PRO: CO 267/66, Desp. 91, Turner to SS, Dec. 20, 1825.

33. PRO: CO 879/35/411, Collection of Treaties, p. 87.

34. PRO: CO 267/47, Desp. 156, Gov. MacCarthy to SS, July 20, 1818. SLA: Colonial Secretary's Letter Books, 1820–1840; Governor's Letter Books, Local Letters, 1808-1839.

35. Watt's Journal. PRO: CO 270/8, Mr. Bright's Journal. Adam Azfelius, *Sierra Leone Journal 1795-1796*, ed. Alexander Peter Kup (Uppsala: 1967) (hereafter called Azfelius's Journal).

36. PRO: CO 267/27, Testimony of Dalu Mohammed, p. 43. Dala Modu Dumbuya claimed to be the headman of all Muslim strangers who came to the colony for trade, and the Muslim title alimami set him apart from other Muslims who lived in the colony. During the period 1820-1841 he was the dominant economic and political figure in the small kingdoms of Kafu Bullom and Loko Masama.

37. PRO: CO 267/132, Desp. 103, Gov. H. Campbell to SS, July 11, 1836.

38. Skinner, "Development of Islam"; idem, "Mande Settlement." PRO: CO 267/132, Desp. 63, H. Campbell to SS, May 2, 1836; CO 267/172, Dr. Madden's Report. CMS: C A1/0192, Rev. C. F. Schlenker, Letters and Reports, Oct. 20 and Nov. 20 and 22, 1840, and Jan. 28 and Feb. 8, 13, and 15, 1844.

39. PRO: CO 879/35/411, Collection of Treaties, pp. 92-95; see also pp. 98-104 for the extension of the stipend system and British involvement in African politics.

40. Ibid., pp. 104-8.

41. PRO: CO 267/132, Desp. 63, H. Campbell to SS, May 2, 1836.

42. CMS: C A1/047, Dr. E. W. Blyden, 1871-1872. SLA: Colonial Secretary's Office no. 894/1869, Report of Mr. W. W. Reade. PRO: CO 267/316, Gov. Pope Hennessy, Sept. 1, 1872, encl. "Report of the Expedition to Falaba, Jan.-March, 1872," E. W. Blyden, March 26, 1872.

43. SLA: Governor's Letter Books, 1808- ; Colonial Secretary's Letter Books, 1820- ; Colonial Secretary's Office, Letters Received, 1850-1869; Governor's Letter Book to Native Chiefs, 1862-1867; Colonial Secretary's Letter Book to Native Chiefs, 1871-1881. PRO: CO 879/35/411, Collection of Treaties.

44. PRO: CO 267/253, Desp. 137, Gov. Hill to SS, May 29, 1856, encl. from Lawson, May 19, 1856. SLA: Local Letters to Gov., Lawson to Gov. Blackall, Dec. 30, 1863; Lawson Memorandum,

Aug. 28, 1869; Lawson Memorandum, Sept. 28, 1869. PRO: CO 267/193, Desp. 119, Gov. Macdonald to SS, July 13, 1846; CO 267/293, Desp. 47, Gov. Kennedy to SS, May 15, 1868, encl.

45. PRO: CO 267/193, Desp. 119, Gov. Macdonald to SS, July, 14, 1846.

46. J. Hargreaves, "The Evolution of the Native Affairs Department," *Sierra Leone Studies*, new series, no. 3, Dec. 1954; D. Skinner, "The Arabic Letter Books as a Source for Sierra Leone History," *Africana Research Bulletin* 3, no. 4, 1973; D. Skinner, "Thomas George Lawson: Government Interpreter and Historical Resource," *Africana Research Bulletin* 4, no. 4, 1974.

47. PRO: CO 267/53, Desp. 14, Gov. Grant to SS, Sept. 24, 1881, encl. O'Beirne's Journal, p. 3.

48. Ibid., p. 18.

49. Ibid., p. 192.

50. PRO: CO 879/24/318A/35, Gov. Rowe to SS, Jan. 23, 1886.

51. PRO: CO 879/35/411, Collection of Treaties.

52. SLA: Colonial Secretary's Letter Books, Cole to alkali, Jan. 25, 1834; April 24, 1834; and Sept. 18, 1834; Campbell to alkali, Dec. 22, 1836; Macdonald to alkali, May 26, 1841.

53. SLA: Colonial Secretary's Letter Books, Campbell to alkali, Dec. 22, 1836.

54. SLA: Colonial Secretary's Letter Books, Macdonald to alkali, May 26, 1841.

55. Ibid.

56. SLA: Colonial Secretary's Letter Books, 1820-1862; Governor's Letter Book to Native Chiefs, 1862-1867; Colonial Secretary's Letter Book to Native Chiefs, 1871-1881.

57. PRO: CO 879/25/332, "Sierra Leone: Desp. from Administrator-in-chief," p. 25; CO 879/35/411, Collection of Treaties, pp. 170-174. SLA: Colonial Secretary's Letter Book, Gov. Hill to Saddo Kamara, Feb. 4, 1859; Gov. Hill to Prince Kindo Bangura, Feb. 7, 1859.

58. British Museum: Parliamentary Accounts and Papers,

Colonies, Session: December 12, 1854-August 14, 1855, vol. 37: Correspondence Relative to the Recent Expedition against the Moriah Chiefs in the Neighbourhood of Sierra Leone, pp. 341-371, Dougan to SS, Dec. 12, 1854.

59. Ibid., Right Hon. Sidney Herbert to the Officer Administering the Government, Feb. 22, 1855.

60. Ibid., Dougan to SS, June 12, 1855.

61. British Museum: Parliamentary Accounts and Papers, Colonies, Session: January 31-July 29, 1856, vol. 42, p. 418.

62. See the Appendix for a list of the kings of Moriah in the eighteenth and nineteenth centuries.

63. PRO: CO 267/253, Desp. 137, Gov. Hill to SS, May 29, 1856; CO 267/254, Desp. 200, Hill to SS, Sept. 19, 1856.

64. PRO: CO 267/260, Desp. 23, Hill to SS, Feb. 13, 1858.

65. PRO: CO 879/35/411, Collection of Treaties, pp. 176-78; see also CO 267/260, Desp. 3, Jan 1, 1858; Desp. 15, Jan. 19, 1858; CO 267/263, Desp. 46, April 2, 1859; Desp. 61, April 18, 1859.

66. Governors were under almost no direct control by the Colonial Office in London. Communication between West Africa and Great Britain was slow—taking up to six months for an exchange of letters—and governors could be selective in the information they provided to the Colonial Office. The important duty of a governor was to promote British interests at the least possible expense and difficulty. Dougan would not have been suspended had his military expedition succeeded, for governors often mounted similar expeditions without Colonial Office sanction and no action was taken against them. Political and economic relations were conducted between African rulers and the colony government in Freetown, not the Colonial Office in London. Therefore, an African ruler considered a treaty with Freetown to be immediately effective, and colony governors were quick to exploit the situation. In later years even the Colonial Office used invalid treaties as the basis for claiming spheres of influence in African territories. Furthermore, colonial officials in the interior often promoted British interests and interpreted colonial policy without the authorization of the government in Freetown or of the Colonial Office, and their actions helped to shape the development of colonial policy in Sierra Leone. Thomas George Lawson was such a colonial officer: he fervently pursued an activist interpretation of the imperial mission. See, for

example, SLA: Local Letters to the Governor, Aborigines Minute Papers, nos. 90, 107, 613, and 634 of 1865. Although colonial officials often described wars as "tribal" in origin—i.e., "Susu-Temne"—they were the result of territorial, economic, and personal ambitions and usually were fought by ethnically mixed armies.

67. PRO: CO 267/270, Desp. 74, Gov. Hill to SS, April 20, 1861, encl. T. G. Lawson to SS, April 18, 1861.

68. SLA: Local Letters to Governor, Lawson to Blackall, Dec. 30, 1863.

69. SLA: Local Letters to Governor, Report by Lawson, Dec. 17, 1868.

70. PRO: CO 267/320, Mr. Lawson's Report on his Mission to the Scarcies and other Rivers, Oct. 17, 1872.

71. SLA: Local Letters to Governor, Report by Lawson, Dec. 17, 1868; Reports by Lawson, March-May 1872.

72. SLA: Local Letters to Governor, List of Chiefs to have an Interview with His Excellency, Aug. 31, 1869, and May 5, 1868. See also *Sierra Leone Weekly News*, Sept. 13, 1884, p. 2.

73. Part two of this study contains many examples of the various roles and services performed by Mr. Lawson, in particular some of his detailed reports and evaluations of the situation in the interior.

74. SLA: Local Letters to Governor, Muslim Leaders to Lawson, Aug. 23, 1872.

75. PRO: CO 267/270, Desp. 74, Gov. Hill to SS, April 20, 1861.

76. PRO: CO 267/355, Desp. 46, Tarleton to SS, Feb. 27, 1884.

77. PRO: CO 267/363, Desp. 160, Gov. Rowe to SS, May 18, 1886.

78. PRO: CO 267/365, Desp. 354, Gov. Hay to SS, Sept. 25, 1886, encl.

79. Ibid., T.T. Pinkett.

80. Ibid., T. R. Griffith, Colonial Secretary and Treasurer.

81. Ibid.

82. PRO: CO 267/372, Desp. 373, Gov. Hay to SS, Nov. 19, 1888.

CHAPTER THREE

1. W. Rodney, *A History of the Upper Guinea Coast, 1545 to 1800* (Oxford, 1970).

2. I am preparing a study on the Northern Rivers region that draws on a large body of archival, oral, and Arabic documentation, as well as printed works. There are, understandably, conflicts between the different oral and written versions about the history of the peoples and states of the region. In the forthcoming study I will present the Arabic documents and their translations along with the oral-history materials. The version in Chapter three is a composite of several sources that I have reconciled to present as clear a history as possible. Among the most valuable sources are: M. Bangura, "Contribution a l'histoire des Sosoe du 16e au 19e siècle (Conakry, 1971-1972); El-Hadj D. S. Toure, "Histoire du Moreah," typescript (Conakry, 1975); Al-Hajj M. S. Fofana, "Ta'rikh al-Muriah," manuscript copy of a document written by Ibrahim Kondittu Fofana during the late eighteenth century (Gbile, 1976); the memoranda and letter books of Thomas George Lawson, Sierra Leone Government Interpreter, 10 vols., 1873-1889 (extracts are given in Part two); and more than forty interviews conducted in Sierra Leone and Guinea during 1969, 1973, and 1976. Other valuable resources are collected in the Church Missionary Archives (London), British Museum (London), Public Record Office (Kew, England), les Archives Nationales—Section Outre Mer (Paris), les Archives Nationales (Dakar, Sénégal), and the National Archives of Sierra Leone (Freetown).

3. A. Howard, "Big Men, Traders, and Chiefs: Power, Commerce, and Spatial Change in the Sierra Leone-Guinea Plain, 1865-1895" (Ph.D. diss., University of Wisconsin, 1972); D. Skinner, "The Development of Islam in Sierra Leone During the Nineteenth Century" (Ph.D. diss., University of California, Berkeley, 1971); C. Quinn, *Mandingo Kingdoms of the Senegambia* (London, 1972); D. Skinner, "Mande Settlement and the Development of Islamic Institutions in Sierra Leone," *International Journal of African Historical Studies* 11, 1978; P. Curtin, "The Western Juula in the Eighteenth Century," Conference on Manding Studies (London, 1972); L. Kaba, "The Maninka-Mori of Bate, Guinea: A Preliminary Survey for Research in Ethno-history," Conference on Manding Studies (London, 1972); L. Sanneh, "The Origin and Dispersion of the Diakhanke: An Introductory Study," Conference on Manding Studies (London, 1972).

4. Sanneh, "Origin and Dispersion"; idem, "The Diakhanke
and the Ummah al-Muhammadiya: A Preliminary Study in the Clerical
and Educational Role of the Diakhanke," Conference on Manding
Studies (London, 1972); idem, "The Origins of Clericalism in West
African Islam," *Journal of African History* 17, 1976; L. Sanneh,
The Jakhanke, (London, 1979), chap. 1. P. Curtin, *Economic
Change in Precolonial Africa*, (Madison, 1975), pp. 75-83; Kaba,
"The Maninka-Mori of Bate, Guinea." J. Surat-Canale, "Touba in
Guinea—Holy Place of Islam," in *African Perspectives*, edited by
C. Allen and R. Johnson (London, 1970). Although scholars dis-
agree somewhat on the origin of Mande family names, it seems
clear that many of the so-called Mandingo and Susu families in
the Northern Rivers were originally Soninke/Sarakuli.

5. Howard, "Big Men, Traders, and Chiefs"; Sanneh, "Origins
of Clericalism"; idem, *The Jakhanke*; Skinner, "Mande Settlement";
idem, "Islam and Education in the Colony and Hinterland of Sierra
Leone (1750-1914)," *Canadian Journal of African Studies* 10, 1976;
Curtin, *Economic Change in Precolonial Africa: Senegambia in the
Era of the Slave Trade* (Madison, Wisconsin, 1975). See also
Papers of the Conference on Manding Studies (London, 1972) and
C. Hodge (ed.), *Papers on the Manding* (Bloomington, Ind., 1971).

6. C. Fyfe (ed.), *Sierra Leone Inheritance* (London, 1964),
pp. 49-53. The Susu are a subgroup of the Mande-speaking peoples. They originated from the Soninke or a closely related
group. There are two main groups of Susu: the coastal Susu in
Guinea/Sierra Leone and the Yalunka (or Jalonke) of northeast
Sierra Leone and contiguous areas of Guinea: they are distin-
guished only by their geographical separation and by the greater
influence of Islam among the coastal Susu. In general, the
identification of ethnic origins is difficult because of the
many long migrations and the extensive intermarriage between
groups. I asked one of my informants why he called himself a
Susu. He said: "Originally, the Yansane were Sarakuli. When
they passed into Guinea they were speaking Maninka and when they
came to Guinea and settled they intermarried with Susu and spoke
Susu. Today they call themselves Susu" (interview with Alfa
Soriba Yansane of Laya, Freetown, March 4, 1976).

7. The tendency to telescope genealogies and attribute a
very long life span to the founder of a king group are problems
that prevent precise dating of migration and settlement. A
comparison of the current versions of several genealogies indicates that the late seventeenth century is the period when many
kin groups were established in the Northern Rivers; others
arrived in the early eighteenth century.

8. According to oral tradition, the Kamara of Tambakka are

descendants of Fore Firigi Kamara of Manden and Farana (Ray
Ganga's interview with Ousman Kamara, Musaia [Sierra Leone],
April 10, 1973). I want to thank Ray Ganga for the oral his-
tories he sent me and for his ideas.

9. Please see note 2 of this chapter for some of the main
sources I used to reconstruct the history of Moriah and neighboring states. The principal interviews are listed in the
Bibliography.

10. One version of the oral tradition says that Fode Mamudu
Katibi Ture married Mangabe Wonde Bangura of Sumbuya. This would
ally the Ture group with the Bangura family in the Northern Rivers. All other oral and written traditions identify Fode
Mamudu's wife as a Kamara. Both versions could be true, of
course, as Fode Mamudu may have had more than one wife.

11. Interviews with Alimami Sorie Sankoh, Tawiya, April 15,
1969, and with Kolea Sankoh, Tawiya, Feb. 28, 1976. See
also, Skinner, "Mande Settlement"; and idem, "Development of
Islam," pp. 112-24. The four Sankoh alimami of Port Loko between about 1760 and 1815 were Namina Modu, Modu Serie, Amara,
and Brima Konkori.

12. Sierra Leone, Kambia District Archives: Susu-Limba File
(Kukuna), Report by E. F. Sayers, District Commissioner of Karene
District, June 29, 1926 (hereafter called Sayers's Report).

13. Interview with Kemokho Dumbuya and Kande Sadu Dumbuya II,
Kukuna, Feb. 26, 1976; Ray Ganga's interview with Lamina Kamara,
Kukuna, May 13, 1973.

14. Sayers's Report; Toure, "Histoire du Moreah"; and Fofana,
"Ta'rikh al-Muriah."

15. See the list of alimami or kandeh at Kukuna in the Appendix. The alternation of ruling houses is not uncommon, but such
a neat list is still suspicious.

16. Interview with the elders of the Dumbuya family,
Dalamodia, Lungi, March 21, 1976; Alusine Yilla's interview
with Alimami Sindamore Dumbuya, Bolobinneh, April 10, 1976;
Skinner, "Mande Settlement"; idem, "Development of Islam"; PRO:
CO 270/8, Mr. Bright's Journal; Azfelius's Journal, pp. 118,
120, 122, 138.

17. Yula is the Susu word for jula. All informants were
unanimous in their identification of the "yula tribes." See
also Lawson's documents in Part two, Military Matters and
Lawson's Roles and Attitudes.

18. PRO: CO 270/8, Mr. Bright's Journal, p. 52.

19. Information on slavery in the Northern Rivers was gathered from interviews with Kemokho Dumbuya and Kande Sadu Dumbuya II, Kukuna, Feb. 26, 1976; with Kolea Sankoh, Tawiya, Feb. 28, 1976; and with Shaikhu Luseni, Gbile, March 26 and April 15, 1969; Feb. 25, 28, and 29, 1976. See also Afzelius's Journal; and PRO: CO 270/8, Mr. Bright's Journal. For recent examinations of the problem of slavery in Africa see S. Miers and I. Kopytoff (eds.), *Slavery in Africa* (Madison, Wis., 1977); M. Klein, "The Study of Slavery in West Africa," *Journal of African History*, vol. xix, no. 4, 1978, pp. 599-609; and F. Cooper, "The Problem of Slavery in African Studies," *Journal of African History*, vol. 20, no. 1, 1979, pp. 103-125.

20. Afzelius's Journal, pp. 122, 123, 126.

21. PRO: CO 879/25/332, "Sierra Leone: Desp. from administrator-in-chief," pp. 8 ff. See also Lawson's documents in Part two, Political Affairs. The implications of the Bilali revolt will be discussed later in this chapter. According to archival sources, Lamina Bilali was a son of Alimami Namina Sheka Dumbuya (who died about 1837-1838) of Kukuna and his Koranko concubine. He was raised as a free son by Alimami Namina Sheka and was promised his freedom and the freedom of his mother and siblings upon the death of the alimami. Instead, Lamina Bilali and his slave kin were treated as the property of the alimami—to be distributed as part of the inheritance. Bilali gathered his family and those slaves who wished to join him and fled in 1838 to Tonko Limba, where he established a refuge for escaped slaves and continued his activities against the Susu into the 1880s.

22. N. Owen, *Journal of a Slave Dealer* (London, 1930), pp. 92-93, 96, 100, and 101; Y. Person, "Ethnic Movements and Acculturation in Upper Guinea since the Fifteenth Century," *International Journal of African Historical Studies* 4, 1971; and Interviews with Shaikhu Luseni, Gbile, March 26 and April 15, 1969; Feb. 25, 28, and 29, 1976. It is difficult now to ascertain the authenticity of this *jihad*.

23. See, for example, N. Levtzion, *Ancient Ghana and Mali* (London, 1973).

24. Person, "Ethnic Movements"; E. F. Sayers, "Notes on the Clan or Family Names Common in the Area Inhabited by Temnespeaking People," *Sierra Leone Studies* 10 (old series), December 1927. Interviews with Alfa Soriba Yansane, Freetown, Mar. 4 and 8, 1976.

25. Interviews with Kolea Sankoh, Tawiya, Feb. 28, 1976;

Alfa Soriba Yansane; and Shaikhu Luseni.

26. See Part two, Political Affairs and Military Matters. Al Hajj M. S. Fofana, "Ta'rikh al Muriah"; El-Hadj D. S. Toure, "Histoire du Moreah." SLA: Local Letters to the Governor, Oct. 9, 1863, from Alimami Fannah and Alimami Sannussee; and Local Letters to the Governor, July 5, 1870, from Alimami Sori Feekeh. The jula are the yula tribes referred to in the oral traditions.

27. D. Skinner's interviews with: Shaikhu Luseni; Kolea Sankoh; Alfa Soriba Yansane; and Alhaji Muhammad Sanusi, Tawiya, Feb. 28, 1976. At its largest, the kingdom of Moriah extended from Sumbuya in the north down to the Kolente River across from Kambia and from the Atlantic to Bena in the east. It covered an area of approximately 1,500 square miles and had a population of perhaps 100,000 people.

28. See the list of kings of Moriah in the Appendix.

29. Archives Nationales, Paris: Sénégal IV, Dossier 56a, June 14, 1868. Archives Nationales, Dakar: 7-G-18, Mellacorée, Aug. 13 and 14, 1879. SLA: Government Interpreter's Letter Books, Nov. 3, 1879.

30. See Part two, Political Affairs and Military Matters. These disputes will be discussed further later in this chapter.

31. See the following section, British Relations with the Northern Rivers.

32. B. Harrell-Bond, A. Howard, and D. Skinner, *Community Leadership and the Transformation of Freetown* (The Hague, 1978), chapters 2 and 3.

33. Any town with a substantial Muslim population had a prayer field or *sallekene*. See Skinner, "Islam and Education in the Colony and Hinterland of Sierra Leone, 1750-1914," *Canadian Journal of African Studies* 10, no. 3, 1977; idem, "Mande Settlement and the Development of Islamic Institutions in Sierra Leone," *International Journal of African Historical Studies* 11, 1978. Quranic schools were called *karanthe* or *karande*, while mosques were known as *jami* or *msiri*.

34. Afzelius's Journal, p. 140.

35. Ibid., pp. 140-41.

36. Watt's Journal, p. 123.

37. J. Mathews, *A Voyage to the River Sierra Leone* (London, 1788).

38. Skinner, "Mande Settlement"; idem, interviews with Shaikhu Luseni. Archives Nationales, Dakar: 7-G-20, Mellacorée, April 11, 1875. CMS: C A1/0 47, E. W. Blyden to Venn, June 19, 1872. SLA: Native Affairs Department Minute Papers, 570/ Dec. 1895, encl. B. Although described by colonial officials as a Susu-Temne conflict, it was part of a wider struggle for political hegemony and economic control.

39. CMS: C A1/E1/115c, Rev. Renner's Journal, Jan.-Mar., 1807.

40. Ibid. CMS: C A1/0 192, Rev. Schlenker's Journal, Nov. 2, 1850. Skinner, "Mande Settlement."

41. Mathews, *Voyage*; Watt's Journal; and The Papers of Governor Zachary Macaulay, Huntington Library, San Marino, California.

42. PRO: CO 270/8, Mr. Bright's Journal, Sept.-Oct. 1802; CO 270/8, Mr. Smith's Journal, Dec. 1802.

43. PRO: CO 268/8, Three Arabic Letters, 1810; CO 267/38, Desp. 52, Gov. Maxwell to SS, May 1, 1814. Sierra Leone Company, *Substance of Report* (London, 1791); idem, *An Account of the Colony of Sierra Leone from its First Establishment in 1793* (London, 1795); idem, *Substance of the Report Delivered by the Court of Directors* (London, 1804).

44. PRO: CO 267/72, Desp.57, Gov. Macaulay to SS, July 4, 1826.

45. Archives Nationales, Paris: Sénégal IV, Dossier 28a, Revue Coloniale, 1845, p. 374.

46. SLA: Governor's Letter Books, Local Letters, Acting Gov. Dougan to Commodore Adams, Oct. 30, 1854. See also Chapter two.

47. Watt's Journal, pp. 119a-20.

48. PRO: CO 267/53, Desp. 14, Gov. Grant to SS, Sept. 24, 1821, encl. O'Beirne's Journal.

49. PRO: CO 268/8, 1810, Three Arabic Letters. Amara Ture (sometimes called Omaru) was a son of Alimami Fode Morani (Imran)

Ture, a king of Moriah after Alimami Mangaba Abu Bakari, probably in the 1760s or 1770s. See the list of kings of Moriah in
the Appendix.

50. PRO: CO 267/38, Desp. 52, Gov. Maxwell to SS, May 1,
1814, encl. from Amara Ture to Gov., Mar. 2, 1814.

51. Ibid.

52. A. Laing, *Travels in the Timannee, Kooranko, and
Soolimama Countries in Western Africa* (London, 1825). PRO:
CO 267/82, Confidential, Gov. N. Campbell to SS, July 28, 1827,
encl.

53. PRO: CO 267/82, Confidential; CO 879/35/411, Collection
of Treaties with Native Chiefs, etc., on the West Coast of
Africa, 1892, p. 90.

54. PRO: CO 879/35/411, Collection of Treaties, pp. 70-71.

55. Ibid., pp. 83-86.

56. Ibid., p. 86. PRO: CO 267/72, Desp. 57, Gov. Macaulay
to SS, July 4, 1826.

57. PRO: CO 270/8, Mr. Bright's Journal, Sept.-Oct. 1802.

58. PRO: CO 879/35/411, Collection of Treaties, pp. 108-48.

59. SLA: Colonial Secretary's Letter Books, to King Stephen,
Mar. 8, 1850; to Quia Fode, Mar. 14, 1850; to Fode Wise, Dec. 11,
1852; to Lamina Bamoi, Mar. 23, 1853; and to Fode Wise, Apr. 3,
1861. During the 1860s the Sierra Leone government vigorously
pursued a policy of incorporating Moriah into the colonial system
that was contrary to directions from the Colonial Office. Earlier treaties were used to justify Sierra Leone's annexation of
the territory. See SLA: Local Letters to the Governor, Aborigines Minute Papers, no. 90, Gov. to SS, Aug. 19, 1865, and
no. 107, Gov. to SS, Oct. 18, 1865; and responses from the
Colonial Office to the Governor, nos. 613 and 634.

60. SLA: Colonial Secretary's Letter Books, to King Stephen,
Mar. 8, 1850; to Quia Fode, Mar. 14, 1850; to Fode Wise, June 26,
1851; to Fode Wise, Dec. 11, 1852; to Ali Foray, Dec. 19, 1852;
and to Fode Wise, July 5, 1855. PRO: CO 879/35/411, Collection
of Treaties, pp. 135-36.

61. For example, the conflict of Maligia described in Chapter two.

62. See Chapter two for a discussion of the Kambia conflict.

63. PRO: CO 879/25/332, "Sierra Leone: Desp. from Administrator-in-chief," pp. 8-9. SLA: Colonial Secretary's Office, Letters Received, Ward to Smyth, May 20, 1856.

64. Mathews, *Voyage*, p. 18.

65. Skinner, "The Development of Islam in Sierra Leone During the Nineteenth Century" (Ph.D. diss., University of California, Berkeley, 1971), pp. 98-105; Bai Farima Bangura, "History of Kambia," (Typescript, Oct. 28, 1938).

66. PRO: CO 267/253, Desp. 137, Gov. Hill to SS, May 29, 1856. Skinner, "Mande Settlement." SLA: Colonial Secretary's Letter Books, to Alimami Wise, Sept. 15, 1858.

67. PRO: CO 879/35/411, Collection of Treaties, pp. 142-44. SLA: Colonial Secretary's Letter Books, to Sattan Lahai, "King of Kambia," Dec. 8, 1852. Archives Nationales, Paris: Sénégal IV, Dossier 115e, M. R. de Joux, July 11, 1883.

68. PRO: CO 267/254, Desp. 200, Gov. Hill to SS, Sept. 19, 1856.

69. PRO: CO 267/260, Desp. 3, Hill to SS, Jan. 1, 1858. See also Chapter two.

70. PRO: CO 267/260, Desp. 23, Hill to SS, Feb. 13, 1858; CO 267/263, Desp. 46, Hill to SS, April 2, 1859; CO 267/263, Desp. 61, Hill to SS, April 18, 1859; CO 879/35/411, Collection of Treaties, pp. 176-80.

71. SLA: Colonial Secretary's Letter Books, to Ansumana Sanasi, June 18, 1856; to Ansumana Sanasi, Dec. 24, 1856; to Ansumana Sanasi, Feb. 15, 1858. SLA: Colonial Secretary's Office, Letters Received, Ward to Smyth, May 20, 1856. Moribaya was a small state between Sumbuya and Moriah that had long tried to maintain its independence. See PRO: CO 270/8, Mr. Bright's Journal.

72. SLA: Colonial Secretary's Office, Letters Received, Alkali Bamba Sennah and Alkali Bukhari to Gov. Hill, Sept. 29, 1860. Archives Nationales, Dakar: 7-G-18, Mellacorée. During the 1860s groundnuts were a major product of the region, amounting to about one million bushels each year.

73. Interviews with Shaikhu Luseni, Gbile. This was the general practice in Islamic political systems in Guinea/Sierra

Leone. The ceremony was performed on several occasions at Port Loko in the presence of Sierra Leone government officials, and it is still used in Sierra Leone.

74. SLA: Governor's Letter Book to Native Chiefs, Blackall to Bukhari, July 16, 1866. PRO: CO 267/293, Desp. 47, Gov. Kennedy to SS, May 15, 1868; CO 267/293, Desp 58, Kennedy to SS, May 27, 1868; CO 879/25/332, "Sierra Leone: Desp. from Administrator-in-chief," pp. 13-15. Archives Nationales, Paris: Sénégal IV, Dossiers 55b and 55c. Archives Nationales, Dakar: 7-G-19, Mellacoree, 1865-1868. According to British and French documents, the French government strongly supported Maligi Gbaily in his struggle with Bukhari. By the 1860s the French had become directly involved in Moriah affairs and were competing with the British for access to markets. The British sphere of influence was gradually being pushed south, to the north bank of the Kolente River. By the early 1880s the British had acknowledged French authority over Moriah.

75. See Part two, Political Affairs, Military Matters, and Trade Information. Archives Nationales, Dakar: 7-G-21, Mellacorée/J-a-69, Jan. 16, 1882 and May 6, 1882; Dakar, 7-g-22, Mellacorée/J-a-70, Mar. 18, 1883. One of Alimami Bukhari's most important war chiefs was called Kibali. He fought with Bukhari during the 1860s and also during the civil war of 1877-1883. Kibali was a native of Kasseh who later became the *bai bureh* there and led an anticolonial uprising in 1898: see L. Denzer, "Bai Bureh," *West African Resistance*, edited by M. Crowder (London,1970).

76. PRO: CO 267/320, Lawson's Report, Oct. 17, 1872. Archives Nationales, Dakar: 7-G-20, Mellacorée, 1873-1878. SLA: Government Interpreter's Memoranda, 1873-1876: July 24, 1875, and May 18, 1876.

77. J. Hargreaves, "The French Occupation of the Mellacourie, 1865-67," *Sierra Leone Studies*, new series, no. 9, Dec. 1957; H. Gailey, "European Rivalry and Diplomacy in the Mellacourie, 1879-1882," *Sierra Leone Studies*, new series, no. 15, Dec. 1961. Archives Nationales, Dakar: 7-g-18, Mellacorée, 1845-1886: Traités. Archives Nationales, Paris: Sénégal IV, Dossiers 55 and 56.

78. PRO: CO 267/320, Lawson's Report, Oct. 17, 1872.

79. PRO: CO 879/35/411, Collection of Treaties, p. 215.

80. PRO: CO 267/320, Lawson's Report, Oct. 17, 1872.

81. Archives Nationales, Dakar: 7-g-20, Mellacorée, Jan 22, 1873.

82. Alimami Bukhari was a strict Muslim who was allied with powerful Muslim families in the Northern Rivers, principally the Yansane of Furikaria and Kalimodia and the Fofana of Gbile and Furikaria. Bukhari studied Arabic and Islamic law in Futa Jalon, and he was literate in West African Arabic. He justified his actions against his detractors during the civil war on the basis of Islamic law, and he portrayed his enemies as hypocrites or backsliders: SLA: Arabic Letter Books, vol. 1: from Alimami Bukhari to Gov. Rowe, Jan 26, 1880, pp. 117-18; from Bukhari to Rowe, Jan 26, 1880, pp. 119-20; from Bukhari to Rowe, Feb. 25, 1880, pp. 121-22; from Bukhari to Rowe, Mar. 3, 1879, pp. 21-23; from Alimami Sattan Lahai, Bai Farima, and Bai Yinka to Rowe, Dec. 31, 1880, pp. 220-21; vol. 2: from Bukhari to Gov. Havelock, Jan 25, 1882, pp. 101-06; from Bukhari to Havelock, Mar. 23, 1882, pp. 173-77; from Bukhari to Havelock, Aug 15, 1882, pp. pp. 253-60; Aborigines Minute Papers 64, Lawson to Col. Sec., Sept. 28, 1883. Archives Nationales, Paris: Sénégal IV, Dossier 55c, Requin to Gov., Dec. 18, 1865. Alimami Bukhari accused his opponents of attacking the mosque at Famoria and killing Fode Ibrahim Tarawali while he was praying. However, the political leaders who were fighting Bukhari reported that his forces attacked and burned the Friday mosque at Fode Bukaria (Furikaria). There were many devout Muslims on both sides, and by using non-Muslim mercenaries Bukhari did not strengthen his argument that he was the pure Muslim who was trying to uphold the law of Allah. The evidence is too slim to describe this civil war as a jihad.

83. See Part two, Lawson's Roles and Attitudes.

84. See Part two, Military Affairs. Archives Nationales, Dakar: 7-G-20, 7-G-21, 7-G-22, Mellacorée, 1879-1883. Archives Nationales, Paris: Sénégal IV, Dossiers 115 and 116. Alimami Bukhari attempted to obtain the aid of the western military forces of Alimami Samori Ture. In the early 1880s there were reports that Alimami Samori Ture's army in northeast Sierra Leone was planning to join forces with Alimami Bukhari Ture to promote Islam and trade, but Samori's army did not reach the lower Kolente River region. Samori's advance to the coast was opposed by local African interests and the British and French governments. Eventually, Samori was forced to abandon his interest in the Sierra Leone-Guinea coast. See Y. Person, *Samori: une révolution dyula*, 3 vols., (Dakar, 1968, 1971, and 1977); idem, "Samori et la Sierra Leone," *Cahiers d'Etudes Africaines*, vol. 7, no. 25, 1967, pp. 5-26.

85. Archives Nationales, Paris: Sénégal IV, Dossier 116; Guinée I and IV. Alimami Dawda's primary rival for the kingship

was Alkali Yallan Fode Ture of Famoria.

86. SLA: Aborigines Minute Papers 79/1879; 80/1879.

87. SLA: Aborigines Minute Papers 81a/1879, notes taken by T. G. Lawson during meetings on June 29 and 30 and July 1 between the governor and African rulers.

88. Ibid.

89. Ibid.

90. SLA: Aborigines Minute Papers 56/1882, notes taken by T. G. Lawson during a meeting with African rulers on May 18.

91. The process of treaty making continued, and between 1888 and 1892 the Sierra Leone government incorporated fifty additional African rulers into the colonial system. These treaties and earlier ones formed the basis on which the protectorate was proclaimed in 1896. PRO: CO 879/35/411, Collection of Treaties, pp. 246-89. The formation of the frontier police and the establishment of police stations in 1890 became an important part of the incorporation process and presented new difficulties for the African rulers: "You know Mr. Parkes, I am tired of these constables, those that were in my country presently did not take my words, that is they do not care about my words" (SLA: Native Affairs Department Minute Papers 385, from Alimami Suluku to Gov., Aug. 13, 1895; see also Native Affairs Department Minute Papers 513/1891, Report on disturbance against police at Kambia).

Bibliography

PUBLISHED SOURCES

Books

Arcin, A. *Histoire de la Guinée française*, Paris, 1911.
Azfelius, Adam. *Sierra Leone Journal, 1795-1796*. Edited by Alexander Peter Kup. Uppsala: 1967.
The Commissioners for Trade and Plantations. *Journal*. London, 1759 to 1763.
Corry, J. *Observations Upon the Windward Coast of Africa*. London, 1807.
Crowder, M. *West Africa under Colonial Rule*. London, 1968.
Curtin, P. *Economic Change in Precolonial Africa: Senegambia in the Era of the Slave Trade*. Madison, Wis., 1975.
Duncan, J. *Travels in Western Africa in 1845 and 1846*. 2 vols. London, 1847.
Field, M. *Social Organization of the Ga People*. London, 1940.
Forbes, F. *Dahomey and the Dahomans*. 2 vols. London, 1851.
Fyfe, C. *A History of Sierra Leone*. London, 1962.
————·, ed. *Sierra Leone Inheritance*. London, 1964.
Hargreaves, J. *West Africa Partitioned*. Vol. 1: *The Loaded Pause, 1885-89*. London, 1974.
Harrell-Bond, B., Howard, A., and Skinner, D. *Community Leadership and the Transformation of Freetown (1801-1976)*. The Hague, 1978.
Hodge, C., ed. *Papers on the Manding*. Bloomington, Ind., 1971.
Laing, A. *Travels in the Timannee, Kooranko, and Soolimania Countries in Western Africa*. London, 1825.
Levtzion, N. *Ancient Ghana and Mali*. London, 1973.
The Lords of the Committee of Council appointed for the Consideration of all Matters relating to Trade and Foreign Plantations. *Report*. London, 1789.
Machet, J. *Les rivières du Sud et le Fouta Djallon*. Paris, 1906.
Madrolle, C. *En Guinée*. Paris, 1895.
Manoukian, M. *Akan and Ga-Adangme Peoples of the Gold Coast*. London, 1950.

Marty, P. *L'Islam en Guinée*. Paris, 1921.

Mathews, J. *A Voyage to the River Sierra Leone*. London, 1788.

Meillassoux, C., ed. *The Development of Indigenous Trade and Markets in West Africa*. London, 1971.

Miers, S., and Kopytoff, I., eds. *Slavery in Africa*. Madison, Wis., 1977.

Owen, N. *Journal of a Slave Dealer*. London, 1930.

Person, Y. *Samori: une révolution duyla*. 3 vols. Dakar, 1968, 1971, 1977.

Peterson, J. *Province of Freedom: A History of Sierra Leone, 1787-1870*. London, 1969.

Quinn, C. *Mandingo Kingdoms of the Senegambia*. London, 1972.

Rodney, W. *A History of the Upper Guinea Coast, 1545-1800*. Oxford, 1970.

Sanneh, L. *The Jakhanke*. London, 1979.

Sibthorpe, A. *The History of Sierra Leone*. London, 1970 [1st ed. 1868].

Sierra Leone Company. *Substance of Report*. London, 1791.

Sierra Leone Company. *An Account of the Colony of Sierra Leone from Its First Establishment in 1793*. London, 1793.

Sierra Leone Company. *Substance of the Report Delivered by the Court of Directors*. London, 1804.

Walker, J. *Black Loyalists: The Search for a Promised Land in Nova Scotia and Sierra Leone, 1783-1870*. New York, 1976.

Winterbottom, T. *An Account of the Native Africans in the Neighbourhood of Sierra Leone*. Vol. I. London, 1803.

Articles

Cooper, F. "The Problem of Slavery in African Studies." *Journal of African History*, vol. 20, no. 1, 1979, pp. 103-125.

Curtin, P. "The Western Juula in the Eighteenth Century." Conference on Manding Studies, London, 1972.

Denzer, L. "Bai Bureh." In *West African Resistance*, edited by M. Crowder. London, 1970, pp. 233-67.

Gailey, H. "European Rivalry and Diplomacy in the Mellicourie, 1879-1882." *Sierra Leone Studies*, new series, no. 15, Dec. 1961, pp. 135-47.

Hargreaves, J. "The Evolution of the Native Affairs Department." *Sierra Leone Studies*, new series, no. 3, Dec. 1954, pp. 168-84.

————. "The French Occupation of the Mellacourie, 1865-67." *Sierra Leone Studies*, new series, no. 9, Dec. 1957, pp. 3-15.

Kaba, L. "The Maninka-Mori of Bate, Guinea: A Preliminary Survey for Research in Ethno-history." Conference on Manding Studies, London, 1972.

Kaké, I. "Touba, un haut lieu de culture islamique des Diakhanké de Guinée," Conference on Manding Studies, London, 1972.

Klein, M. "The Study of Slavery in Africa." *Journal of African History*, vol. 19, no. 4, 1978, pp. 599-609.

Person, Y. "Ethnic Movements and Acculturation in Upper Guinea since the Fifteenth Century." *International Journal of African Historical Studies* 4, 1971, pp. 669-89.

—————. "The Dyula and the Manding World." Conference on Manding Studies, London, 1972.

—————. "Samori et la Sierra Leone." *Cahiers d'Etudes Africaines*, vol. 7, no. 25, 1967, pp. 5-26.

—————. "Samori and Islam," in J. Willis, ed., *Studies in West African Islamic History*. Vol. 1: *The Cultivators of Islam*. London, 1979, pp. 259-77.

Sanneh, L. "The Diakhanke and the Ummah al-Muhammadiya: A Preliminary Study in the Clerical and Educational Role of the Diakhanke." Conference on Manding Studies, London, 1972.

—————. "The Origin and Dispersion of the Diakhanke: An Introductory Study." Conference on Manding Studies, London, 1972.

—————. "The Origins of Clericalism in West African Islam." *Journal of African History* 17, 1976, pp. 49-72.

Sayers, E. "Notes on the Clan or Family Names Common in the Area Inhabited by Temne-speaking People." *Sierra Leone Studies* 10, old series, 1927, pp. 14-108.

Skinner, D. "The Arabic Letter Books as a Source for Sierra Leone History." *Africana Research Bulletin* 3, no. 4, 1973, pp. 41-50.

—————. "Thomas George Lawson: Government Interpreter and Historical Resource." *Africana Research Bulletin* 4, no. 4, 1974, pp. 51-59.

—————. "Islam and Education in the Colony and Hinterland of Sierra Leone, 1750-1914." *Canadian Journal of African Studies* 10, no. 3, 1976, pp. 499-520.

—————. "Mande Settlement and the Development of Islamic Institutions in Sierra Leone." *International Journal of African Historical Studies* 11, 1978, pp. 32-62.

Suret-Canale, J. "Touba in Guinea—Holy Place of Islam." In *African Perspectives,* edited by C. Allen and R. Johnson. London, 1970, pp. 53-81.

ARCHIVAL COLLECTIONS

National Archives

France (Paris):
    Guinée I
    Guinée IV
    Sénégal IV.

Sénégal (Dakar):
    7-G-18 to 7-G-22, Mellacorée.

Sierra Leone (Freetown): (SLA):
    Aborigines Minute Papers, 1877-1890
    Arabic Letter Books, 1877-1901
    Colonial Secretary's Letter Books, 1820-
    Colonial Secretary's Letter Book to Native Chiefs, 1871-1881
    Colonial Secretary's Office, Letters Received, 1850-1869
    Governor's Letter Books, 1808-
    Governor's Letter Book to Native Chiefs, 1862-1867
    Government Interpreter's Letter Books (GILB), 1876-1889
    Government Interpreter's Memoranda (GIM), 1873-1876
    Local Letters to the Governor
    Native Affairs Department Minute Papers, 1891-1898.

United Kingdom, Public Record Office (London): (PRO):
    Colonial Office (CO) 267, Original Correspondence, Sierra
      Leone
    Colonial Office 268, Entry Books
    Colonial Office 270, Sessional Papers
    Colonial Office 272, Sierra Leone Blue Books
    Colonial Office 879, Confidential Prints
    Foreign Office (FO) 84, Slave Trade
    Foreign Office 881, Confidential Prints: numerical series
    30/29, Granville Papers.

Regional Archives

Kambia District Archives, Kambia, Sierra Leone.

Libraries

British Museum (London), Parliamentary Accounts and Papers,
    Colonies.
British Museum (Colindale), *Sierra Leone Weekly News*, Freetown.
Church Missionary Society (CMS; London), C A1, Sierra Leone
    Missionary Reports, Diaries, and Letters.
Rhodes House (Oxford) Manuscript Collection, Journal of Mr. James
    Watt in his Expedition to and from Teembo in the year 1794.
Huntington Library (San Marino, California), The Papers of
    Governor Zachary Macaulay.

UNPUBLISHED SOURCES

Theses

Bangura, M. "Contribution à l'histoire des Sosoe du 16e au 19e siècle." Memoire de Diplome de Fin d'Etudes Superieures, Institute Polytechnique Gamal Abdel Nasser, Conakry, 1971-1972.
Howard, A. "Big Men, Traders, and Chiefs: Power, Commerce, and Spatial Change in the Sierra Leone-Guinea Plain, 1865-1895." Ph.D. dissertation, University of Wisconsin, 1972.
Ijagbemi, E. "A History of the Temne." Ph.D. dissertation, Edinburgh University, 1968.
Skinner, D. "The Development of Islam in Sierra Leone During the Nineteenth Century." Ph.D. dissertation, University of California, Berkeley, 1971.

Papers

Bangura, Bai Farima. "History of Kambia." Typescript, October 28, 1938.
Toure, El-Hadj D.S. "Histoire du Moreah." Typescript. Conakry, 1975.
Fofana, Al-Hajj M. S. "Ta'rikh al-Muriah." Manuscript. Gbile, n.d.

Interviews

Conducted by Ray Ganga

Lamina Kamara, Kukuna, May 13, 1973.
Ousman Kamara, Musaia, April 10, 1973.

Conducted by David Skinner

Kande Ibrahim Conteh, Freetown, Mar. 3, 1976.
Kemokho Dumbuya and Kande Sadu Dumbuya II, Kukuna, Feb. 26, 1976.
Elders of the Dumbuya Family, Dalamodia, Lungi, Mar. 21, 1976.
Alkali Kalay Musa III, Kambia, Mar. 26, 1969.
Shaikhu Luseni, Gbile, Mar. 26, and April 15, 1969, Feb. 25, 28, and 29, 1976.

Alimami Sorie Sankoh, Tawiya, April 15, 1969.
Kolea Sankoh, Tawiya, Feb. 28, 1976.
Alhaji Muhammad Sanusi, Tawiya, April 14, 1969, and Feb. 28, 1976.
Alfa Soriba Yansane, Freetown, Mar. 4 and 8, 1976.
Alimami Mori Fode Turay II, Kambia, Mar. 25, 1969 and Feb. 28, 1976.

Conducted by Alusine Yilla

Abu B. Contah, Laya, April 10, 1976.
Alimami Sindamore Dumbuya, Bolobinneh, April 10, 1976.
Ibrahim Fofana, Famoria, April 19, 1976.
Alhaji Mohamed Fofana, Taigbe, April 18, 1976.
Abu Bakar Sillah, Furidugu, May 2, 1976.
Abu Suma, Musaia, April 12, 1976.
Nabie Ture, Furikaria, April 14, 1976.
Nabie Ture, Maligia, April 17, 1976.
Soriba Ture, Yankissa, April 20, 1976.

Index

About the Author

David E. Skinner is Associate Professor of History at the University of Santa Clara (Calif.). He received his doctorate in history from the University of California at Berkeley and fellowships for travel and research in Africa from the National Endowment for History, the Mabelle McLeod Lewis Memorial Fund, and the Social Science Research Council. Previous publications include articles in *Africa, Africana Research Bulletin, Canadian Journal of African Studies, International Journal of African Historical Studies,* and *West Africa* and the monograph *Community Leadership and the Transformation of Freetown, 1801-1976* (co-author).